AF332979

Rebels and Bureaucrats

STUDIES OF THE EAST ASIAN INSTITUTE
COLUMBIA UNIVERSITY

JOHN ISRAEL   •   DONALD W. KLEIN

Rebels and Bureaucrats

China's December 9ers

UNIVERSITY OF CALIFORNIA PRESS
BERKELEY • LOS ANGELES • LONDON

University of California Press
Berkeley and Los Angeles, California

University of California Press, Ltd.
London, England

ISBN 0-520-02861-9
Library of Congress Catalog Card Number: 74-18757
Printed in the United States of America

To Mary, Sue, Nym

Contents

Tables

Acknowledgements

This book would have been impossible without the assistance of hundreds of people during our two decades of research and writing about Chinese students and leadership. Some, such as John K. Fairbank and Eugene Wu, have aided us in every stage of our work. Among those who gave support and encouragement, few were more helpful than John Ma, formerly of the Hoover Institution at Stanford University. In research for this book, as well as other projects of both authors, John has been generous with his time and talents. We also wish to acknowledge our debt to many others who are not listed by name but who have shared in the production of this manuscript.

We consulted and interviewed scores of December 9th participants, as well as their friends and schoolmates and outside observers. Some are mentioned in footnotes; others wish to remain anonymous. Thanks to their help, we have been able, we hope, to clothe the bare bones of historical figures with flesh and blood.

We have received generous assistance from three institutions. Columbia University's East Asian Institute in particular must be singled out. It provided bed and board for one of us for six years. Thanks to the efforts of the then Director, the late John

Lindbeck, we were able to collaborate there for a summer. Our labors were expedited by the Institute's excellent facilities and congenial intellectual atmosphere. Still more important, the Institute provided us with three first-rate research assistants: Lois B. Hager, Susan Horsey, and Jane L. Lieberthal. They ferreted out and collated thousands of facts, and we are particularly grateful for this work because we know full well the tedium involved.

In addition to Columbia, Harvard University's East Asian Research Center and the University of Virginia's Wilson Gee Institute were also generous in their support.

John S. Service of the University of California's Center for Chinese Studies read the manuscript in its entirety and offered detailed and valuable advice, both substantive and editorial. Professor Philip West of the University of Indiana, author of a forthcoming book on Yenching University, gave us useful criticisms on the section dealing with that institution, as did former Yenching Professor Randolph Sailer. Thanks are also due Carl E. Dorris (Ph.D., history, University of Kansas, 1975), who shared with us data unearthed in dissertation research on the Shansi-Chahar-Hopei Border Region.

Our prose has benefitted enormously from the close reading and incisive critique of Dr. James A. Brussel, who further demonstrated his generous (if not foolhardy) disposition by volunteering to do the index.

This book is dedicated to three women who have given unselfish aid and encouragement to the authors: Mary Israel, Sue Klein, and Helen Foster Snow. Mary Israel was especially helpful in the final stages, performing such grubby but essential chores as reading copy and checking footnotes. We owe a special word of appreciation to our friend and editor, Mervyn Adams Seldon. Mervyn went far beyond the usual painstaking editorial duties. She made manifest myriads of miracles on multitudinous messy matters and included among her charitable works a draft index and a list of abbreviations, to say nothing of unbounded encouragement. But for her sound judgment, the entire book might have resembled this paragraph.

Mrs. Snow, better known to her friends as "Peg" and to the reading public by her pen name, Nym Wales, merits a special note of thanks. Without her accounts as a foundation and backdrop, our description of the student movement would have been pale indeed. While in China, she and her former husband, the late Edgar Snow, exemplified the best of the participant-observer tradition of journalism. Subsequently, by publishing her China notes instead of leaving them to gather dust, she performed a great service to a later generation struggling to know secondhand the China that she learned about firsthand and understood so well. Helen Foster Snow has never received the recognition she has long deserved, and so it gives us special pleasure to dedicate this book to her.

Abbreviations

ACFDY   All-China Federation of Democratic Youth

ACFLAC   All-China Federation of Literary and Art Circles

CCP   Chinese Communist Party

CPPCC   Chinese People's Political Consultative Conference

CSMAC   Central-South Military and Administrative Committee

CYL   Communist Youth League

GAC   Government Administration Council

KMT   Kuomintang

NCPG   North China People's Government

NDYL   New Democratic Youth League

NLVC   National Liberation Vanguards of China

PLA   People's Liberation Army

PSNSU   Peiping Student National Salvation Union

PRC   People's Republic of China

U.N.   United Nations

WFDY   World Federation of Democratic Youth

Notes

CKJML   Kuo Hua-lun, chief ed., *Chung-kung jen-ming lu* [Chinese Communist personalities] Taipei: n.p., 1967.

CNCH   *Ch'ing-nien ch'ien-hsien* [Front line of youth]. Hankow.

CWR   *China Weekly Review*. Shanghai.

IECHIL   Li Ch'ang and others, *"I-erh chiu" hui-i lu.* *See* Bibliographic Note.

IECYT   Jen-min ch'u-pan she, ed., *I-erh chiu yun-tung. See* Bibliographic Note.

NCSM   Nym Wales [Helen F. Snow], *Notes on the Chinese Student Movement, 1935–36. See* Bibliographic Note.

PTCK   *Pei-ta chou-k'an* [Peita weekly]. Peiping.

RON   Chiang Nan-hsiang and others, *The Roar of a Nation. See* Bibliographic Note.

SCMM   *Selections from China Mainland Magazines*

SECCNCNTK   Yen-ching ta-hsueh hsueh-sheng tzu-chih hui, ed., *Shih-erh chiu chou-nien chi-nien t'e-k'an* [December 9th first anniversary memorial issue]. Peiping: n.p., 1936.

SECTK   *Shih-erh chiu t'e-k'an* [December 9th special]. Peiping.

SNIC   John Israel, *Student Nationalism in China, 1927–1937. See* Bibliographic Note.

SNL   Min-hsien-tui [National Liberation Vanguard of China], ed., *San-nien-lai ti min-hsien* [Three years of the Vanguard]. n.p., October 1938.

URI   Union Research Institute

WMTTW   Chung-hua min-tsu chieh-fang hsien-feng tui tsung-tui-pu [NLVC headquarters], *Wo-men ti tui-wu* [Our corps]. n.p., March 15, 1937.

YTCK   *Yen-ta chou-k'an* [Yenching weekly]. Peiping.

Introduction

On December 9, 1935, some two thousand college and high school students demonstrated in Peiping's streets and outside the city wall. This event, still little known in the West, has been dubbed epoch-making by Mao Tse-tung; indeed it was. For Chinese youths, it marked the end of nearly four years of silence. Intimidated by government suppression, patriotic young people had swallowed their anger while Japan's military adventurers moved inexorably from recently conquered Manchuria toward the heartland of North China. Finally pent-up fury no longer could be contained. The December 9th outburst was followed on December 16 by a second demonstration, four times as large. News of the Peiping uprising electrified students, intellectuals, professionals, and even factory workers in cities throughout China. These patriotic forces coalesced in a National Salvation movement powerful enough to halt Chiang Kai-shek's appeasement of Japanese aggression and to transform his anti-Communist extermination campaign into a united front against the aggressor.

December 9 was no less epochal for the students themselves. Having discarded passivity for a posture of defiant *engagement*, many of them moved steadily leftward. Less than two months after December 9, the radical student leadership was absorbed into the National Liberation Vanguards of China (NLVC), which was to become an adjunct of the Communist Youth League (CYL). The following summer a few December 9 veterans embarked on the long dangerous journey to the Communist base in the barren reaches of Northwest China. In the summer of 1937, when Japanese troops occupied Peiping, this trickle of youthful pilgrims became a flood. The December 9ers had cast their lot with the forces of Mao Tse-tung.

Three decades later, seventeen years after Mao's seizure of power, another crisis was about to find resolution in a more famous movement, the Great Proletarian Cultural Revolution. Once again a deceptive calm preceded the storm. On December 9, 1965, ten thousand well-behaved youths filed into Peking's Great Hall of the People to dutifully commemorate a historic event. Conspicuous among them were the greying heads of a dozen middle-aged bureaucrats whose historic deeds were being extolled. Thirty years before, as university and high school students, they had braved freezing winds and club-swinging police to storm the citadels of the old order. Now, in their late forties and early fifties, they were at the threshold of power. The Mao Tse-tung generation was aging and soon would pass from the scene; the mantle of national leadership would quite possibly fall upon their shoulders. Yet, within months this promising group of loyal functionaries would be attacked by teen-age revolutionists including, no doubt, many of those who had filled the Great Hall to applaud their exploits. Their authority was to be challenged by young rebels just as they had once challenged that of their elders. Accused of opposing Mao, they would be forced from office by militant Red Guards. By late 1966, all but a handful would have disappeared from the public stage.

The saga of this "December 9th generation"—the young intelligentsia drawn into the Communist camp during the anti-Japanese crusade of 1935–37—poses a series of important questions for historians and social scientists. Chinese student movements invite comparative study. A dominant motif, the age-old theme of young Hotspurs versus cautious elders, frequently recurs in the clash of student nationalists and practitioners of appeasement: "The president, who has taken a stern stand against student demonstrations in recent weeks, was asked to send his army to the borders to fight the Israelis rather than to beat up students in Beirut."[1] The president is Suleiman Franjieh, the students Lebanese, the year 1973, but with the change of only a few nouns it could be Chiang Kai-shek versus the December 9ers in 1935.

Unfortunately, comparative study is in its infancy despite intense interest in student movements during recent years. Student movements have attracted attention because of their importance, their dramatic appeal, and their intimate relationship to a panoply of other issues. Scholars have sought to understand the sources of these phenomena, the composition of student movements, and their impact upon the contemporary political and social order. However, many have interpreted these outbursts as destructive forces—intrusions in the normal pattern of academic life and disruptions of the established political system. For example, Louis S. Feuer has observed that student movements can undermine academic freedom and liberal institutions.

Less studied have been the positive and constructive functions of these movements. In stable democracies, young people often enter political life through student branches of established political parties. In colonial and semicolonial societies, however, students are introduced into the adult political world through participation in revolutionary movements. In the recent history of Burma, Indonesia, Cuba, China, and other countries, national leaders received their political baptism in student politics. Men like Castro, Sukarno, and Mao first became aware of their political talents and experimented with techniques they would later use to mobilize millions of their fellow citizens.

[1] *The Washington Post*, April 13, 1973.

Hence, student movements have provided apprenticeships for future political elites. For adult revolutionary movements (whose leaders may have developed from earlier generations of student activists), campuses have been a valuable source of recruits. In countries where educated talent is at a premium, these recruits may mean the difference between life and death for aspiring political organizations.

In traditional China, where a rigid multi-tiered examination system compelled students to spend the better part of their lives mastering prescribed texts, there was neither time nor incentive for young people to become politically involved. Still less did a system based upon rote learning and orthodox interpretations provide a reward for rebels. But however great the pressures for scholastic achievement, an even deeper strain of Confucianism emphasized the moral and political responsibility of the scholar. Confucius had insisted that learned men judge their rulers' behavior (as well as their own) by a higher ethical code. Accordingly, students who buried their heads in books and ignored the conduct of government violated a key precept of the Master. The fact that many "students" in imperial China were in their thirties and forties, had passed the lower examination, and had assumed political burdens, blurred still further the line of demarcation between students and officials. For these reasons, Chinese student protest has a history of more than two millennia.

Another tradition is the quest for literati support by both imperial aspirants and established rulers. In the twentieth century, both Nationalists and Communists, during their rise to power, have courted China's educated elite. Sun Yat-sen's career reached a turning point in 1905 when he was able to join with Chinese students in Japan. The early leaders of the Chinese Communist Party (CCP) emerged from the student movement of May 4, 1919 against appeasement of Japan's imperial ambitions.

Founded in 1921 by students, teachers, and other young intellectuals, the CCP gained a further influx of educated youths who joined the Party in reaction against the incident of May 30, 1925, when demonstrators were mowed down by British police in Shanghai. However, the CCP's urban base—both student and proletarian—was decimated by Chiang Kai-shek's purges after April 1927. Other survivors of the early years lost their lives during the epic 6,000-mile Long March of 1934–35. Meanwhile, the Party reconstituted itself with peasant recruits: by 1933, the Communist movement in China had become almost exclusively rural. Hence, the Communist organization that emerged in the hills of Shensi late in 1935 was radically different from the coterie of young intellectuals that had met in a Shanghai home in 1921. During these years, survivors among the original leaders had shed naïve idealism and proclivities for abstract discussions. They had been pursued by ruthless enemies and thrown upon the primitive resources of rural China. Hardened by warfare, cold, hunger, fatigue, medical neglect, and the deaths of comrades and loved ones, they had become professional revolutionists.

To these tough warriors came a new group of disciples. From the summer of 1936 until the tightening of the Nationalist blockade around the Communist base area in 1939, student volunteers flocked to the Northwest to fight beside Mao. This was the first sizable student group in a decade to join the Communist movement. In special schools in Yenan and elsewhere, they were trained, indoctrinated, and absorbed into the Party before being sent to work among the masses. Like their predecessors of earlier generations, many perished during the 12 years of war from 1937 to 1949, but survivors emerged in the vanguard of the new order.

The story of these students, of their career patterns and their relationship with other elements in the Communist movement, suggests a highly ambivalent relationship between a generation of ardently patriotic urban intellectuals and Mao Tse-tung's rural-based disciples. An examination of the complex and unstable symbiosis between these two groups should help us to understand the past and future of Chinese communism.

Formidable historiographic problems confront the chronicler of the December 9th generation. A mass movement cannot easily be described in terms of individual participants even if all biographical data are available. In this case the data emphatically are not available. Unlike the anti-Japanese movement of 1931, when names of prominent leaders appeared regularly in the Chinese press, that of 1935 was described in much less personal terms—when censors allowed it to be reported at all. Harsh repression had taught student activists the necessity for anonymity.

As a consequence, only occasionally can we identify individuals among the masses. We know by name—and sometimes only *as* names—a few hundred individuals who participated in the December 9th movement and only two hundred or so of them have since become prominent in Peking. They are but a fraction of the estimated 2,000 students who marched on December 9, 1935 and 7,775 who demonstrated on December 16. They constitute an even smaller proportion of Peiping's 13,517 college students and the nearly 25,000 college and high school members claimed by the Peiping Student Union.

What were our criteria for including individuals in this study? Several prominent December 9th leaders in our narrative did not, in fact, rise to prominence after 1949 but either died or disappeared from view during and after the Sino-Japanese War. We include them in order to shed light upon the nature of student activism at various Peiping universities and on the reasons why certain promising young radicals failed to emerge in high places. These individuals are not, however, counted in our quantitative analysis of Party and state leadership. Several other Peiping college students, duly noted in our account, were not known to have been politically active in 1935–36 but later became prominent in the Communist order. We cannot omit them because the impact of the December 9th experience was so formidable that few who were on the scene could have escaped its influence. Hence we judge them "guilty" of membership in the December 9th generation unless proven "innocent."

A somewhat larger group first appears in the historical record as members of the National Liberation Vanguards of China, a body composed almost entirely of December 9th leftists. These people fall within our parameters even though their educational affiliations often remain unknown. We are aware of the possibility that one or two of them were not students at the time, but here too we must err on the side of inclusion. A few may have attended institutions outside of Peiping, but since Peiping's demonstrations evoked nationwide response, there is no reason to exclude them from our study. As a matter of fact, it is noteworthy that identifiable December 9ers from cities other than Peiping are rather rare. The December 9th spirit may have been nationwide, but the cadre it spawned was concentrated in the old city of culture.

Even though the general thrust of the December 9th movement was leftward, a number of December 9th veterans later occupied prominent positions in the Nationalist establishment on Taiwan. Among them are Minister of Foreign Affairs Shen Ch'ang-huan (Yenching University), Vice-Minister Yang Hsi-k'un (Peking University), *China Post* publisher Nancy Yü-Huang (Yenching), sociologist Chü Hao-jan (Tsinghua University), and Hung T'ung, a former leftist who is now dean of students at Tsinghua University in Hsinchu and prominent in the Anti-Communist National Salvation Youth Corps. Still others enjoy varying degrees of renown in Hong Kong intellectual and commercial circles and in the American academic world. However, only the December 9ers who joined the Communists have collectively left their mark on history, and it is to this group that the term "December 9ers" is confined.

An indefinite number of December 9th veterans remain undiscovered and uncounted. No doubt there are many in official posts whose names have not appeared in news media available to us. Many of those of whom we do hear are little more than names and titles. Others have adopted revolutionary *noms de guerre* and are unrecognizable. Nonetheless, our 200-odd sample is a very distinguished group or, rather, was so until the

Cultural Revolution. It would be fallacious to interpret the group's limited size as evidence of insignificance.

Our study is akin to the increasingly popular form of collective biography that Lawrence Stone calls "prosopography"—"the investigation of the common background characteristics of a group of actors in history by means of a collective study of their lives."[2] The prosopographer's method is:

> to establish a universe to be studied, and then to ask a set of uniform questions—about birth and death, marriage and family, social origins and inherited economic position, place of residence, education, amount and source of personal wealth, occupation, religion, experience of office, and so on. The various types of information about the individuals in the universe are then juxtaposed and combined, and are examined for significant variables. They are tested both for internal correlations and for correlations with other forms of behavior or action.[3]

Available data on the December 9ers, however, are too crude and incomplete to permit such a disciplined study. Hence we must adopt a less precise, more suggestive approach to identify and characterize a group sharing similar origins, social experience, and career patterns. Since December 9ers are not typical of China's leadership as a whole, generalizations about them cannot be projected on to the entire elite. Nor can we single out a particular biographical factor—such as class interests, family background, or school ties—that shapes their thoughts and behavior. We contend, rather, that the coincidence of many things—time, place, socioeconomic characteristics, relationships to other groups, and unique historical events—defines the subject, invites collective analysis, and opens the way to comparative study.

---

[2] Lawrence Stone, "Prosopography," in Felix Gilbert and Stephen R. Graubard, eds., *Historical Studies Today* (New York: W. W. Norton & Co., 1972), p. 107.

[3] *Ibid.*

[4] See Julián Mariás, "Generations: The Concept" and Marvin Rintala,

We refer to the December 9ers as a "generation." Since much ink has been spilled over this term,[4] let us explain what we do and do not mean. We obviously are not speaking of a "biological" generation consisting of all the people born on the same day or during the same year. Nor are we speaking of a generation in the metahistorical sense, in the way that the term "World War I Generation" is commonly used to refer to the millions of men and women in many countries whose lives were shaped by that great event. The December 9ers are a *political generation* in the narrowest sense. Our study does not extend to all Chinese college and high school students of the mid-1930s or even to all those for whom the anti-Japanese movement was a formative experience. Instead, it is focused upon those who subsequently gained prominence under the Communists. If the term "generation" is more broadly understood, the December 9ers would have to be labeled a generational *subgroup* defined not only as those of a similar background swept up by the same events but, further, as those who responded to those events in a fundamentally similar way and with similar consequences.

The December 9ers command our attention because they constitute the most sharply defined group of leaders in post-1949 China. One can speak of a "Long March" generation, but it includes individuals of the most divergent backgrounds who joined the movement over the course of 14 years. The December 9th generation overlaps with what John Gittings calls the "Yenan Generation"—the "thousands of military and civilian cadres" who were graduated from Lin Piao's Resistance University (K'ang-jih ta-hsueh or K'angta) during the war years.[5] Yet, in spite of the crucible of wartime experience, these graduates constitute a heterogeneous conglomerate, internally

---

"Political Generations," *International Encyclopedia of the Social Sciences* (New York: Macmillan and the Free Press, 1968), 6: 88–96.

[5]John Gittings, "The Spirit of Yenan," *Far Eastern Economic Review* 72, no. 23 (June 6, 1971): 59.

rift by divergent social origins, formative experiences, political alliances, and career patterns. The December 9th group is a unique distillate of a historical movement. It is an elite united by age, socioeconomic background, and education. These men and women share a formative experience, resulting in a sense of nationalistic dedication, some similarities in career patterns, and, perhaps, a common fate.

I

The Environmental Crucible

The December 9ers were profoundly affected by the historic drama that unfolded during their childhood years. Most were born during the era of the 1911 revolution. In this epochal event converged many social forces. Their common denominator was resurgent nationalism, a shared conviction that China could not survive the rule of a corrupt and decadent dynasty. During subsequent years the nationalist theme was reiterated time and again. When Republican dreams were obliterated by warlord realities, patriotic wrath was turned against China's new rulers who seemed even less able than the old to build a viable state.

Ultimate targets of nationalistic indignation were foreign nations that had humiliated China. Japan, however, was increasingly singled out for criticism. While status quo powers such as England and the United States professed moral outrage, Japanese late-comers to the imperialist arena behaved with adolescent aggressiveness. Their encroachments on China's sovereignty in 1915, 1919, and 1928 inspired youthful indignation. During the blitzkrieg conquest of Manchuria in 1931, many December 9ers were old enough to share the psychological burdens of China's humiliation.

During this era of outraged nationalism China was simultaneously undergoing a cultural revolution. From 1917 to 1923, her intellectual world displayed breadth and vitality reminiscent of the florescence of the hundred schools during the third century B.C. Within a few years after 1911, it was widely agreed that political solutions had failed, that mere institutional reforms were inadequate, that China must be shaken to its roots before meaningful changes could emerge. Iconoclasm was in order. Nothing remained sacred. Buddhism and Taoism were scarcely worthy of the critic's pen; a two-thousand-year-old Confucian orthodoxy was caricatured as a "man-eating" doctrine. Footbinding was denounced for crippling young girls' limbs, filial piety for shriveling young men's souls. Only upon a foundation of liberated youth could a new China be built. Up with the young, down with the old—this was the order of the day.

After the student demonstration of May 4, 1919, the New Culture movement became more politicized. Intellectual leaders, inspired by the upsurge of youthful energy, turned to politics. In this spirit, the radical professors Ch'en Tu-hsiu and Li Ta-chao welcomed Comintern agents and helped them to found the Chinese Communist Party. Also aided by Comintern agents, Sun Yat-sen set out to revitalize the Kuomintang (KMT) and to give it, for the first time, a truly mass base.

Coincident with these cultural and political upheavals was a social revolution stemming from the post-Opium War Western impact. By the turn of the century, the old landlord-gentry elite was forced to share power with, and to assimilate, new urban groups—merchants, financiers, industrialists, scientists, technicians, lawyers, doctors, and teachers. Some of these men had been trained abroad; all had been influenced by Western and semi-Western commercial and educational institutions. No longer was landholding the only respectable investment and the examination system the only prestigious path to fame. On China's seaboard fringes, a pluralistic urban society was developing. Its repercussions reached inland provinces like Hunan, where the young Mao Tse-tung read translations of foreign political philosophers and fell under the spell of a new breed of teachers. Although Confucian attitudes continued to receive verbal acquiescence in the home, they were less functional in the new environment. No longer was it self-evident that life-long experience endowed family patriarchs with wisdom relevant to the younger generation. New patterns of family relationships were emerging.

The little we know of December 9ers' family backgrounds permits us to sketch but a rough composite picture. Because of the expense of attending college, or even high school, their families had to be among the economic elite. In 1933, only 3.6 percent of China's college students came from working-class homes. Almost 17 percent listed the family occupation as agriculture, but most of these farmer fathers must have been landlords or very wealthy peasants. Approximately two out of three students came from homes of businessmen, educators, and government officials.[1] This general picture is confirmed by the survey Olga Lang conducted between 1935 and 1937 of 1,164 college students.[2]

From the findings of Richard H. Solomon, who interviewed 91 middle- and upper-class Chinese men in Taiwan and Hong Kong in 1965, we can attempt to extrapolate the overall family life structure of the December 9ers.[3] Their early childhoods were marked by indulgence, especially when it came to feeding.

[1]*Ch'üan-kuo kao-teng chiao-yü t'ung-chi* [National Statistics on higher education] (Nanking, 1933), Table 55, p. 88. Reprinted in Philip West, "Yenching University and Sino-American Relations, 1917–37," (Ph.D. dissertation, Harvard University, 1970), p.373.

[2]Olga Lang, *Chinese Family and Society* (New Haven, Conn.: Yale University Press, 1946), p. 365.

[3]Richard H. Solomon, *Mao's Revolution and the Chinese Political Culture* (Berkeley: University of California Press, 1971), pp.1–93, *passim*. Solomon's interview sample resembles the profile of the December 9th generation both in economic background and in geographical origin, with a heavy concentration on China's central and southern coastal provinces. However, only some two dozen of his respondents were chronological contemporaries of the December 9ers and only half of these had received any higher education. None was a

Weaning came late; toilet training was casual. Once the age of indulgence had passed, however, they soon discovered the authoritarian side of the benevolent paternalism they had experienced. Lines of command were clear and hierarchical. Fathers were remote, frequently engendering awe by their very presence. Sentiments of love, though not lacking, were stifled by fear as well as by the onus placed on overt emotional expression. Elder brothers, too, were to be obeyed without question. The word of older male authorities was equivalent to law. Given scant opportunity for remonstrance, children sought outlets in blind tantrums, but even these failed to evoke the desired response. Attitudes toward authority that emerged from such a family experience were profoundly ambivalent—on the one hand a deep sense of dependence, on the other a veiled but profound feeling of hostility.

A fundamental premise of Solomon's study is that modes of interpersonal relations are much more resistant to change than are consciously held values. Nonetheless, parents of the December 9th generation were by no means part of an unchanging and unadulterated Chinese tradition. Disproportionate numbers of Peiping's college students hailed from China's eastern and southern seaboard, the area most exposed to outside influences. Their families were members of the new urban commercial classes or belonged to those elements of the old gentry elite that were coming to terms with the new culture. The fathers of nearly three-fifths of the college students in Lang's sample had graduated from modern colleges or high schools.[4] As young men, they had been exposed to the full impact of the new nationalism and the new culture. One who was forty in 1935 might well have protested the 21 Demands and endorsed the iconoclastic essays of Ch'en Tu-hsiu. A man of sixty

---

woman. (See Table 1, p. 15; also, Appendix 5, pp. 541–58.) His findings, therefore, are highly suggestive but far from conclusive for our study.

[4]Lang, *Chinese Family*, p. 365.

might have witnessed K'ang Yu-wei's "Petition of the Examination Candidates," urging China to resist Japan's draconian terms of settlement after the Sino-Japanese War of 1894–95. More than one could recall father-son disputes on questions of marriage, education, and career. Even those with traditional educations were sufficiently sympathetic to the changing scene to see that their children received more modern training than the fathers had received.

Hence, by the late 1930s, we find less evidence of intergenerational conflict than might be expected in a rapidly changing society. Candid autobiographical essays by student leaders and others at Yenching University revealed "very little preoccupation with revolt against parents."[5] In Olga Lang's survey, youngsters were asked to report disagreements with parents on a list of issues including marriage, education, profession, religion, Western culture, politics, friends, hygiene, fashions, recreation, and participation in the student movement. The average proportion of disagreement on a given issue was less than 20 percent, and a full 20 percent of those with college-educated fathers reported no differences of opinion at all. (Interestingly, children whose parents had had a traditional education were more radical than those with college-educated parents. This correlation may reflect higher incomes, treaty-port attitudes, and Kuomintang affiliations of the college-educated, as well as divisive pressures in more tradition-bound homes.)[6] Even if we allow for reluctance to air family problems in public, the December 9th generation did not appear to be preoccupied with family rebellion.

But appearances may deceive. Lewis S. Feuer argues that radical students generally sublimate the generational conflict at home and act it out against father surrogates on campus and in society at large.[7] Was this the case in China? Available evidence

[5]Former Yenching professor, letter to John Israel, August 24, 1970.

[6]Lang, *Chinese Family*, p. 367.

[7]Lewis S. Feuer, *The Conflict of Generations* (New York: Basic Books, 1969).

provides scant support for such a view. Olga Lang found that "the proportion of sons with purely negative attitudes toward their fathers was not larger among the radical students than among those with conservative and moderately democratic political views." She unearthed no support for "the theory that an unfriendly home atmosphere with a severe father and inharmonious family relations is particularly favorable to the development of radicalism in the young."[8]

However, Lang did find distinct characteristics in the *style* of family relationships among Chinese students who became radicals. They "did not dislike their parents more than the other students, but they criticized them more often and more openly" and "took their parents into their confidence less frequently than the others." Moreover, "distaste for staying at home was more pronounced in the radical than the nonradical students," and "the proportion of radical students who did not think changes in the Chinese family system necessary was smaller than in any other political group." Lang concluded that the higher instance of rebellion against family authority among radicals "was caused not by early childhood experiences but by the influence of their environment outside the family."[9] This militates still further against Feuer's sublimation thesis.

Why were family revolts, so prominent in the older generation of Communist leaders such as Chu Te and Mao Tse-tung, so rare among December 9ers? Part of the answer is that so little is known about the family situations of the latter. Further knowledge might reveal that some, indeed, were rebels at home

---

Feuer's theory has a "heads-I-win-tails-you-lose" quality that makes it difficult to handle. Feuer seizes upon Mao Tse-tung as a classic example of the son who rebels against an authoritarian father and continues his rebellion against society (p.182). On the other hand, unable to find evidence of conflict in the close-knit family of Berkeley rebel Mario Savio, he assumes that "the university constituted a surrogate father against whom all the emotions of generational revolt could be channelized" (p. 444).

[8]Lang, *Chinese Family,* p. 319.

[9]*Ibid.,* pp. 319–20.

before they became rebels on campus. Another part of the answer lies in the nature of the group. The December 9 leaders were college students. College education was too expensive for a young man or woman to bear without parental support. Scholarships were few, and working one's way through college was beneath the dignity of these latter-day literati. Whatever incipient conflict of generations there may have been, few students who dared to break with their families could have made it through college.

Students who joined the CCP were, of course, more radical than most of their classmates, and perhaps more impoverished. Though evidence is far from conclusive, Lang's survey suggests that a disproportionate number of them came from less affluent backgrounds. Radical students, she writes, tended to be "sons of small landlords and peasants who were wealthy according to the village standards but infinitely poorer than industrialists, bank directors, professionals, or high officials." But ideological radicalism per se did not automatically produce political activism. Nor was low income the most positive variable in determining the radical student. "The most important," writes Lang, "seems to have been the atmosphere in the college," and it was the students in North China who were most inclined to transmute ardent nationalism into a sympathy for the Communists.[10] It was not accidental that the movement erupted in North China's major university center—Peiping.

In terms of values, one is impressed with the broad range of agreement between generations. Students, like parents, were urbanites who admired Western culture and were staunchly nationalistic in their politics. In its modern, urban-oriented aspects, the Kuomintang government reflected the views and aspirations of this class. The mid-1930s, moreover, were the Kuomintang's most promising years. Although military campaigns against Communists and warlords continued, survival of the government seemed assured. Administrative and financial

[10]*Ibid.*, p. 318.

reforms had restored a measure of stability to the educational world. Fiscal reforms had unified the currency, and monetary deflation provided a comfortable standard of living for officials, teachers, students, and others on fixed stipends. For students of a scholarly bent and for the many who hoped to pursue careers in public life within the existing social structure, this was not an unhopeful period.

But by 1935, the government's slogan, "Save the Nation through Study," was beginning to ring hollow. Students became alarmed as Chiang Kai-shek's policies of appeasement bared North China to aggression. This apprehension was shared by their families in treaty ports where Japanese overwhelmed Chinese competitors by smuggling and special privileges backed by military and political coercion. Hence, the Anglo-American-oriented commercial classes (the kinds of people who sent their children to Tsinghua and Yenching Universities) were not inclined to oppose their sons' and daughters' anti-Japanese activities. Only when the students' nationalism drew them toward the Communists did parental disapproval become more serious.

In any event, not until the later stage of the movement did large numbers of students move decisively toward the left. Their early demands for civil liberties and national resistance were addressed to the national government. Spokesmen invariably made it clear that they would whole-heartedly support Chiang if he led them against the foe. After the outbreak of war, most of them were as good as their word. Of course the students in our highly selective group eventually reached radical conclusions and most of their parents probably reacted accordingly. As Olga Lang observed:

Once these young people adopted radical ideas, which usually happened during their college years or in the higher grades of high school, their relations to their families changed. Their views encountered strong opposition from their parents because the young people advocated a new political and economic system which threatened the privileged position of the father. Furthermore, the whole ideology of Communism was a flagrant contradiction of the old Chinese tradition.[11]

However, to parents seeing sons and daughters off to college in September 1935, nothing would have seemed more ridiculous than the suggestion that these children would soon be in the ranks of the Red Army. That many would before long lie buried side by side with simple peasants in remote parts of China was unthinkably absurd. In September 1935 scarcely anybody knew where the Red Army was. So far as one could tell, it had disappeared into the wilds of western China, harried into oblivion by the forces of Chiang Kai-shek. Why should solid citizens of Shanghai, Foochow, and Canton worry about the "Red bandits"? Had they known that the CCP's leaders had survived the Long March, they could not have cared less. Shensi was far away. Had they heard of the August 1 proclamation in which the Communists called for a national united front against the Japanese, they would have dismissed it as blatant propaganda.

Nothing suggested the advent of an unusual session on campus. For several years there had been concern over intellectual unemployment: college graduates were unable to secure positions commensurate with their qualifications. But for graduates of prestigious Peiping institutions with excellent family connections, the future seemed reasonably secure. It seemed as if students and teachers alike had taken to heart Tsinghua Chancellor Mei I-ch'i's exhortation at the opening exercises of the previous school year:

As we meet today we must bear in mind that tomorrow is September 18. Three years ago tomorrow began a period of gravest crisis for our nation. Last year I said that I didn't know when you would stop your study and work because of outside agitation. Happily a year has passed in peace without incident, but from this year on you must still bear this thought in mind if you are to be able to put everything you have into your studies. This is not an attempt on my part to frighten you; it is the hard truth. My generation of intellectuals occupies a posi-

[11]*Ibid.*, p. 320

tion of leadership. We have no way of knowing what may happen to make us lose our heads and panic, despite our intentions. Therefore, we must all knuckle down to work and apply ourselves with all our might to study, preparing for the day when we can wipe clean our nation's shame . . .[12]

Mei obviously assumed that "saving the nation by study" had not lost its persuasive power—and who could prove him wrong? Close observers, however, might have noticed a widening gulf between the beliefs of the May 4th generation, which dominated the ranks of teachers and administrators, and the credo of the young. The former clung to Western models in education and other realms of national life and retained faith in the efficacy of gradualism. The latter saw a need for national self-reliance, recognized a necessity for mobilizing the rural masses, and regarded revolution as essential.[13] But radical student values had yet to be translated into action.

No shocking headlines about campus unrest had disturbed parents of China's students during the previous academic year. Radical student leaders who had stormed the bastions of Nanking in 1931 had graduated or disappeared. The last three years had been peaceful and 1934–35 had been the quietest year in a decade.

Yang Hsueh-ch'eng, a freshman at Tsinghua, resembled anything but the fiery patriot who a decade later would fall exhausted from political battles and succumb to the ravages of disease. His classmate Chiang Nan-hsiang recalled in later years:

At first he was very studious, and was not at all interested in politics. Nearly every day, he could be seen books tucked under his arm, arriving at the library to diligently study and look up reference material. He

[12]Paraphrased in the *Ta-kung pao (l'Impartial)* (Tientsin), September 18, 1934. Cited in Chü Hao-jan, "Chi Shih" (Class history), in Chü Hao-jan, ed., *Ch'ing-hua shih-chi pi-yeh san-shih nien chi-nien t'e-k'an* [Special thirtieth anniversary volume of Tsinghua's tenth graduating class] (Taipei, n.p., 1968), p. 9.

[13]West, "Yenching University," p. 429, makes this point in regard to Yenching. It also applies to Peking University, Tsinghua, and other institutions. China College, where the faculty may have been more radical than the students, was a possible exception.

was very quiet and reserved, attracted little attention, and seldom participated in extra-curricular activities. He was considered a careful, ideal student of the "orthodox" type.[14]

If young Yang had any unorthodox ideas, he wisely kept them to himself. (Classmates who organized a Modern Lecture Society were arrested following a police raid that also struck neighboring Yenching).[15] During the summer of 1934, Yang spent a great deal of time at the swimming pool. But, "by the summer of 1935," noted Chiang Nan-hsiang, "a change had come over him, and he was often in the reading-rooms avidly reading the contents of the daily newspapers."

Yang's newly-found interest in national affairs arose from a situation that Peiping's students could scarcely ignore. Japanese expansion southward and westward across the Asian continent had proceeded spasmodically. After the conquest of Manchuria in 1931, and again after the thrust south of the Great Wall in 1933, there had been a pause. Each time the Nanking government had acquiesced to further losses of territory, sovereignty, and national pride. Now once more, in the summer of 1935, aggressive elements of the Japanese military were on the move, this time in the heartland of North China. Still unprepared to resist, Chiang Kai-shek sent Minister of War Ho Ying-ch'in to buy more time. The price was the Ho-Umetsu agreement of July 6, 1935: withdrawal of Nationalist political and military forces from the Peiping-Tientsin region and suppression of anti-Japanese activities.

The Ho-Umetsu accord left a political and military vacuum in North China. To fill it, Japanese expansionists conjured up a "North China Autonomy Movement" under which five provinces—Shantung, Hopei, Shansi, Suiyuan, and Chahar—would be placed under a puppet regime. "Spontaneous" proautonomy demonstrations were staged, and conspicuous troop movements and low-flying bombers suggested that

---

[14]*RON*, p. 147. *See*, List of Abbreviations.

[15]*Yen-ching hsin-wen* (Yenching news), March 19, 1935.

Chinese cooperation was imperative. The only Chinese military force in the area was the 29th Army under General Sung Che-yuan, a former subordinate of warlord Feng Yü-hsiang. Sung had no desire to surrender his independence—to Japan or Nanking—but he was unprepared to stand alone against the armed might of Japan. By late October, it appeared that North China might soon become another Manchukuo with the sacred old city of Peiping as its capital.

WHY YENCHING?

"All Yenching Graduates are Communists."
—JAPANESE POLICEMAN, 1937

National Peking University (Peita) was nationally recognized as the fountainhead of the modern Chinese student movement. China's first modern national university, famed for the quality of its faculty and students, Peita was the birthplace of the New Culture, initiator of the May 4th movement, source of the radical current in the 1931 crusade to Nanking. Peita undoubtedly would be in the center of anything that happened in the student world.

A less likely source of political initiative was Yenching University, a mission school overseen by a New York board. Set in a tastefully landscaped campus graced by stone lions and tree-lined pools, Yenching was reputed to offer a "palatial education" for "aristocrats."[16] High tuition and Christian tradition reinforced the image of an academic playground for the hedonistic, English-speaking scions of South China's treaty-port bourgeoisie and wealthy emigré businessmen. For anxious parents Yenching offered security from the "alleged moral laxity and political radicalism" of the government universities.[17]

---

[16]Hsu Pao-ch'ien, "Erh-shih nien lai hsin-tao ching-yen tzu-shu" [My twenty years' religious experience], *Chen-li yü sheng-ming* [Truth and life] 1, no. 4 (June 1934): 183, quoted in West, "Yenching University," p. 369.

[17]West, "Yenching University," p. 377.

Although four applicants were turned away for every one admitted,[18] its students were, in fact, drawn disproportionately from a select group of mission-operated high schools and were scarcely of the same quality as the select survivors of Peita's highly competitive entrance examinations. In spite of some first-rate teachers, Yenching's faculty was uneven and underrated.

By 1935, however, Peita had lost its political vitality. As a government school situated inside Peiping's city walls, it easily succumbed to pressures of local and national authorities. Though maintaining its reputation for scholarly excellence, Peita, in the firm hands of Chancellor Chiang Monlin, had become a political backwater. Gone were the excited and dissonant voices of the New Culture period, gone the brave banners of radical protest. This time the political initiative would have to come from elsewhere.

That Yenching helped to fill the vacuum left by Peita obviously requires some explanation. If for no other reason, Yenching might have been disqualified for such a role by its Christian origins. Only a decade earlier, missionary schools had been targets of an anti-Christian movement supported by both the Kuomintang and the Communists. After Chiang Kai-shek's alliance-by-marriage to the Methodist Soong family, the breach between the KMT and the Christian community had closed. So much less reason, it would seem, for radical activists to congregate at a place like Yenching. Nonetheless, the fact remains that Yenching played a key role in the December 9th movement. Some of the reasons are succinctly set forth by Jessie G. Lutz:[19]

1. *Yenching's sense of separation and its efforts to compensate for this by*

[18]Figures for 1936 were 295 accepted out of 1,487 applicants. Of those accepted, 64 percent had been graduated from Christian and other "accredited" private schools and 13 percent from government schools. West, "Yenching University," p. 381.

[19]Jessie G. Lutz, "December 9, 1935: Student Nationalism and the China Christian Colleges," *Journal of Asian Studies* 26, no. 4 (August 1967): 632–37. Paraphrased except where quotation marks indicate otherwise.

assertions of national identity. Yenching was separated from Peiping not only physically (the campus was 5 miles northwest of the city walls) but by "the missionary origin, the foreign support, the large number of Western teachers, and the heavy dependence on English." Furthermore, college administrators had striven "to build a cohesive campus community in the tradition of church-related colleges in the United States." Since 1925 a movement toward acclimation to the Chinese environment had resulted in a stridently nationalistic attitude as if to deny the university's sense of separateness.

2. *Semiextraterritorial status,* which gave Yenching a certain degree of legal and political immunity.

3. *The affluent urban commercial background of Yenching's students.* "It was urban China which felt the threat of Japan most keenly, and it was the business community which had been hurt by the flow of Japanese goods into north China via Manchuria."

4. *Because of moral constraints upon the government and the influential family connections of the students, demonstrations could be held with some degree of impunity.*

5. *"Yenching students had been made conscious of their Chineseness* by their frequent contact with Westerners and Western learning, by their subordination to Western administrators, and by their apparent status as protégés of Christianity."

6. *Unlike most other institutions, the "Christian college students had a functioning student government to channel nationalistic fervor."*

7. *Yenching students enjoyed the sympathy of their college administration.*

8. *The admission of a number of Manchurian refugee students,* whose ardent nationalism fed the fires of the December 9 outburst.

9. *Yenching's school of journalism* conveyed to its students the Western tradition of a free press, made them aware of the power of the press, taught them modern techniques of publicity, and placed them in contact with a number of sympathetic Western correspondents.

"It is no coincidence," writes Lutz, "that several of the initiators of the December 9 demonstration were simultaneously

Tungpei (Manchurian) refugees, journalism majors, leaders in Yenching's student government, and staff members of the student newspaper."[20] Nor is it coincidence that nearly all activists whose academic majors are known were enrolled in journalism and other "soft" disciplines rather than in "hard" scientific and highly technical professional school programs. Early in the movement, at least five junior premedical students at Yenching transferred to history and journalism so that they would have more time to devote to radical political activities.[21]

Not only were these disciplines less rigorous and time-consuming, but exposure to them—in those days before the social sciences were captured by the positivists and absolute relativists—helped students to develop an acute awareness of social injustice. The Chinese had never viewed the social sciences and humanities as "value-free" disciplines. History, traditionally, was a "mirror for viewing the present in light of the past." The most esteemed literature was frankly didactic, and even ancient poetry such as the *Book of Odes* was valued largely for its veiled moral messages. In modern times, Chinese continued to find instrumental moral values in liberal education. Treaty-port professionals might master medicine, law, or accounting for careerist purposes, but history, sociology, and political science were seen as instruments for ethical and social change. John Dewey's disciplines, like the followers of Marx and Lenin, believed in the social value of learning. For students of the humanities and social sciences, all approaches—traditional, liberal, and radical—led to a critical analysis of man and society. From such disciples came the leaders of the December 9th movement.

Yenching was a bastion of American liberalism. It was scarcely accidental, then, that the December 9th movement started with a civil libertarian orientation. The first student broadside, drafted at Yenching, decried governmental suppres-

---

[20]*Ibid.*, p. 637.

[21]Li Min to Edgar and Helen F. Snow, undated, in *NCSM*, p. 148.

sion of free speech and publication. The later shift in leadership from Yenching to government schools coincided with the change in emphasis from civil liberties to the substance of foreign policy.

What, if any, impact did Christian doctrine have on student politics at Yenching? Helen F. Snow, who was especially close to several YWCA people at Yenching, was impressed by "the tremendously progressive influence of the YWCA and other Christian institutions and schools on the women's movement in China." Writing in 1939, she observed

that even today a majority of the revolutionary and progressive students, both boys and girls, were influenced by Christian idealism at one time or another—though it is fashionable now to deny it. However, it was the philosophical and ethical nature of Christianity, rather than its purely religious side, that interested these young Chinese. And most of those who were really influenced by Christian thought, like those who joined the Communists, originally had humanitarian instincts and a sense of justice for the oppressed. In its early influence, Christianity, especially Protestantism, was a very revolutionary concept in China.[22]

Mrs. Snow overstated the case. Only a minority of December 9 leaders were from Yenching or other Christian institutions. Furthermore, only a minority of Yenching students were Christian. In 1931, Christian students constituted 39.8 percent of Yenching's men and 58.3 percent of its coeds—45.1 percent of the entire student body.[23] By 1935, this figure had dropped to less than 32 percent.[24] Even these students are described as being "of Christian affiliation" or "with a Christian background," suggesting that many of them may have been Christians by virtue of family or education rather than conviction or practice. Most of Yenching's practicing Christian students were mem-

[22]Nym Wales [Helen F. Snow], *Inside Red China* (New York: Doubleday, 1939), p. 171.

[23]Dwight W. Edwards, *Yenching University* (New York: United Board for Christian Higher Education in Asia, 1959), p. 317.

[24]West, "Yenching University," p. 412.

bers of the Christian Fellowship, numbering about 30 percent of the enrollment.[25]

Christian students by no means dominated the December 9th movement. Only at Yenching is correlation between Christianity and politics evident, and there the record is ambiguous. A coed who had acted as a secret agent for the police reportedly did so "out of Christian conviction," and a left-wing Yenching activist charged that most of the school's "reactionary students" were Christian.[26] On the other hand, a number of left-wing students had Christian affiliations. Of the ten Yenching leaders about whom we have relevant information (most of it thanks to Mrs. Snow), two of the five men and four of the five girls came from Christian homes or had been educated in Christian secondary schools. The only ones known to have been active in Christian affairs after they entered college, however, were two girls later associated with the YMCA.

The transition from Christianity to Communism was facilitated by at least a few Yenching faculty members. On a recent visit to Peking, one former Yenching teacher was reminded by a December 9er, now prominent in the government, that he had introduced her and others to the *Communist Manifesto* and various writings on Russia. Though his purpose had been simply to acquaint students with diverse schools of contemporary thought, his liberal pedagogy had bred radical results.[27]

By the mid-1930s, many Chinese Christians were trying to come to terms with Marxism. It appears that Christians who were attracted to communism found their place in the liberal, social action wing of the Chinese Christian movement, centering in the YMCA and YWCA. In seeking national salvation they, like YMCA leaders Wu Yao-tsung and Chiang Wen-han, agonized over the challenge that revolutionary Marxism posed

[25]Edwards, *Yenching University*, p. 333.

[26]Han Suyin, *A Mortal Flower* (New York: Putnam, 1965), p. 369; Li Min to Edgar and Helen F. Snow, *NCSM*, p. 148.

[27]Former Yenching professor, letter to John Israel, September 15, 1974.

to Christian reformism. With varying degrees of reluctance, they accepted atheism and materialism and finally embraced the Communist movement as the only viable means of express- ing humanitarian aspirations while disavowing the imperialist tradition that tainted even the most liberal wing of the Chinese churches. As Yenching alumnus Tan Leeton later explained to Han Suyin:

I was a member of the Christian Fellowship, looking to God for China's salvation, and finding God deaf. Like scores of Yenching's Christian students, I ended by turning to the Red Army, and it did what God had not done. After that I was still a Christian, but I felt that God only helps those who help themselves.[28]

The fact that the December 9th movement started at Yenching and that most of its early leaders entered the Com- munist fold should not, then, mislead us into sweeping con- clusions about the philosophical affinity between Christianity and Marxism. Nonetheless, these young Chinese contributed significantly to the Christian-Marxist dialogue that began in the 1920s and continued into the 1950s.

[28]Han Suyin, *Mortal Flower*, p. 369.

II

Faces in the Crowd

"In the beginning," wrote a December 9 veteran, "there were no more than a few dozen students who positively participated in the work of national salvation."[1] In fact, the chain of events leading to the historic demonstration of December 9 was precipitated by an anonymous Tsinghua University student identified in the record by the initial "R."

One October day "R" visited some friends at nearby Yenching University. Something had to be done, he said, to protest the Nanking government's suppression of civil liberties. His friends agreed: at this critical juncture in the nation's history the Japanese could sever North China from the rest of the country while the voices of patriotism were gagged.[2]

YENCHING

The response was unanimous: Draft a resolution! The issuance of a manifesto—the classical milksop tactic of cautious academics—was a daring proposal in the repressive atmosphere

[1] Yuan I, "Shih-erh chiu i-lai chih yen-yuan" [The Yenching campus since December 9], in *SECCNCNTK*, p. 17.

[2] X.A.N. (pseud.), "Shih-erh chiu hui-i-lu" [Reminiscences of December 9th], in *Ibid.*, p. 2.

of 1935 Peiping. The manifesto was drafted by a young man named Wang Ju-mei, of whom we shall hear more. To convey Wang's ideas in the most forceful and disciplined manner the students then chose Kao Ming-k'ai.[3] Kao was a twenty-two-year-old junior from Pingtan, a seaside town in Fukien, a province that produced many Yenching students. After graduating from Foochow High School ("Anglo-American College"), he entered Yenching in the fall of 1933 and concentrated on philosophy and French literature. He later studied in France and was a classical scholar until his death in 1965. Noted for his literary virtuosity and known to have liberal sympathies, Kao was too unassuming and scholarly to take the initiative. Yet his schoolmates realized that their ideas would have maximal impact if expressed in Kao's incisive prose. The ancient and highly prized virtue of recognizing and utilizing "human talent" had evidently survived among these latter-day literati. Kao's broadside expressed the wrath of his schoolmates with an elegance that, unfortunately, is lost in translation:

After the establishment of the government at Nanking, according to newspaper reports, the number of youths slaughtered totaled no less than three hundred thousand and the number of those who have disappeared and been imprisoned cannot even be estimated. Killing was not enough, they were buried alive; imprisonment was not enough, they were even subjected to torture; hell itself has been brought to humanity![4]

Kao's resolution asked the ruling party to respect "the rights of free speech, press, assembly, and association" and to halt "illegal arrests of students." Approved by a student assembly and endorsed by a handful of other schools, the document was

---

[3]Kao Ming-k'ai has heretofore been given credit for authorship of the manifesto. See *Ibid*. However, in an interview in New York on March 28, 1972, Helen Snow revealed that Wang Ju-mei (alias Huang Hua) had written the original draft, which was then "polished" by Kao. Mrs. Snow's source of information is a well-informed December 9er who chooses to remain anonymous.

[4]*NCSM*, pp. 13–14.

sent off to the KMT plenum then in session.

Chang Chao-lin

The same meeting elected a new student body president, Chang Chao-lin. Chang was the obvious candidate for the position. Tall, handsome, outgoing, and good-natured, he was extremely popular, especially among coeds. He was a born leader, possessing intellectual and physical courage.[5] In addition, Chang had one other important attribute: he was from Manchuria. A photograph by Helen Snow confirms a friend's description of his "broad, honest, typically Northeastern face."[6] Having fled his homeland during Japan's 1931 invasion, Chang was not one to look on with folded hands while North China was absorbed into the realm of the Rising Sun.

But Chang Chao-lin was as confused as he was angry. As a journalism student, he felt especially frustrated because the Chinese press, censored of anti-Japanese sentiments, provided not the slightest clue to the fate of North China. What were the facts behind persistent rumors that Sung Che-yuan was about to give in to Japanese intimidation? Only foreigners, Chang surmised, could have access to the facts. This line of thinking brought him to the door of his journalism teacher, Edgar Snow.

Edgar Snow was a twenty-nine-year-old free-lance writer and part-time lecturer at Yenching. His wife, Helen, was a writer and part-time student. To these sympathetic young Americans Chang Chao-lin bared his soul. Edgar Snow confirmed the rumor: Sung Che-yuan was indeed ready to capitulate. Chang wept.

In Chang's footsteps came a steady stream of young visitors. Their anxious voices filled the Snow house during the twilight afternoons of late autumn. As left-liberals reacting to the international scene of the mid-1930s, the Snows saw a world threatened by fascism. In China, this menace took the form of

⁵*Ibid.*, p. 1.
⁶James Bertram, *First Act in China* (New York: Viking, 1938), p. 167.

an internally repressive but externally pusillanimous Kuomintang regime capitulating to the demands of aggressive Japanese militarism. Yet the Snows, no doctrinaire ideologues, were groping toward their own world views. Helen Snow drew upon the liberal Protestantism of her New England heritage and her still recent experience as a high school student leader. Her husband's sympathetic identity with the students was tempered by the newsman's professional skepticism. Between them, the young couple helped the Yenching students sift through ideas and grope toward a solution.

Huang Hua

Among this group of gilded Yenching youths, one burdened by poverty was destined to rise higher than most of his affluent schoolmates. Then known as Wang Ju-mei, he has since gained fame as the distinguished diplomat, Huang Hua. A native Hopei senior majoring in economics, Huang was chairman of the Executive Committee of the Yenching Student Council. He "spoke in a slow, quiet, deep voice" but "flushed easily," recalls Helen Snow.[7] Though less extroverted than Chang Chao-lin, he was highly effective in behind-the-scenes operations. Mrs. Snow remembers him as a "proud, moody, self-possessed boy, with sad and serious eyes . . ., reserved in comparison with the other leaders, who tended to be friendly and affectionate."[8] Yet when Edgar Snow was gathering material in Communist territory and needed an interpreter with "discretion, courage, and intelligence," his wife unhesitatingly chose Huang Hua.[9]

On December 6, 1935, Huang Hua's article, "The Present State of the Chinese Fascist Movement," appeared in a special "fascism" issue of the *Yen-ta chou-k'an* (Yenching weekly).[10] Here

---

[7] *NCSM*, p. 112. Information on Huang's native province, heretofore in doubt, has been supplied by an anonymous December 9er. See Chapter 2, note 3, above.

[8] *NCSM*, p. 60.

[9] *Ibid.*

[10] Huang Hua, "Chung-kuo fa-hsi-ssu yun-tung hsien-chuang" [The pres-

we find a theoretical basis for the bitterness against Kuomintang repression that Huang had expressed in the manifesto to the KMT plenum. The article demonstrates that Huang had learned quite early to analyze large social phenomena in terms of Marxist-Leninist categories. Although Huang did not join the Communist movement until early 1936,[11] he shared the penchant for Marxist analysis so common among avant-garde Chinese intellectuals of that time. Huang argued that Chiang Kai-shek was trying to develop a fascist state in the Hitler-Mussolini image and predicted his failure: "Aside from squeezing out the last few drops of national territory and the lives of four hundred million people to give to the imperialists, Chinese fascism has no future," he wrote. "It lacks a mass base; its structure is extremely unstable; its political and economic contradictions deny it any possibility of development."[12] Unable to free itself from imperialist, capitalist, and warlord masters, he continued, Chinese fascism would disintegrate under pressure from the revolutionary movement of peasants and workers and the nearly universal demand for resistance against Japan. Huang's conclusion called for a "heroic struggle for our own salvation."[13] Three days later, he and fellow students carried their demands to the streets.

Recent observers bear witness to Huang Hua's many-sided personality. Western diplomats regard him as a "tough negotiator" but have found him on occasion "affable and an interesting conversationalist . . . well-versed in a number of non-political topics" including American toys and games.[14] Helen Snow notes that Huang was the only member of the Yenching

---

ent state of the Chinese fascist movement], *YTCK* 6, no. 9 (December 6, 1935): 12–14.

[11] Information provided by an anonymous December 9er. See Chapter 2, note 3, above.

[12] Huang Hua, "Chung-kuo fa-hsi-ssu yun-tung hsien-chuang," p. 14.

[13] *Ibid.*

[14] Donald W. Klein and Anne B. Clark, *Biographic Dictionary of Chinese Com-*

coterie to display any antiforeignism. In 1949, however, this did not prevent him from deftly handling Chinese Communist relations with his former college president, American Ambassador John Leighton Stuart.[15] In 1956, James Bertram found it possible to discuss foreign policy with Huang in a way that was impossible with members of the post-Liberation generation. "I knew he spoke as a disciplined and trusted Party member," Bertram observed, "but he did not talk Party jargon, and he was aware of my own point of view."[16] The secret of Huang's success, declares a Kuomintang writer, is that he combines the qualities of the doctrinaire Communists who lack rapport with Westerners and those of the "intellectual-type diplomats" who can establish rapport but lack impeccable Party credentials.[17] Another KMT source describes him as "sincere and forthright" in appearance but "extremely narrow-minded and prejudiced, selfish and self-seeking, the very model of a member of the petit bourgeois class."[18] Yet even this hostile account pays tribute to his organizational and agitational skills.

Huang is unquestionably a man of many talents and varying moods. Perhaps the background of poverty that made him wary and defensive in the Yenching environment sharpened his wits and enabled him to make the most of opportunities. Huang was the first of the Yenching students to meet Mao Tse-tung and other high-ranking Communists. Yet, when Helen Snow saw him in Yenan in May 1937, she discovered that he and his chum Ch'en Han-po "had taken on the airs of mandarins."[19] But in

---

munism, 1921–1965 (Cambridge, Mass.: Harvard University Press, 1971), 1:395.

[15]John Leighton Stuart, *Fifty Years in China* (New York: Random House, 1954), pp. 248–58.

[16]James Bertram, *Return to China* (London: Heinemann, 1957), p. 121.

[17]L. Chen, "Peiping to U.S. via Huang Hua," *Free China Weekly* 12, no. 34 (August 29, 1971): 2.

[18]*CKJML,* p. 488.

[19]*NCSM,* p. 78.

September 1939, Edgar Snow found him "greatly matured . . . a man of quiet self-confidence," though "full of duties."[20] These contrasting assessments may reflect the divergent values and personalities of the two Snows, or it may mean that two years as a "mandarin" had enabled Huang to play the role more smoothly.

In any case, Edgar Snow's description of Huang is remarkably similar to James Bertram's comments on Chang Chao-lin, whom he too had known in Peiping:

Meeting him again in Sian (in December 1936) I was struck once more by the sudden maturity that the Chinese often show when they exchange the rather sentimental atmosphere of college life for a responsible position. Chang had always been a responsible person, but almost overnight he had become a very serious man of affairs.[21]

We must bear in mind that the life of Peiping student activists was not a frivolous one and thus should not exaggerate the changes that occurred in moving on to responsible adult roles. The transition from Peiping to Yenan was not a matter of playful collegians suddenly become somber bureaucratic paperpushers. The December 9th movement had served as a political apprenticeship for the heavy duties that these young men and women would soon have to shoulder.

From the late 1930s to the late 1940s, little more was heard of Huang Hua and Chang Chao-lin, but it is obvious that Huang was advancing in a way that Chang was not. We know that Huang worked under Communist luminaries Chu Te, Chou En-lai, and Yeh Chien-ying during and after the war. During the Marshall Mission of 1946–47, an Executive Headquarters was established in Peiping to bring about a nationwide ceasefire. Within each organ under the Executive Headquarters were representatives from the American, Nationalist, and Communist sides. Huang was assigned the task of setting up the

[20]Edgar Snow, *The Battle for Asia* (New York: Random House, 1942), p. 282.

[21]Bertram, *First Act*, p. 167.

press unit for the Communist side. In 1949, while Chang Chao-lin was no more than a petty functionary in the Information Department of the Ministry of Foreign Affairs Huang negotiated with the American ambassador. Huang has since risen to the top while Chang, since the early 1960s, has labored in obscurity in the field of education. He currently teaches at Kirin University in Changchun. Huang led China's negotiating team to Panmunjom in 1953 and played an important role at the Geneva Conference in 1954. In 1960, he became ambassador to Ghana, which was then China's major diplomatic base in West Africa. Indicative of Huang's strong personal position is the fact that he remained at his post in Cairo during the Cultural Revolution, the only Chinese ambassador who was not summoned home. After diplomatic relations between Peking and Ottawa were established in October 1970, Huang was named ambassador to Canada (July 1971). But soon afterward, following the seating of the P.R.C. in the United Nations, Huang was transferred to New York to assume his new post as Peking's first permanent representative to the Security Council (November 1971).

Ch'en Han-po

While Huang Hua pursued his diplomatic career in Accra and Cairo, his former classmate Ch'en Han-po served on the council of the Asia-Africa Society of China. It is quite possible that Huang had recommended Ch'en for the position. The two friends had much in common. Prior to the December 9th movement, Ch'en, Huang, and Chang Chao-lin, among others, had belonged to a youth group sponsored by Young Marshal Chang Hsueh-liang, then under the influence of Italian fascism. The group was later taken over from within by the left.[22] Ch'en shared Huang's taciturn qualities. As editor of the school weekly collecting material for an article on fascism, he appeared at

[22] *NCSM*, p. 2, and information from an anonymous December 9er. See Chapter 2, note 3, above.

the Snows' house, a bespectacled intellectual, "skeptical, cool and critical, dignified rather than outgoing like Chang Chaolin."[23] Both he and Huang scornfully rejected the idea of a public demonstration when it was first suggested by Helen Snow. Huang doubted that a demonstration would ever get into the streets; the students would simply be arrested and labeled Communists.[24] Ch'en was "completely defeatist and pessimistic": aside from a few students from Manchuria, nobody else would lift a finger. When he left, Helen Snow reports, "he was so sensible that I felt like a scatterbrain with such a wild idea."[25]

Ch'en's cool intelligence has served him well in his career as journalist and propagandist. Like many young Chinese, he moved around a good deal during the early war years. In June 1938 he was reported unemployed in Kiangsu; in March 1939 he was said to be in Chengtu.[26] He next appeared after V-J Day as editor of a prominent Shanghai publication.[27] In 1949, when the new government was formed, he was giving a course at the Yenching School of Journalism and was deputy director of the Peking Press School under the national government.

December 9 and Women's Lib

The December 9th movement was, among other things, a chapter in the liberation of Chinese women. Having been released from the ties of bound feet and admitted to coeducational colleges, many of these modern girls became leaders in the struggle for social and political reform. A Yenching Discussion Group on Women's Problems met at least four times before December 9 and was sometimes joined by members of a sister society at Tsinghua. At one such gathering, reports were presented on the status of women in five kinds of society—feudal,

<hr>

[23]*NCSM*, p. 2.

[24]Edgar Snow, *Journey to the Beginning* (New York: Random House, 1958), p. 142.

[25]*NCSM*, p. 3.

[26]*Ibid.*, pp. 198–99.

[27]*Ibid.*, p. 78.

semifeudal and semicolonial (China), capitalist, fascist, and socialist. Discussants concluded that "only under socialism could the life of women be most rational and ideal" and agreed that "we women who have received a higher education bear the responsibility of promoting the new society."[28]

From the very outset of the December 9th movement women were prominent. Three of the ten signatories of Kao Ming-k'ai's manifesto were girls' middle schools; a fourth was a women's normal college. Four of the nine institutions active in the inaugural meeting of the reconstituted Peiping Student Union were girls' schools.

Kuo Ming-ch'iu

The union's most important female leader was eighteen-year-old Kuo Ming-ch'iu of the prestigious First Girls' Middle School. Kuo presided over the resurrection of the long-defunct organization and served as its first chairman. Her charismatic personality and penetrating speeches left audiences spellbound.[29] She was regarded by fellow students as "a theoretical giant."[30] Kuo was not known to be a Communist at that time, but by April 1936 she and her future husband, Lin Feng, were considered the ablest lieutenants in Peiping of Liu Shao-ch'i, head of the CCP's newly-reestablished Tientsin-based North China Bureau. Liu reportedly found Kuo "clever, able, and very useful to the revolution" and, incidentally, politically stronger than Lin.[31] Her father, presumably less impressed with her political and intellectual acumen, was said to have placed her in

---

[28]Li Min, "Nü-sheng wen-t'i t'ao-lun hui pao-kao," [Report on the discussion group on women's problems], *YTCK* 6, no. 9 (December 6, 1935): 44–45. See also the report of the group's subcommittee on Chinese women, "Pan-feng-chien pan-chih-min-ti ti Chung-kuo fu-nü" [The semi-feudal, semi-colonial Chinese woman], *ibid.,* pp. 46–48.

[29]X.A.N., "Shih-erh chiu hui-i-lu," pp. 10–11.

[30]*NCSM,* p. 27.

[31]"A Chronicle of Events in the Life of Liu Shao-ch'i (1899–1967)," *Current Background,* no. 834 (August 17, 1967), p. 4.

confinement after the December 9 demonstration.[32] This may explain why a Yenching student activist who greatly admired Kuo saw little of her after the early days of the movement.[33]

Li Min

At Yenching, a remarkable circle of coeds gathered around warm and sympathetic Helen Snow. Closest to Mrs. Snow was Li Min, Secretary of the Student Council's Supervisory Committee and of the Discussion Group on Women's Problems. "Small, quiet, loyal, . . . very affectionate and lovable," Li seemed to exemplify the best of Confucian virtues.[34] Her father had been a progressive official of the late Ch'ing dynasty and an admirer of the reformer Liang Ch'i-ch'ao. His death reduced the family to poverty. With the aid of scholarships, Li Min managed to get through the missionary-run True Light Middle School in Canton and to enter Yenching in 1933.

Reverent toward her father's memory, totally devoted to her friends, relating with ease to people of alien cultures, Li Min might, under other circumstances, have been enrolled in the traditional annals of virtuous women if not in the roster of Christian saints. But at Yenching University in 1935, these qualities of loyalty and dedication drew her toward the left. "She was ready to fight physically for Chang Chao-lin and Wang Ju-mei," reports Helen Snow, a contention born out by Li Min's own testimony (somewhat out of line with her beatific characteristics) that she "almost wanted to smash the face of a Christian girl who sat by me and called [Chang Chao-lin] 'dictator' and 'stupid.' "[35] The salient word is "almost."

Li Min was moved by human suffering and injustice, recalling Agnes Smedley's autobiography as "a landmark" in her thinking. As a passionate admirer of Franklin D. Roosevelt, Li

[32]*NCSM*, p. 27.

[33]X.A.N., "Shih-erh chiu hui-i-lu," p. 10.

[34]*NCSM*, p. 3.

[35]*Ibid.*, pp. 77, 148.

later disseminated the ideas of the Atlantic Charter and the Four Freedoms during her career as a teacher. "I never taught Marxism as I did not know it," she wrote. "Nevertheless, my husband [Yeh Te-Kuang] and I were arrested on June 1, 1947, in Chungking on the campus with another six of the faculty members and 23 students on the charge of being Communists." Having experienced wartime and postwar China as "a mere struggle for a living and the fear of getting killed without ever being able to see a real democratic China,"[36] Li Min remained on the mainland after 1949. In 1958, she was a member of the Executive Committee of the Kiangsu Women's Federation.

Kung P'u-sheng and Kung P'eng

The best-known of Helen Snow's circle of coeds are the Kung sisters, P'u-sheng and P'eng. They came from a prominent Christian family in Hofei, Anhwei Province. P'u-sheng was born in Shanghai on September 6, 1913; her sister in 1914. Their father, a Nationalist Army officer, sent the girls to St. Mary's (Episcopal) School in Shanghai. Here, as in other cases, we find fundamental differences between generations unaccompanied by any sign of rebellion or hostility. Though disagreeing with his daughters' ideas, Kung was proud of his girls and did nothing to interfere with their careers. The sisters were also very close to each other and observed the amenities of family loyalty even though they followed rather different paths.[37]

P'u-sheng entered Yenching in the fall of 1932 and P'eng (then known as Wei-hang) the following year. P'u-sheng, a sociology major, was active in the Christian Fellowship and subsequently in the YWCA, an organization that attracted many dedicated young social reformers from the modern urban elite. Embracing both Christian universalism and Chinese nationalism and prepared to channel humanitarian concerns into radical politics, P'u-sheng personified new forces at work on the

[36] *Ibid.*, p. 4.
[37] *Ibid.*, pp. 5, 77.

Yenching scene. Typical was her appearance as chairwoman of the International Women's Day celebration on March 8, 1936. While an older speaker extolled the virtues of a pleasant family life and healthy children, Kung's comments, according to a participant's notes, stressed nationalism and social change and related these to the status of women:

The chairman said we wanted to save the nation and mankind from war and China from degradation and Fascist suppression; our half of the world must save the world from this. She told about the China [*sic*] movement and said at present the universities and progressives must spread their influence to the whole country; that the status of women could only be solved as part of the national problem; it is not psychological but bound up with the whole system.[38]

P'u-sheng served as vice-president of the Yenching student body whose president was her boy friend, Chang Chao-lin. After graduation, she continued her career in China and the United States in international "Y" activities. In September 1937, two months after the outbreak of war, she was appointed co-executive secretary of the Shanghai Student Relief Committee, which provided funds, jobs, and shelter to young people fleeing the Japanese invader. Subsequently, as YWCA national student secretary, she worked among Kunming's wartime student refugees. After conducting a survey to determine their subsistence needs, she wrote an article describing self-help projects sponsored by the YWCA.[39]

In September 1941, P'u-sheng was admitted to Union Theological Seminary in New York. In her master's essay, "Student Christian Movement in Wartime China, 1937–1941," she told of the movement's struggle against official suppression of civil liberties and excoriated "the Fascist tendency of [the KMT] party machine which controls the Chinese govern-

---

[38] *Ibid.*, p. 181.

[39] "Kunming Students Meet Hard Times with Self-Aid Projects; Group Blazes Way in 'Hit' Stage Show," *CWR* 95, no. 3 (December 21, 1940): 98. Kiang Wen-han, "Emergency Student Relief in China" (Manuscript, Changsha, January 18, 1938; YMCA Archives, New York), p. 3.

ment."[40] During the summer of 1942 she studied religion in Columbia University's School of General Studies. She went back to China but returned to the United States soon after V-J Day—against the wishes of the YWCA, which wanted her to continue working in China. On September 29, 1945, she was readmitted to the School of General Studies as a special student but withdrew before the end of the semester after registering for a course on professional writing. From 1946 to 1948 she worked at Lake Success as a researcher with the U.N. Human Rights Commission. She returned again to China in 1949.[41]

In July 1949, P'u-sheng married Chang Han-fu. Like Kung P'eng and her husband Ch'iao Kuan-hua, Chang was part of Chou En-lai's English-speaking press coterie in wartime Chungking. With Chou as Foreign Minister, the foursome pursued diplomatic careers. Chang eventually became a vice-minister of Foreign Affairs. P'u-sheng served on Peking's special mission to the U.N. Security Council during the Korean crisis of 1950 and has since been active in the Chinese Red Cross, the National Women's Federation, the Sino-Indian Friendship Association, and the Chinese People's Institute of Foreign Affairs. "Highly civilized and cultivated, with great charm and dignity, admired by her friends and disarming to her enemies," she would, according to Helen Snow, be a good choice for ambassador to the United States or delegate to the U.N. "in the Madame Pandit and Mrs. Roosevelt tradition."[42] She was not, however, appointed to China's first U.N. delegation headed by her brother-in-law Ch'iao Kuan-hua.

While Kung P'u-sheng worked in cosmopolitan Shanghai and New York in the service of humanity, her younger sister was rising to eminence in the service of the CCP. Although she did not join the Party until sometime in 1936, Kung P'eng's

---

[40]"Student Christian Movement in Wartime China," (Master's essay, Union Theological Seminary, 1942), p. 22.

[41]*NCSM*, p. 77, and Pusheng Kung, Columbia University transcript.

[42]*NCSM*, p. 77.

Marxist proclivities, like those of many of her contemporaries, antedated the December 9th movement. In 1972 Kung P'u-sheng told Helen Snow that it was Randolph Sailer, a popular Yenching psychology professor, who had introduced her, Kung P'eng, Li Min, and others to books on the Soviet Union.[43] In the *Yen-ta chou-k'an* special issue on fascism, which was published three days before the historic demonstration, she wrote an enthusiastic review of R. Palme Dutt's *Fascism and Social Revolution*. Among portions that she deemed worth quoting in the original English was this bit of deathless doggerel: "The last fight let us face; the internationale unites the human race."[44]

Kung P'eng made a strong impression upon those who knew her, but so diverse were these impressions that one sometimes wonders if her acquaintances were talking about the same person. According to Han Suyin, Kung P'eng was the "most brilliant of all" the freshmen she knew at Yenching in 1933.[45] Another classmate portrays her as one who adjusted imperfectly to the Yenching scene. Though prettier than her sister, she is said to have reacted strongly against the superficialities of Yenching life, such as the preoccupation of many students with dancing and clothes and the widespread preference for English over Chinese. The same classmate reports that Kung P'eng "didn't like the type of student which Yenching produced."[46] P'eng, unlike P'u-sheng, did not call upon the Snows,[47] but she was very close to a popular American professor, now retired and living in the United States. When he read the above description of Kung P'eng, he wrote:

[43]Helen F. Snow to John Israel, August 24, 1974.

[44]Lung Chou [Kung Wei-hang, alias Kung P'eng], "I-pen kuan-yü 'fa-hsi-ssu chu-i chu wen-t'i'ti shu chieh-shao" [Introducing a book on "Some Problems of Fascism"], *YTCK* 6, no. 9 (December 6, 1935): 44–45. Dutt's book was published in 1935 by International Publishers in New York.

[45]Han Suyin, *A Mortal Flower* (New York: Putnam, 1965), p. 257.

[46]John Israel, interview with Charles Lo, New York, July 28, 1968.

[47]*NCSM*, p. 5.

Wei-hang seemed to us a rare combination of perfect sincerity, deep conviction and sensitivity, and modesty, plus of course her great charm. When before the December 9 trip to town she said very naturally "If I come back . . . ," and later told us of being chased over the roofs by a policeman, it didn't seem in the least histrionics. I wouldn't agree that she "adjusted imperfectly to the Yenching scene," or that she was governed by her dislike though I don't remember her showing any interest in going to the United States. . . . To us she was pretty pure gold. When she dropped in on us after the [communist] take-over she had no guard with her, as [another young official] did, and when I asked her why she said "Oh I'm only a small potato," though I would imagine she outranked him a good deal.[48]

Whatever Kung P'eng's inner nature, the Communists quickly recognized her talents, especially her knack for getting along with foreigners. After serving in the Communist-dominated National Liberation Vanguards of China, she graduated from Yenching in 1937 and went to Yenan. There she became personal secretary to Chou En-lai, another figure whose enigmatic qualities have led to widely divergent impressions. Her first marriage ended tragically with the death of her husband, possibly of peritonitis.[49] With her second husband, Ch'iao Kuan-hua (Tsinghua, 1933), she served in Chou's Chungking liaison office during the war. *New York Times* correspondent Tillman Durdin found the young couple to be "highly capable press and public relations representatives." The "shapely and beautiful" Kung P'eng, Durdin recalls, carried out her duties with consummate skill:

From Chinese Communist sources to which she was privy she always had revealing, if slanted, packets of information on political affairs in Chungking and elsewhere in the country.

The door of the Ch'iao's small apartment in the government sector was always open to foreign visitors, and the Ch'iaos themselves were frequent guests of foreigners at dinners and receptions.[50]

[48]Former Yenching professor, letter to John Israel, August 22, 1970.

[49]John S. Service, letter to Donald Klein, September 3, 1969.

[50]Tillman Durdin, "Kung P'eng, Press Spokesman for Chou En-lai, Dies in Peking," *New York Times,* September 24, 1970, p. 50.

After the war the Ch'iaos continued as members of Chou En-lai's entourage in Nanking and served as his public relations agents while the Marshall Mission's mediation efforts tried to prevent the outbreak of civil war. After the breakdown of the mission, they carried on similar activities in Hong Kong.

In 1949 Kung P'eng was named Director of the Information Department of the Foreign Ministry. She gained worldwide prominence at the Geneva conference of 1954 and was a spokesman for the Chinese delegation at the Geneva meetings on Laos in 1961. By that time, reports Durdin, "Miss Kung's beauty had faded. . . . She had become heavy, almost fat, and features that once were radiant and expressive had settled into a mask."[51]

Perhaps the mask-like features of Chinese representatives in Geneva in 1961 were not unrelated to John Foster Dulles's icy refusal to shake hands with Chou En-lai in the same city seven years earlier. Kung P'eng's austere demeanor was more than an individual idiosyncracy. In 1956, James Bertram had found his old roommate, Huang Hua, an unsmiling bureaucrat of "composed features," strikingly different from "the eager young student of twenty years before."[52] But, as the Snows had observed in the late 1930s, a year or two in Sian or Yenan was sufficient to transform Huang, and even the outgoing Chang Chao-lin, into very serious young officials. There may have been a measure of calculation in all this. Certainly alumni from such a "bastion of reaction" as Yenching would have been unwise to have greeted foreign friends with backslapping bonhommie. Moreover, the difficult and dangerous decades after their graduation would likely have brought out the serious side of the most ebullient personality. We would be ill advised to interpret Kung P'eng's "mask" as part of a Chinese Communist plot to eradicate all vestiges of sex appeal.

Whatever may have become of her charm, Kung P'eng lost none of her talent. In April 1964 she became assistant minister

---

[51] *Ibid.*   [52] Bertram, *Return to China,* p. 169.

of Foreign Affairs. She survived the rigors of the Cultural Revolution but died, probably of cancer, on September 20, 1970.[53] Her adeptness in the realm of officialdom was noted by a Kuomintang writer who described her as one who "moves with the tide and is good at following the inside track."[54] Her ability to maneuver with ease along the interstices of Chinese and Western cultures reflected her Yenching heritage. At times she displayed the virtues of the humane extroverts Chang Chao-lin, Li Min, and Kung P'u-sheng. Yet, like Huang Hua, she was totally devoted to the Communist cause. Thus she achieved high status in a profoundly nationalistic and revolutionary milieu.

Liang Szu-i and Chang Shu-i

Among the coeds in the Snow circle were two others now prominent in international cultural relations and social welfare activities. Liang Szu-i, daughter of Liang Ch'i-ch'ao, entered Yenching as a premedical student in 1933. In class she sat next to Han Suyin, who describes her as "a sturdy beetle-browed girl of great character . . . very straightforward."[55] "Large, healthy and efficient-looking," as Helen Snow recalls her, Liang was afraid neither "of ideas nor of action."[56] She married fellow student Chang Wei-hsun (Arthur Chang), son of a California lettuce-grower. He impressed Han Suyin as "a hard-working, honest young man with great courage and simplicity" who devoted himself to learning the Chinese language from which he, like many overseas Chinese, had been cut off.[57] Arthur's sister, Constance, was also active in the student movement but is better known as the mother of Nancy T'ang, Peking's chief interpreter for President Nixon's visit. Nancy was born in New

---

[53]Durdin, "Kung P'eng."

[54]*CKJML*, p. 748.

[55]Han Suyin, *Mortal Flower*, p. 278; also p. 256.

[56]*NCSM*, p. 5.

[57]Han Suyin, *Mortal Flower*, p. 270.

York City where her father, T'ang Ming-chao, edited the *Overseas Chinese Daily*. Liang Szu-i also lived in the United States while her husband taught and practiced pediatrics at the New York University College of Medicine and in the Children's Medical Service at Bellevue Hospital in New York City. The Changs returned to China around the time of the Communist take-over. Chang Wei-hsun and several Yenching classmates were among the seven young American-trained doctors who took up work at Tsinan's Bethune Medical Center, named for the Canadian surgeon who gave his life while serving Chinese guerrillas in 1939. Though Chang and his colleagues used sophisticated equipment and instructional material donated by American friends, they sought to make their skills available to the masses in accordance with Maoist precepts. Both Changs became active members of the China-Cuba Friendship Association organized in December 1962, and Liang Szu-i took part in the China-Afghanistan Friendship Association as well. Chang was director of pediatrics and deputy director of the then called China-Soviet Union Friendship Hospital when the Cultural Revolution broke out.[58]

Li Min's friend, Chang Shu-i, appeared to Helen Snow as "a pretty, apple-cheeked girl with dimples and a slow, quiet manner."[59] To the tormented Eurasian freshman, Han Suyin, Chang was "a lovable, sweet person in third year, who wanted to be a social worker, was engaged in many student activities [and] tried to interest me in something other than myself."[60] Chang, too, visited the United States in the mid-1940s. She has served as deputy secretary-general of the Chinese People's National Committee for the Protection of Children and deputy director of the International Liaison Department of the

[58]*NCSM*, pp. 5–6; Helen Snow, interview, March 28, 1972; Chang Wei-sun (Arthur Chung; i.e., Chang Wei-hsun, Arthur Chang), "Doctors Serve, Teach and Learn," *China Reconstructs*, July-August 1952, pp. 40–44; Edgar Snow, "Report from China, III," *New Republic*, May 1, 1971, p. 23.

[59]*NCSM*, p. 5.

[60]Han Suyin, *Mortal Flower*, p. 287.

National Women's Federation.

Like Kung P'u-sheng, Chang Shu-i's social interests in the late 1930s focused on the YMCA. Both sympathized with the Chinese Industrial Cooperatives (Indusco) program of small-scale industry, in which Helen Snow, Rewi Alley, and others were involved. Both women and their husbands established strong American connections during the 1940s and contributed their abilities to the New China in 1949. Neither moved to the center of power, though Kung, as director of the International Affairs Department in the Foreign Ministry, rose to a much more influential position than did Chang Shu-i. What personal turmoil, if any, they may have experienced in making the transition from the YWCA to communism remains a matter for conjecture.

The Yenching student leaders obviously were not cast from a single mold. In spite of missionary school training, their attitudes toward Christianity varied. Though predominantly from affluent and influential families, they by no means accepted the social and political status quo. One thing that united them was the leftist milieu of China's intellectual world of the 1930s. Marxist literature was in vogue. Best-sellers encouraged rebellion against authority. Since the beginning of the decade, the dominant tone in the *Yen-ta yueh-k'an* (Yenching monthly) had been Marxist.[61] The enthusiastic response to Huang Hua's manifesto made it evident that liberal issues such as freedom of expression were capable of winning broad popular support if couched in militant terms and linked with the question of national salvation. But liberalism failed to provide a satisfactory frame of reference for social analysis, and liberal views were losing ground to radical critiques.[62] "The Communist model," writes Philip West, "increasingly shaped [students'] perception of the good society."[63] These generaliza-

61West, "Yenching University," p. 479.
62*Ibid.*, pp. 394–95, 459–65.
63*Ibid.*, pp. 376–77.

tions apply not only to Yenching but to universities throughout China. A former Yenching professor later recalled

a strong strain of student interest in . . . Communist theory and Communist practice, Communism as a nose-thumbing at the Western powers who felt themselves so superior to China, some elements probably of real sympathy with the common people, that grew so rapidly later on, the appeal of idealistic turning back on the selfish, grafting inefficiency of the warlords and then the KMT.[64]

But communism remained very much an abstraction. Hungry for detailed information, Yenching students deluged a visiting Soviet ambassador with more than a hundred questions.[65] Some, like Huang Hua, could turn out impressive Marxist analyses of the current scene. But of the Chinese Communists, recently emerged from the Long March, they knew little or nothing. The Snows may well be correct in believing that none of their Yenching friends was a Party member at the time of the December 9 demonstration. These students were just beginning, as Edgar Snow has noted, "to become aware of Communist alternatives in terms of *nationalist* aims," which they learned about through the underground "mosquito press" and clandestine reports of the August manifesto.[66] They wanted to make contact with experienced Communist leaders, but in November 1935 most Peiping Communists were in jail. Yet, when the New Zealand writer James Bertram moved into a Yenching dormitory several months later, he found his roommate Huang Hua

a quiet, well-behaved youth who was a model scholar. From time to time he received ingeniously transmitted reports from the remote hinterland where moved a mysterious Red Army of peasants and workers. He kept his own counsel. When the students of Peiping poured out onto the broad streets of China's old capital, lifting their

[64]Former Yenching professor, letter to John Israel, August 22, 1970.

[65]*Yen-ching ta-hsueh hsiao-k'an* (Yenching University weekly), June 8, 1934; cited in *SNIC*.

[66]Edgar Snow, "Comment," *The China Quarterly*, no. 26 (April-June 1966), p. 172. Italics in original.

banners and shouting their slogans beneath the faded pink walls of the Forbidden City, he was usually to be found somewhere nearby in a rickshaw, wearing a . . . merchant's gown and looking like a bored spectator.

"I last saw him years later," Bertram recalled, "lean and brown in the blue cotton uniform of a political commissar of the Eighth Route Army."[67]

TSINGHUA

For American scholars, China's Christian colleges are more accessible than its governmental universities. Thanks to the New York City Archives of the United Board for Christian Higher Education in Asia, a series of monographs has appeared on these institutions. Preeminent among the Christian colleges and politically unique, Yenching has received special attention.[68] On the other hand, no non-Christian university has received comparable treatment.

One should not suppose, however, that the relative importance of institutions and their students is proportional to our knowledge about them. In terms of identifiable December 9 participants active on the mainland since 1949, Yenching, with about a dozen, ranks a poor second to Tsinghua University, which has produced at least twice as many.

Tsinghua opened in 1911 as a preparatory school for students planning to study in the United States under the Boxer Indemnity. Located near Yenching among scenic surroundings close to the ruins of the old Summer Palace, it combined the Taoist concept of a peaceful refuge for contemplation with the American notion that colleges should be isolated from distracting urban influences. Academically, American principles prevailed from the onset. Chou I-ch'un, who served as

[67]James Bertram, *Beneath the Shadow* (New York: John Day, 1947), p. 6.

[68]*See* Hubert Freyn, *Prelude to War* (Shanghai: The China Journal Publishing Co., 1939), and previously cited works by Helen F. Snow (Nym Wales), Edgar Snow, Dwight Edwards, Jessie Lutz, Philip West, and John Leighton Stuart.

chancellor from 1913 to 1918, was a graduate of St. John's in Shanghai and Yale University.[69] Dubbed "Tsinghua University" in 1925, the school became a full-fledged national university in 1929. From then on, a Tsinghua degree no longer carried with it an automatic fellowship to America. However, the tradition of postgraduate study in the United States continued into the 1930s. The change came with students of the December 9th generation who pursued post-graduate work on the battlefields of China.[70]

The Boxer endowment made Tsinghua less subject to the vicissitudes of funding than were other government universities and enabled it to build a physical plant second to none in China. In 1932, Tsinghua's top-ranking library had more than 310,000 volumes—one out of nine of all the books in China's university libraries. (Peita with 210,000 was third; Yenching

[69]Liu Ch'ung-hung, "Kuo-li ch'ing-hua ta-hsueh" [National Tsinghua University], in Chang Ch'i-yun and others, eds., *Chung-hua min-kuo ta-hsueh chih* [Annals of universities in the Republic of China] (Taipei: Chung-hua wen-hua ch'u-pan shih-yeh wei-yuan-hui, 1954), 1:76 (hereafter cited as *Ta-hsueh chih*).

[70]However, old traditions died hard—witness this confession by alumnus Ch'ien Wei-ch'ang: "During the December 9th movement, I was motivated by a narrow nationalism to participate in the mass movement. But there were contradictions in my thinking. On the one hand, the petty bourgeois sense of righteousness and youthful revolutionary ardour, and on the other a selfish personal desire to study abroad and become a professor. Because of this every time a movement started I participated with enthusiasm, but once it had settled down I quietly sneaked back to the laboratory to prepare for class. . . . As one group after another of old friends bravely left school to take up their positions in the work of the revolution, they would always hope I would go, and I was amenable to the idea, but when it came time to depart I had apprehensions about the difficulty of revolutionary work so I vacillated and ended up not going. To comfort myself I said that there had to be a "division of labor" in our work, some going into revolution and others into science, and that science would also be very important after the success of the revolution."

Ch'ien got his American Ph.D. and became a professor. Some of the guilt in his confession may have been induced, but the career pattern is a familiar one. Ch'ien Wei-ch'ang, "Wo t'iao-ch'u-le ti-kuo chu-i ti hsien-ching" [I Escaped from the imperialist trap], Kuang-ming jih-pao, ed., *Ssu-hsiang kai-tsao wen-hsien* [Selected documents on thought reform], (Shanghai: Kuang-ming jih-pao, 1952), 4:76.

with 190,000 was fourth.)[71] The scenic campus, a garden during the imperial period, was studded with sturdy Western-style buildings, and new construction was ever in evidence. Between 1932 and 1935, while Peita's student body remained around the 1,000 level, Tsinghua's increased more than 200 percent, from less than 600 to more than 1,200.

By 1935, under the direction of Mei I-ch'i, Tsinghua had become a preeminent center of learning, second, perhaps, to Peita in the humanities and social sciences, superior in the natural sciences, and the equal of Shanghai's Chiaot'ung (China's M.I.T.) in engineering. Such an institution could afford to be highly selective. Of approximately 3,000 annual applicants, only about 300 were admitted.[72] One reason for the flood of applicants was the low tuition—about 20 Chinese dollars per year in 1936 in contrast to 40 at Peita and 110 at Yenching.[73] (In 1936, the Chinese dollar was worth U.S. 30 cents.) Low fees enhanced Tsinghua's appeal to relatively impoverished but highly-qualified applicants. Compared with Yenching, it drew more students from families of educators and government officials, fewer from those of businessmen.[74]

[71]Chung-kuo hsueh-sheng she, *Ch'üan-kuo ta-hsueh t'u-chien* [An illustrated introduction to the nation's universities], Shanghai: Shang-hai liang-yu t'u-shu yin-shua kung-ssu, 1933), p. 10.

[72]John Israel, interview with Charles Lo, July 28, 1968.

[73]Philip West, "Yenching University and Sino-American Relations, 1917–1937," (Ph. D. dissertation, Harvard University, 1970), p. 377. Figures for 1930 differ somewhat but confirm low estimates for the cost of a Tsinghua education. Annual expenses for a typical Tsinghua student totaled $273.40 Chinese dollars, a figure that could be equalled at Peita only with financial aid and extreme self-denial. A median level of subsistence at Peita was calculated at $400. At Yenching, it was considered "possible" to hold annual expenses to $350. See Hsin ch'en pao ts'ung-shu shih, ed., *Pei-p'ing ko ta-hsueh ti chuang-k'uang* [The condition of Peiping's universities], rev. ed. (Peiping: Hsin ch'en pao yin-shua pu, 1930), pp. 40, 135, 158 (hereafter cited as Hsin ch'en pao, *Chuang-k'uang*).

[74]*Ch'üan-kuo kao-teng chiao-yü t'ung-chi*, Table 55, p. 88, reprinted in West, "Yenching University," p. 373; John Israel, interview with former Tsinghua student. A reporter noted as early as 1930 that "Tsinghua is no longer the

Tsinghua's faculty and curriculum reflected the school's American origins. In 1937, 69 of 94 full professors had studied in the United States.[75] Tsinghua's students lived in modern dormitories and participated in an array of extracurricular activities that would have looked impressive on any American campus. One favorite pastime was bridge. Tsinghua students had a reputation for taking their sports seriously. Even though up-to-date facilities were provided for the school's highly-vaunted athletic program, in the cold of winter male and female students attired in shorts could be seen doing outdoor calisthenics to the call of a physical education instructor. Every day at 4:00 P.M. young athletes descended en masse upon the well-equipped gym with its all-weather swimming pool and hot showers. They demonstrated a positive mania for basketball; so heavily used were the courts that, it was said, not even a drop of water could penetrate the crowds. The school slogan (in English) was "Fight to the finish and never say die."[76]

Nonetheless, politically, socially, and ideologically, Tsinghua was far less Americanized than Yenching. Fewer students were graduates of Christian high schools, fewer still were practicing Christians. Rarely was English spoken outside the classroom. Long gowns were more numerous, Western-style suits less so. Whereas Yenching attracted a disproportionate percentage of students from Kwangtung and Fukien (old centers of Protestant missionary activity), Tsinghua drew its largest numbers from the lower Yangtze provinces of Kiangsu and Chekiang (the political-economic base of the Nationalist government). Instead of Tsinghua's passion for basketball, Yenching students preferred the aristocratic, individualistic game of tennis.

Tsinghua College of old; Tsinghua University already has no small number of impoverished students." Hsin ch'en pao, *Chuang-k'uang*, p. 134.

[75]Y. C. Wang, *Chinese Intellectuals and the West* (Chapel Hill: University of North Carolina Press, 1966), p. 180.

[76]Chung-kuo hsueh-sheng she, *T'u-chien*, p. 73.

Tsinghua, which boasted a long tradition of military training,[77] was more nationalistic, and the style of life there was more rigorous than at the neighboring missionary institution.

Li Ch'ang

A crucial link between the December 9ers and the Communist youth movement was Tsinghua's Li Ch'ang. Of Li's pre-Tsinghua life, barely anything is known. We first discover him, according to his own account, gritting his teeth in the face of an icy sandstorm during the January 1936 propaganda trek through the North China countryside. He tells us that he joined the Communist Youth League in April, the CCP in May, and assumed general command of the NLVC in August. We can only surmise what personal qualities enabled him to advance so rapidly. An impression of Li on the eve of the Cultural Revolution comes from Diana Lary, an English instructor in 1964–65 at Peking's Second Foreign Languages Institute:

At the . . . Institute where Li was President, he was held in high regard, and his record during the December 9th Movement was used as an example to the students by members of the school leadership who had studied with him then. He had by the middle 1960s become a rather weighty gentleman, conscious of his dignity and of his revolutionary record. He had about him an *hauteur* which was lacking in many of the school's lower cadres; unfairly perhaps, the thought occurred that he had become fat, literally and metaphorically, on the success of the Revolution.[78]

A Kuomintang source describes Li as short, near-sighted, pockmarked, and with several gold teeth.[79] Which of these features he had during his student days is unknown. Adding to the confusion, a KMT writer who heard him speak during the height of the united front in 1938 described him as "young and strong" and a forceful orator.[80] In any case, it would be ill-

---

[77]John Israel, interview with T. K. Tong, New York, July 28, 1969.

[78]Diana Lary, letter to Donald W. Klein, August 2, 1972.

[79]*CKJML*, p. 130.

[80]Hsiao Kai, "Kuo-chi fan-ch'in-lueh yun-tung hsuan-ch'uan chou

advised to portray Li the young student leader in terms of Li the middle-aged bureaucrat.

Whatever Li's youthful characteristics, the history of the December 9th movement is inextricably intermeshed with the NLVC, and the development of that organization is identified with the career of Li Ch'ang. Li is one of the preeminent figures of his generation.

Lu Ts'ui

Quite another style of leadership was provided by Lu Ts'ui, Tsinghua's "Joan of Arc." While the movement was still in progress and Li Ch'ang was unknown outside of his circle of friends and comrades, this charming, romantic, and impulsive young woman had already gained international renown. Lu was born in 1914 in the northern Chekiang town of Huchow.[81] Her family had been subject to radical fluctuations in fortune. Her great grandfather had been a shopkeeper and her grandfather's failure in the official examination had left him in the ranks of the unemployed. Fortunes evidently improved for her father, who is variously described as a banker or as a high government official in the province.

Vivacious and petite, Lu Ts'ui had been a popular student leader at Soochow University in Shanghai. After expulsion for political activities, she transferred to Tsinghua, where she was among a dozen students arrested for organizing a Sit-and-Talk Society. However, she was not a particularly good speaker and was better known socially than politically. Among her close friends was Liu Wu-kou, daughter of the famous left-wing Kuomintang poet, Liu Ya-tzu; the Lius came from the southern Kiangsu city of Soochow, located in the same lower Yangtze estuary as Lu's native Huchow. Before the December 9th move-

chung-kuo ch'ing-nien k'ang-jih ta-hui su-hsieh" [Notes on the Chinese youth rally for the international antiaggression movement propaganda week] *CNCH*, no. 4 (February 15, 1938), p. 23.

[81]*NCSM*, p. 110.

ment broke out, Lu was a principal in a locally famous triangular love affair, the other members of which were engineering student Chu Min-sheng and a graduate student in economics named Tai Shih-kuang. Fellow basketball stars, Chu and Tai were also close personal friends. Of the two, Lu preferred Chu, who was strong, handsome, and the more intelligent, but both eventually went abroad, leaving her heartbroken. One can only speculate whether disappointment in romance helped to drive Lu deeply into politics. An early leader of the December 9th movement, she represented Tsinghua on the steering committee for that day's demonstration. Late that afternoon, she stood and addressed a thousand Tsinghua and Yenching demonstrators who had waited in front of the Hsichih Gate since 8:00 A.M., having been locked out of the city.[82]

Lu Ts'ui's historic moment came on December 16. Once again a locked gate stood between demonstrators inside and outside the city walls. On this occasion, however, an element of treachery fed the fires of youthful indignation. Lu had led 5,000 followers to the Shunchih Gate on the explicit guarantee by the police that they would be granted access. When they arrived, however, they found the gate barred while police on the inside brutally assaulted several hundred fellow demonstrators from Peita. At this point, Lu ran to the massive gate, rolled under the narrow opening and was seized by startled police as she tried to slide the bolt. When foreign correspondents arrived, they found her quite articulate even while being pummeled by half a dozen policemen:

Not at all dismayed, Miss Lu began to lecture them furiously upon various aspects of their relation to the national patriotic movement in the present crisis but was silenced and, after exchanging a few words with the correspondents, the tiny victim was hauled off to headquarters for "questioning" in great triumph by the Captain of the "riot squad," a maniacal gendarme, who had been observed through the

<hr>

[82]*Ibid.*, pp. 106, 111. John Israel, interview with one of Lu's Tsinghua schoolmates, Hong Kong, December 18, 1973.

day flailing the students with almost berserk fury.[83]

A sit-down strike by Lu's supporters finally secured her release, and at 7:30 that night she was allowed to roll back under the gate and lead them on the long march to Tsinghua.[84]

The movement now had a heroine. Male students flocked to her dormitory to inquire about Lu's welfare. Foreign correspondents sought further information. American readers had a good look at her in a photograph accompanying Helen Snow's article, "Students in Rebellion," in the July 1936 issue of *Asia*.[85] The photograph makes it clear why she could capture the hearts of fellow students, the press, and eventually her future husband, Jao Shu-shih. She is shown standing with the winter's sun shining on her oval face. Her expression is alert yet somewhat contemplative, as though she were taking the measure of a crowd. Behind narrowed lids, her shining eyes peer into the distance. Her lips are relaxed, slightly parted. Her bobbed black hair is combed back over her right ear. She is wearing a coat with an open fur collar, under which a scarf hangs down loosely over a bulky sweater. Her attitude is that of the aristocratic leader, a combination of poise, dignity, determination, and sculptured beauty. Beneath the photo is the caption:

Miss Lu Ts'ui, diminutive "Joan of Arc," was the leader of the student demonstration [of December 16]. It was she who, when Shunchih [Gate] was closed against them, rolled beneath the gate and very nearly succeeded in pulling the gate-bar before the police caught and arrested her. She was later released, but on February 29, a full regiment made a raid on Tsinghua University to get her and some other leaders.[86]

From then on, Lu was on the move. One of her refuges from the police was the Snows, though she was too irrepressible to

---

[83]*NCSM*, p. 111.

[84]*Ibid.*

[85]Nym Wales (pseudonym for Helen F. Snow), "Students in Rebellion," *Asia* 36, no. 7 (July 1936): 451.

[86]*Ibid.*

obey their injunction to hide in a closet when visitors came.[87] In March, she attended the preparatory meeting of the reconstituted National Student Association in Shanghai. Not one to neglect her filial obligations, Lu took the opportunity to pay a visit to nearby Huchow, where her parents had become frantically concerned over her well-being. However, she did not miss the chance to look up "some comrades in the South" to discuss political problems.[88] Shortly thereafter, she went on to Europe to represent China at the World Youth Congress in Geneva (August 31–September 6, 1936). "Before China is completely liberated from the foreign yoke," she told her fellow delegates, "we Chinese youth can never live in happiness."[89] In Paris she helped establish an overseas branch of the Federation of National Salvation Associations. Lu impressed a fellow worker as somewhat cocksure,[90] but perhaps it would be too much to expect a young woman lionized by classmates and spotlighted by world publicity to be utterly devoid of egotism.

Sometime during 1936 Lu is reported to have joined the Chinese Communist Party.[91] In the spring of 1938, she wrote a column from Paris for the CCP's organ in Wuhan, the *Hsin-hua jih-pao* (New China daily) in which she described preparations for the Second World Youth Congress to be held at Vassar College in August.[92]

Thereafter, Lu's political career, spanning nearly two decades, took her on further travels abroad to attend student, youth, women, and peace conferences. She rose to become a

[87] *NCSM,* p. 52.

[88] *Ibid.,* p. 110.

[89] First World Youth Congress, *Youth Plans a New World* (Geneva, 1936), p. 31.

[90] Hu Ch'iu-yuan hsien-sheng hsu [Mr. Hu Ch'iu-yuan's preface], in Ssu-ma Lu, Tou-cheng shih-pa nien [Eighteen years of struggle] (Hong Kong: Ya-chou ch'u-pan she, 1952), p. 3.

[91] United States State Department, *Biographical Files Report.*

[92] "Ti-erh ts'e shih-chieh ch'ing-nien ta-hui" [Second World Youth Congress], *Hsin-hua jih-pao,* April 15, 1938.

standing committeewoman of the National Women's Federation and director of its International Liaison Department. From about 1938 to 1940, she lived in the United States with her husband, Jao Shu-shih, who apparently edited the weekly *China Salvation Times* in New York. In 1946, she appeared in Peiping as one of four secretaries working under George Hatem, Communist health advisor to the Executive Headquarters of the Marshall Mission. She returned to Yenan on February 2, 1947.[93]

Lu and Jao were a prominent couple during the early years of the new order. Jao, who had narrowly escaped death in the New Fourth Army Incident of 1941, advanced rapidly in the CCP after 1949 and in 1952 was appointed director of the Party's Organization Department. In 1954, however, both Jao and Lu Ts'ui disappeared from public view. The following year, Jao was anathematized as a coconspirator with Kao Kang in an alleged high-level plot against the Party. Kao committed suicide; Jao's fate was not disclosed. Though there are rumors that Lu has remarried, there has been no authentic news of her since 1954.

Jung Kao-t'ang

Lu's schoolmate, Jung Kao-t'ang, then known as Jung Ch'ien-hsiang, had a promising career until the Cultural Revolution. An outstanding guard on the basketball court, Jung was a well-known campus figure before December 9. He was a versatile youth whose talents included playwriting and folk singing. He also appeared on the police list as a Communist suspect. One day in 1933 or 1934, most likely in the small hours of the morning, Jung was taken away, beaten, and thrown into jail. More than a year passed before his release, and a rule requiring special permission for readmission after prolonged absence blocked his attempt to reenter Tsinghua. He finally succeeded

---

[93]*Kuo-fang nien-chien* [National defense yearbook] (Taipei: n.p., 1952), pp. 431, 461.

due to the intercession of Tsinghua's dean, the famous eugenicist P'an Kuang-tan. Jung may or may not have graduated. If he was not politically involved before his arrest, he left no question about his sympathies thereafter. He became an active member of the NLVC, represented the Communists in the Personnel Section and the Administrative Department of the Marshall Mission's Executive Headquarters in 1946, and became an outstanding figure in national and international sports organizations after 1949. As an organizer of the All-China Athletic Federation, Jung was in a position to serve as patron to Tsinghua's former Director of Physical Education, Ma Yueh-han (John Ma), who had befriended him during his student days. While Jung was secretary-general of the federation from June 1952 to October 1956, both he and Ma served as vice-chairmen.[94]

Huang Ch'eng

Another Tsinghua student whose political record antedates December 9 was Huang Ch'eng. A native of Fengjun County in Hopei, Huang had been expelled from Tientsin's Peiyang College of Engineering in 1933 for anti-Japanese activities. Soon after his entrance into Tsinghua the following year, he became chairman of the student association, achieved widespread recognition for his activities after December 9, and was elected chairman of the Peiping Student Union in the spring of 1936. "A man of middle height, dressed neatly and simply," Huang was "dark skinned and pleasant-looking," recalled a schoolmate, "and his deep, bright eyes gave the impression of a very intelligent and modest person."[95] Huang was a natural leader who expressed himself with verve even under trying cir-

[94]*Ibid.*, p. 430; John Israel, interviews with Huang Chung-fu [Jack Huang], Hong Kong, August 1959, New York, July 28, 1969; Li Ch'ang, "Recollections of the National Liberation Vanguard of China," Part II, in *SCMM*, no. 297 (January 22, 1962), pp. 28, 37. Ma Yueh-han (John Ma) is not the same as the John Ma mentioned in the Acknowledgments.

[95]Shih Li-teh, "A Tribute to Huang Cheng," in *RON*, p. 161.

cumstances. While hiding from the police in a professor's home, he wrote:

The night is long, our path ahead is hidden;
The stars hang low, the longed-for dawn is late;
With shame I brood alone on tasks unfinished,
Yet firm in faith desire no better fate.
No more I cling to self or think of safety,
Here in the fight shall all my blood be shed;
Say not the way is long, dawn slow in coming;
Cocks crow, the sun is rising just ahead![96]

Jailed late in December 1936, Huang organized his fellow prisoners and gave them detailed instructions on how to behave. Even though ill with a high fever, sometimes unconscious, and hardly able to speak, he refused to be freed of his fetters until those of his comrades had also been removed.[97] Huang's talents brought him into the Political Department of the New Fourth Army. Captured in the incident of January 1941, he died a martyr's death at the Shangjao concentration camp.[98]

Yang Hsueh-ch'eng

At Tsinghua tension between left and right was severe. The Kuomintang drew strong support from juniors and seniors. In the fall of 1935, a majority of the Student Union Council were KMT members. Among the senior class's delegation were several talented KMT members who attempted to provide non-Communist leadership during the December 9th movement. On the other hand, sophomores of the class of 1938 furnished radical cadres such as Yao I-lin, Huang Ch'eng, Wu Ch'eng-ming, Liu Yü-hang, and Yang Hsueh-ch'eng, and this leftist coterie played a key role beginning with the organization of the December 16 demonstration.[99]

[96]*Ibid.*, p. 160.

[97]*Ibid.*, pp. 165–67.

[98]*Ibid.*, p. 161.

[99]John Israel, interview with a Tsinghua alumnus, class of 1936, Hong Kong, December 18, 1973.

For most December 9 activists, political enlightenment came gradually. The transformation of Yang Hsueh-ch'eng from closet scholar to revolutionary hero was, perhaps, not atypical. Yang entered Tsinghua in 1934. He was politically indifferent until the summer of 1935. Once he became involved, however, Yang's devotion to the cause was uncompromising. During a propaganda crusade to the countryside in January 1936, he kept pace on foot with a vanguard of cyclists. Suffering from overexertion and exposure to frigid winter elements, he became ill. During the war, he worked with similar indifference to his own health while he was in charge of CCP organization in his native Hupei Province. There, at the age of twenty-nine, he died of tuberculosis.[100]

Chiang Nan-hsiang

Chiang Nan-hsiang, author of Yang's eulogy, lived to become president of the university that had expelled him. At the end of the turbulent 1935–36 academic year, Mei I-ch'i, suspecting that Chiang was a "professional student" for the CCP, ousted him and at least two other suspects, including Huang Ch'eng and Wu Ch'eng-ming. Huang transferred to China College of Peiping. Wu, scion of a Hopei banking family, graduated from Peiping University in 1940, earned an M.A. from Columbia University's School of Business in 1946, and became a widely published economist after 1949. It is unclear whether or not Chiang, a junior at the time of his expulsion, ever returned to finish his undergraduate studies.

The lack of a degree would have made little difference in the career of a man with Chiang's abilities. Chiang was highly regarded by schoolmates though he generally skipped classes and avoided demonstrations. He spent much time immersed in Marxist literature but spoke with a notable lack of dogma-

---

[100]Chiang Nan-hsiang, "In Memory of Comrade Yang Hsueh-ch'eng," in *RON*, pp. 160–72, *passim*. Also see Warren Kuo, *Analytical History of the Chinese Communist Party* (Taipei: Institute of International Relations, 1970), 3:517.

tism.[101] Recognized even by Kuomintang biographers as a talented writer and organizer,[102] Chiang probably became a member of the CCP in the spring semester of 1936. One source states that he joined on the personal recommendation of Chou En-lai.[103] After the Marco Polo Bridge Incident of July 7, 1937, Chiang fled successively to Tientsin, Nanking, Linfen, and eventually Wuhan, all the while conducting political activities for the NLVC and the CCP. By January 1938 Chiang was in Wuhan, probably working under Chou En-lai's liaison mission to the Nationalist government. A KMT intelligence communiqué of 1942 identifies him as alias Yü Mo-wen, secretary of the Youth Work Committee of the Party's South China Bureau. He was said to have fled to Yenan after two associates confessed to KMT authorities.[104] After his arrival in the Communist capital in January 1941, he became co-editor of *Chung-kuo ch'ing-nien* (China youth) magazine.

According to one source, Chiang spent the last phase of the war in special service work in Southeast China and, as of V-J Day, was based in Shanghai's eastern suburbs.[105] He is more reliably reported to have gone in September 1945 to Manchuria, where he was instrumental in founding the Northeast Democratic Youth League, a precursor of the nationwide New Democratic Youth League (NDYL). Chiang was an outstanding figure at the NDYL's First Congress in April 1949. He has subsequently held a number of important posts in youth, educational, and cultural affairs. In November 1952 he returned to Tsinghua as president, only to be expelled from his alma mater—for the second time—during the Cultural Revolution.

[101] John Israel, interview with Hung T'ung, Taipei, October 30, 1973.

[102] *CKJML*, p. 662.

[103] URI, *Who's Who in Communist China* (Hong Kong: URI, 1966), p. 114.

[104] Chung-tiao-chü [Chung-yang tiao-ch'a t'ung-chi chü, Central Bureau of Investigation and Statistics], *San-shih-i-nien-tu chien-wei hsueh-yun ts'e-lueh yen-chiu chuan-pao* [Special report on the study of strategy of the traitors' phoney student movement in 1942], (n.p., n.d.).

[105] URI, *Who's Who*, p. 114.

Yao I-lin

Though Tsinghua charged nominal tuition, preparing for and attending a university were an expensive proposition. Few Tsinghua students knew the sting of poverty. Typical was Yao I-lin, a tall, husky young man who belonged to "a prominent and presumably well-to-do" Anhwei household.[106] Yao's father, a distinguished late Ch'ing official who supported Yuan Shih-k'ai, died while his son was an infant. Young Yao studied at a Christian school and considered himself, at that time, a Christian. He later attended a middle school attached to Kuanghua University in Shanghai where he won academic honors and gained a reputation for articulateness. In 1934–35 Yao was elected to represent fellow freshmen on the Council of the Tsinghua Student Union. Soon after December 9, Yao, by then a sophomore history major, held responsible positions in the CCP. He reportedly worked for the Party's Peiping Committee in February 1936 and was secretary-general of the North China Sub-bureau in 1937. By 1949 Yao had become a specialist in economic affairs and in February 1960 he was named minister in the Ministry of Commerce.[107]

Han Ming

During the February 29, 1936, police raid on Tsinghua, Yao I-lin and Chiang Nan-hsiang were briefly held captive before their rescue by fellow students, including Yang Hsueh-ch'eng.[108] A student who played a less heroic role during this incident was Han Ming. A tall, dark, dashing extrovert, the mustachioed Han was something of a campus character. He

[106]Klein and Clark, *Biographic Dictionary,* based on *NCSM,* p. 135. The distinguished Yao family of Tungcheng, Anhwei, mentioned in Arthur Hummel, ed., *Eminent Chinese of the Ch'ing Period* (Washington, D.C.: Government Printing Office, 1943, 1944), 1:239 and 2:900–901, very possibly may be Yao I-lin's.

[107]URI, *Who's Who,* p. 678; John Israel, interview with a schoolmate of Yao's, Hong Kong, December 18, 1973.

[108]*RON,* p. 157.

had once dressed up as Haile Selassie, the Ethiopian emperor much admired for his resistance to Mussolini, and the nickname "Haile Selassie" stayed with him.

Han's reputation as a harmless clown began to sour as Tsinghua students became politically polarized. Mei I-ch'i, who recalled Han as "a very nice young man," delegated him to attend a government-sponsored conference of educators and students in January 1936.[109] When schoolmates learned that he had refused to join them in boycotting this meeting, their amusement turned to wrath. Han fell in with the rightist T'ung-fang pu faction named after the September 18 Memorial Hall (formerly called the T'ung-fang pu) where the rightists held their meetings. (Leftists were known as the Auditorium faction.) On February 29, Han was accused of helping a coed named Chi Yun-shou prepare a list of student radicals, presumably to aid the police. Han allegedly admitted that he had assisted her but said he had done so "just for fun."[110] His schoolmates were not amused.

Han's subsequent political career suggests that he was fundamentally an opportunist without deeply-held convictions. After graduation, he joined the KMT's Central News Agency. Following the war he worked for the *Hsin-min pao* (New people's daily) and followed that paper's publishers leftward during the growing disillusionment with the Nationalists. A friend who met him in 1947 found him extremely pessimistic about the future of KMT China.[111] After Liberation, Han settled down with his pretty wife in a nice Shanghai apartment, attempting to enjoy a bourgeois life while remaining "progressive" in thought. He was a member of the China Democratic League and knew the organization's senior leader, Lo Lung-chi. During the Hundred Flowers period, the League became a source of outspoken

[109] John Israel, interview with Mei I-ch'i, Taipei, November 28, 1959.

[110] *NCSM*, p. 109.

[111] John Israel, interview with Huang Chung-fu [Jack Huang], Hong Kong, August 13, 1959.

criticism and was brutally attacked during the subsequent Anti-rightist movement. In 1957, Han was dubbed the leading rightist in the League's Shanghai Committee.[112]

Although Han's name disappeared from the media, in the early 1960s a Hong Kong schoolmate received a letter from a fellow alumnus reporting him very ill with diabetes. The disease was, no doubt, exacerbated by dietary excesses for Han was a renowned trencherman. A friend recalled his heroic gastronomic feats: consuming a quart-sized container of ice cream even though he trembled afterward; ordering two serving bowls of dessert, one for himself, one for everyone else at the table. A decade later, when his wife wrote to say that Han had died two years before (ca. 1968), Tsinghua alumni in Hong Kong took up a collection to assist the widow and three children of their tragicomic friend.[113]

PEITA

Peking University held a unique position in the Chinese educational world and was equally unique in the history of the student movement. Established in 1898 by the Ch'ing government, it became China's first modern national university. During World War I, under the leadership of Ts'ai Yuan-p'ei, Peita brought together a galaxy of intellectual luminaries and gained a preeminence that it never lost. Events that shook China's educational and political world—the literary revolution, the New Culture movement, and the May 4th student movement—all centered in this institution. Peita suffered under the warlords. In the wake of brutal attempts at police suppression, Ts'ai Yuan-p'ei resigned and many eminent faculty members found it advisable, between 1919 and 1927, to flee to Shanghai.

[112]Entry for Han Ming, U.S. Consulate General, Hong Kong, biographic files.

[113]Much of the foregoing information on Han was furnished by a friend and former schoolmate, interviewed by John Israel in Hong Kong on December 18, 1973.

Nonetheless, the institution preserved its reputation and traditions. In 1929 Chiang Monlin, who had served as acting chancellor after Ts'ai's resignation in 1919, became chancellor. Under his leadership, Peita entered its silver age.

Although the academic prominence of the Peita faculty now rivaled that of the May 4th era, the permissible range of political deviance was narrowed. Helen Snow lamented this in a manuscript entitled, "What Has Become of the May Fourth Revolutionaries?" A note on the back of her draft characterizes the middle-aged May 4th veterans in these words: "Those not buried in ancient literature are now called fascists by the students."[114] Mrs. Snow's pessimism echoed the jeremiads of a Peita writer:

After May 4th, Peita stood at the very center of the nation's educational and cultural world but since then the atmosphere has become increasingly oppressive. Since the success of the Northern Expedition in 1927, though Peita has remained a great revolutionary base, it cannot compare to the earlier period, and the students' power of solidarity has gradually dissipated. Some people have gone so far as to ask, "Has Peita died?" Some were prepared to write its epitaph. During this era . . . professors and students have shown signs of being of two minds: whatever ideas the professors might champion were unlikely to be those of the students. The reason for this, said some, was that during the May 4th period professors and students stood together against the government but today's professors were in the government's camp. There was, no doubt, a good deal of truth to this.[115]

There were, to be sure, some exceptions. The great historian Ku Chieh-kang, who had been steadfastly nonpolitical during the May 4th period, now took time out from scholarship for anti-Japanese propaganda.[116] May 4th leader Hsu Te-heng marched on December 9 and championed student activists. The renowned chemist Tseng Chao-lun contributed an article on

[114]*NCSM*, p. 93.

[115]Chung-kuo hsueh-sheng she, *T'u-chien*, p. 31.

[116]Laurence A. Schneider, *Ku Chieh-kang and China's New History* (Berkeley and Los Angeles: University of California Press, 1971), pp. 5–6.

"National Defense Chemistry" to the *Pei-ta chou-k'an* (Peita weekly), and even KMT stalwart T'ao Hsi-sheng, soon to become an uncompromising critic of student leftists, wrote a brief essay, "Unite under the Great Banner of National Liberation," for the weekly's special December 16th edition.[117]

Chancellor Chiang Monlin, a former student of John Dewey, was opposed to student political activism. He drew strong support from the dean of Peita's Law College, Chou Ping-lin, a fellow member of the Kuomintang. Chiang's right-hand man and chief spokesman for the "save-the-nation-through-study" position was Dewey's most famous Chinese graduate student, Hu Shih, then dean of the College of Arts. Hu had clashed with student militants as early as 1915, when he upbraided those who sought to save their nation by abandoning studies in the United States and returning home to join the political struggle. After December 9, Hu and Professor Ma Hsu-lun rekindled an animosity dating from the May 4th era. Ma was a complex man, a doughty survivor of many political and intellectual campaigns who had opposed the revolutionary movement before 1911, served as an administrator under warlords, and resisted the vernacular literature movement. Now he roused Hu's wrath by siding with student radicals. At the end of the academic session, Ma was one of three Peita faculty members "granted" a year's leave of absence, which he had not requested.[118]

Though May 4 remained an occasion for pious commemoration, Peita never recaptured its earlier position as unchallenged pacesetter for Chinese student movements. Its final hour of

[117]Tseng Chao-lun, "Kuo-fang hua-hsueh" [National defense chemistry], *PTCK*, no. 2 (January 13, 1936), pp. 18–20; T'ao Hsi-sheng, "Tsai min-tsu chieh-fang ta ch'i chih hsia t'uan-chieh" [Unite under the great banner of national liberation], *PTCK*, no. 1 (December 30, 1935, Special December 16th demonstration edition), p. 59. Also see Hsu Te-heng, as told to Chou Chen, "Hui-i i-erh chiu" (Reminiscences of December 9th), *Yen-ching hsin-wen* [Yenching news], December 8, 1947, p. 2. We thank Philip West for calling this item to our attention.

[118]Ma Hsu-lun, *Wo tsai liu-shih sui i-ch'ien* [My life before age sixty] (Shanghai: Sheng-huo ch'u-pan she, 1947), pp. 117–19.

glory had come in 1931 when Peita had provided the radical hard core of Peiping students besieging the government in Nanking. While most young activists remained content to petition their government to declare war on Japan, Peita's Demonstration Corps angrily protested the transparent treachery of Chiang Kai-shek's "reactionary" regime. The ensuing repression fell particularly heavily upon Peita. According to Helen Snow, "at least 50 students" were arrested between 1932 and 1935.[119] After a flurry of protest against Chiang Monlin's "fascist" educational policies in the fall of 1932, all signs of radical activism disappeared from the campus.

Ch'ien Chia-chu

Peita did, however, boast one of the few survivors of the 1931 Demonstration Corps still on the scene and able to play an active role after December 9. He was Ch'ien Chia-chü, a brilliant student of economics who had served as press secretary for the corps.[120] Highly respected for his command of Chinese and English as well as economics,[121] Ch'ien was asked to teach at his alma mater after graduation. Though a faculty member, he was but twenty-five years old in 1935, a contemporary of many of his students. Hence, he should be counted among the members of the December 9th generation. Vivid recollections of 1931 transmitted, no doubt, by Ch'ien and others led Peita writer Chang Ju-p'u to trace the origins of the current national salvation movement to the Nanking demonstration of December 5, 1931, in which 180 members of the Peita Demonstration Corps were arrested.[122]

As observed, one reason why Tsinghua, and even Yenching,

[119]*NCSM,* p. 92.

[120]*SNIC,* pp. 64 ff., especially p. 68.

[121]See Hsu Te-heng, note 117.

[122]Chang Ju-p'u, "I-erh i-liu hsueh-sheng shih-wei yun-tung chih fa-sheng chi ch'i i-i" [The outbreak of the December 16th student demonstration movement and its meaning], *PTCK,* no. 1 (December 30, 1935), p. 4.

overtook Peita in the early stages of the December 9th movement was that these upstart schools—neither of them institutions of higher education in 1919—were located outside the city walls and enjoyed a certain degree of political immunity. Moreover, Yenching and Tsinghua were established on the American model. Students were expected to enroll formally, attend classes regularly, and live in dormitories. American-style extracurricular activities were an established part of the college scene. Also, the relative compactness of these campuses facilitated internal communication while their comparative isolation spared students the distractions of urban life.

Peita, on the other hand, was a sprawling urban complex in the heart of Peiping. Rather than make do with the university's run-down old dormitories, many students lived in off-campus rooming houses and hostels and with private families. Peita drew more heavily upon the Sorbonne model than upon Harvard, Yale, or Oberlin for its organization and style. To enter Tsinghua one had to meet minimum standards in all areas of the liberal arts, but a talented student could gain admission to Peita even if his or her brilliance was confined to a single subject. Once he or she had matriculated, individual creativity continued to win rewards. Once matriculated, a student need not attend classes but could pass courses by doing well on examinations and writing superior papers. Anyone could audit courses. Leisure-time activities also differed from the wholesome extracurricular programs of the colleges outside the city walls. Though Peita men had outlived their pre-May 4th reputation as "the brothel brigade," their diversions included the traditional pastimes of gambling and visiting prostitutes. Parents who insisted upon the security of a more isolated and structured environment sent their children to Tsinghua or Yenching, not Peita. As a result, the latter attracted a highly intelligent but socially motley assortment of students, semi-students, and non-students. "Alongside the showy Yenching students, those from Peita seemed drab and reticent," recalled one-time Yenching matriculant John Paton Davies, Jr.[123] In contrast to the fresh-faced, eighteen-year-old Yenching and Tsinghua freshmen, many began studies at Peita while in their mid-twenties or later. This was reflected in a popular saying among Peiping coeds: *"Pei-ta lao, Shih-ta ch'iung, Yen-ching Ch'ing-hua k'o t'ung-yung!"* (Peita men are too old, Normal U. too poor; get a Yenching-Tsinghua man for sure!)

James Bertram, who returned to Peking in 1956 to find the quasi-rural Yenching campus now a university suburb housing Peita, mused upon the pre-Liberation contrast between the two institutions:

The lovely [Yenching] campus—formerly the neglected villa of a Manchu prince—had been carefully planned and replanted around its lakes and old bridges; and the original buildings remain perhaps the happiest blend yet achieved between modern construction and traditional Chinese palace architecture. Yenching students were mostly the sons and daughters of officials and wealthy merchants. They were charming, graceful creatures—especially the girls, as they cycled round the campus in their slit skirts of coloured silk.

It was different at Peita, the old Peking National University within the walls of the city, where poor students in cotton gowns blew upon their nails in unheated classrooms, and went out perhaps once a week for a good meal of Mongol mutton in a market restaurant. With all its poverty and material shortcomings, it was Peita that had the reputation for scholarship: what was best taught at Yenching, it would not be unfair to suggest, was foreign manners and the art of making useful friends.[124]

The urbanized, unregimented, rather anarchic aspects of Peita life made it difficult to organize student movements. One could not work through free and active student government organization as at Yenching. Many students could not be reached through dormitory communications because they lived off-campus. On December 9, as the swarm of demonstrators passed Peita's gates, its students responded impulsively and the

---

[123]John Paton Davies, Jr., *Dragon by the Tail* (New York: Norton, 1972), p. 144.

[124]Bertram, *Return to China*, pp. 145–46.

birthplace of the May 4th movement was represented by a small contingent that marched under a cardboard box top proudly inscribed with the characters for Peita.

However, once the movement was under way, it was inconceivable that Peita would play anything but a leading role. The meeting of December 10 that voted to initiate a general strike was held, appropriately, at Peita. The same day, Peita became the first post-December 9th school to be raided by police; six students were arrested.[125] Nonetheless, the very loose-knit urban ambiance that frustrated political organizers also made Peita an attractive refuge for "professional" students and other revolutionists. For example, NLVC leader Li Ch'ang studied at Tsinghua but lived at Peita.[126] It is striking that all the students and teachers known to have been Communists before December 9, 1935, were at Peita and other universities within the city walls. The most important and famous of these was a Peita student named Yü Ch'i-wei, better known in later years as Huang Ching.

Huang Ching

Huang Ching was born around 1911 into an influential family in Shaohsing, Chekiang. One uncle, Yü Ta-wei, later held cabinet posts in the Nationalist government; a second became an adviser to the Hopei-Chahar Political Council (prime target of the December 9 and 16 demonstrations), and a third, Tseng Chao-lun, was a famous Peita chemist and supporter of the student movement. In normal times, such a family would have gone on producing learned scholars and loyal ministers but these were not normal times. Huang's younger sister or cousin, Yü Shan, became an actress—and Huang became a Communist.

[125]Pa-li chiu-kuo ch'u-pan she, *Hsueh-sheng chiu-kuo yun-tung* [The students' national salvation movement] (Paris: Pa-li chiu-kuo ch'u-pan she, 1936), p. 139.

[126]Li Ch'ang, "Recollections," Part II, p. 33.

Huang Ching was studying physics at Tsingtao's Shantung University when the Japanese invaded Manchuria in 1931. His earliest recorded political activity was his participation in the student movement that fall. Like Ch'ien Chia-chü and thousands of other young patriots, he carried his protest to Nanking. Back in Tsingtao, Huang joined the Communist Party, became chief of the Propaganda Department in the city's Party committee, and was imprisoned by the authorities. Released on bail, he traveled to Shanghai, where he contacted people in the dramatic world. Huang returned once more to Tsingtao where, according to some accounts, he met a young actress who went under the stage name of Lan P'ing. The two are said to have lived together and may have been married, but politics apparently displaced romance, for Huang left to continue his revolutionary activities in Peiping. Six years, many miles, and one husband later, Lan P'ing arrived in Yenan, moved in with Mao Tse-tung and took the name Chiang Ch'ing. In 1966, after two-and-a-half decades in seclusion, she emerged as the leading Maoist in the Cultural Revolution. Huang Ching's widow, Fan Chin, director of the *Pei-ching jih-pao* (Peking daily), was one of the Cultural Revolution's first victims.

While Lan P'ing recovered from her broken romance and pursued her acting career in Shanghai, Huang Ching carried on his revolutionary activities in North China. He attended classes at Peita, possibly in the mathematics department. According to his own testimoney, during the December 9 movement, he was one of the two Communists in North China still out of jail but he presumably was referring to leadership elements only.

When Yenching students first brought Huang to see the Snows sometime after December 9 he introduced himself as David Yü. "I was struck by his appearance immediately," recalls Mrs. Snow:

He was fairly tall for a Chinese, pale, tired and ill looking, a little unkempt in his long Chinese gown, which all the student leaders wore at that time. His face was handsome and expressive with an easy smile and good teeth. He had a grandfatherly air toward the other students. He was cool and calm and gentle and tolerant. But his hands shook when he held a piece of paper, though he showed no other sign of nervousness. He was well-bred, with a pleasant, likeable manner, and he spoke good English. He had the quality of leadership—it permeated the room as he walked in even though his manner was quiet and shy.[127]

Peita students knew that Huang had a Party "background," but they did not care since this amiable and experienced revolutionist contributed substantially to their anti-Japanese cause. At planning sessions a day or two before demonstrations, Huang would arrive late with intelligence on the positioning of gendarmes and police and the location of their strong and weak points. Nonetheless, despite his skill in underground operations, Huang had no conspiratorial mannerisms to repel the liberals. In demonstrations, he marched with the masses but did not hesitate to step into an exposed position as a leader when the occasion called for it. Running into an old schoolmate and his wife on the street, Huang immediately helped them find a room in which to live.[128]

Huang's attitude toward his fellow students, though not at all condescending, was definitely avuncular. The wisdom and sophistication of this experienced revolutionary contrasted dramatically with the naive enthusiasm of his younger comrades-in-arms. He criticized the Yenching manifesto of November 1 as too leftist—excessively anti-fascist and insufficiently anti-Japanese.[129] In keeping with his scientific training, he loved to analyze politics cooly and rationally. Compared with the Yenan Communists, Helen Snow found him sophisticated about the KMT, which he meticulously categorized in terms of specific interest groups.[130] "I talked with many of the Communist leaders in Yenan," she wrote, "but none of them

[127]*NCSM*, p. 36.

[128]John Israel, interview with a Peita alumnus who wishes to remain anonymous, Hong Kong, December 11, 1973.

[129]*NCSM*, p. 36.

[130]*Ibid.*, p. 41.

had the information or dialectical thinking that impressed me so much as David had, except Mao Tse-tung himself."[131]

Experience had added to these "soft" virtues the toughness and total dedication of a seasoned revolutionist. By the time Huang Ching was twenty-five, more than ten young friends had been executed.[132] Helen Snow recalls him nonetheless as one who enjoyed revolution for its own sake.[133] Though he had a heart condition, he was unconcerned about his personal health. He ate on the run, slept inadequately, and moved every three or four days to avoid the police. "He did not expect to live long," explained Mrs. Snow, "and he wanted to make every minute count."[134]

Huang not only survived the war but advanced fast and was briefly mayor of Kalgan at the end of the Sino-Japanese conflict. After 1949, he served as mayor of Tientsin, rose to membership on the CCP Central Committee, and simultaneously held two ministerial positions. He died on February 10, 1958, while still in his mid-forties.

Lu P'ing

To students of the 1960s, the best known December 9th Peita alumnus is Lu P'ing. Lu was a sophomore in education and still went by his prerevolutionary name, Lu Ti. Big, strong, active in competitive sports, he played the role of a *ta-shou*—bully boy—during demonstrations.[135] Lu was an active member of the National Liberation Vanguards of China and became a member of NLVC Headquarters late in 1937. Together with Liu Chü-ying (later a Shantung guerrilla leader, and after 1949

131 *Ibid.*, p. 140.

132 *Ibid.*, p. 197.

133 Letter to John Israel, April 19, 1971.

134 *NCSM*, p. 36.

135 John Israel, interviews with a classmate of Lu's, Hong Kong, December 11, 1973, and with Wu Chün-sheng, former chairman of Peita's education department, Hong Kong, December 17, 1973.

one of the few December 9 men who remained in the
military—rising to the rank of major-general by the mid-1950s),
and Li Ch'ang (see above), he carried on debates at Peita
against NLVC "rightists" who blamed the leaders for polariza-
tion of the national salvation movement.[136] Lu went on to higher
positions: a top-ranking youth leader, vice-minister in the
Ministry of Railways (1954–57), vice-president of Peita
(1957–60), and then president (1960–66). Like his counterpart,
Chiang Nan-hsiang at Tsinghua, Lu fell victim to a new generation of student radicals during the Cultural Revolution. He was
labeled an anti-Maoist revisionist and was driven from the
presidency of the university where 30 years earlier he had once
led youthful left-wing stalwarts against the alleged tyrannies of
incumbent Chancellor Chiang Monlin.

Ma Ta-yu

Like Lu P'ing, Ma Ta-yu fought in the van and could also be
found up front whenever there was a meeting. Ma, a
Kwangtung native, majored in physics. After graduation, he
received a Ph.D. from Harvard and returned to China to teach
at wartime Southwest Associated University (Hsinan Lienta).
During the December 1st student movement in 1945, he was
beaten by KMT plainclothesmen, but he apparently had
mellowed since his student days, for he is quoted as passing off
the incident as a product of "human nature." Under the Peking
government, he became a member of the Standing Committee
of the All-China Federation of Natural Sciences and later director of the Electronics Research Institute in the Chinese
Academy of Sciences. As a student, he was considered a radical
nationalist rather than a Communist and he seems to have
remained on the non-Communist left. In August 1962, he was
named to the Central Committee of the China Democratic
League.[137]

---

[136]Li Ch'ang, "Recollections," Part II, p. 33.

[137]Interviews (see note 135); Yuan T'ung-li, *A Guide to Doctoral Dissertations*

Ch'en Chung-ching

Lu's schoolmate, Ch'en Chung-ching was a *rara avis*—the December 9er who hated his father. Born in November 1915, Ch'en lost his mother while in infancy. His father, a former Nationalist army officer, remarried, but Ch'en coexisted uneasily with both father and stepmother.[138] A former schoolmate at Peiping Normal University's Associated Middle School attributes Ch'en's quiet, lonely, and rather cold personality to the lack of maternal warmth in his upbringing.

Ch'en came to life in the meeting hall. A born leader, he was one of two freshman class representatives in the Student Union that year when the overriding issue was the Nanking government's failure to resist Japan's invasion of Manchuria.[139] During the December 9th movement, Ch'en frequently chaired mass meetings. Fellow students admired his articulateness, clarity, and analytic ability but saw in him, despite his excellent academic record, the embryonic bureaucrat rather than an intellectual.[140]

When war broke out, Ch'en followed Peita to its temporary refugee campus at Changsha. In 1938, together with Wu Ch'eng-ming and Hung T'ung, both from Tsinghua, he joined Nationalist General Hu Tsung-nan as an officer of the Hunan Youth Field Service Corps. Under Hu's aegis, he rose to deputy commander and finally to deputy provincial secretary of the Three People's Principles Youth Corps. During this time, it is said that he and other future CCP notables in Hu's service confessed their Communist affiliation and renounced the Party,

---

by Chinese Students in America, 1905–1960 (Washington, D.C.: The Sino-American Cultural Society, 1961), p. 164; Hsi-nan lien-ta ch'u-hsi fu-k'an, ed., *Lien-ta pa-nien* [Eight years of Southwest Associated University] (Kunming: Hsi-nan lien-ta hsueh-sheng ch'u-pan she, 1946), p. 199.

[138]Klein and Clark, *Biographic Dictionary*, 1:101.

[139]John Israel, interview with Ch'en's former schoolmate, Hong Kong, December 18, 1973.

[140]John Israel, interview with Peita alumnus who wishes to remain anonymous, Hong Kong, December 11, 1973.

though actually retaining membership status.[141]

By 1945 Ch'en was a member of the corps' National Committee and by 1946 an executive member of Shensi KMT Headquarters. Armed with these impressive credentials, Ch'en went abroad and enrolled in Columbia University's graduate program in economics. He returned to China without an advanced degree after the first semester of the 1948–49 academic year and was assigned to the P.R.C. Ministry of Foreign Affairs. He subsequently fulfilled his schoolmates' prophesy of a bureaucratic future and rose to the position of vice-chairman of the Commission for Cultural Relations with Foreign Countries.

Yao Chung-ming

Another Peita December 9 alumnus who achieved prominence in the diplomatic service is Yao Chung-ming. Yao probably was a year or two ahead of Ch'en Chung-ching, because he graduated from Peita before the outbreak of war whereas Ch'en had to wait until 1942 for an opportunity to complete his degree requirements. Yao was reportedly arrested by the KMT in 1937 for anti-Japanese activities and remained in prison until the outbreak of the Sino-Japanese conflict later that year. After his release, he helped organize a band of peasants and students in Shantung and moved with them to Yenan. There he joined the CCP, attended a Party school, and coauthored a play entitled, "Comrades, You've Taken the Wrong Path!" depicting the "struggle against rightist opportunism in the revolutionary ranks."[142] During the Marshall Mission, Yao served with the Military Mediation Department of the Tsingtao Armistice Team. After 1949 he became, successively, ambassador to Burma and Indonesia.

---

[141]Donald W. Klein, interview with a former subordinate of General Hu Tsung-nan, Hong Kong, January 1964; cited in Klein and Clark, *Biographic Dictionary*, 1:102.

[142]Klein and Clark, *Biographic Dictionary*, 2:997.

CHINA COLLEGE OF PEIPING

For reasons already noted, nearly nine out of ten of the prominent December 9 alumni hail from Yenching, Tsinghua, and Peita. What requires an explanation, however, is the paucity of representatives from China College. Politically, this institution was more polarized than any other Peiping college, with the possible exception of Tsinghua. Founded in the first year of the Republic by Sun Yat-sen, Sung Chiao-jen, and Huang Hsing, China College had historic ties with the Kuomintang. Sung and Huang were its first two chancellors—a position that remained largely an honorary one for prestigious party stalwarts—and Chiang Kai-shek served as an honorary chairman of its board. Its Chancellor since 1922 had been Wang Cheng-t'ing, ex-YMCA leader, former Nationalist foreign minister, and, in 1928 and 1931, target of anti-Japanese student violence. On the other hand, China College "reportedly had the largest number of underground Communist Party members of any college or university in Peiping."[143]

To join the December 9th demonstration, thirty or forty China College stalwarts broke through the school gate, which had been closed by campus police. Leaders chose the college to head one of four marching divisions in the demonstration of December 16. On December 22, China College's Sun Yat-sen Hall hosted more than 2,000 student representatives for an accusation meeting and exhibition at which 500 pieces of demonstrators' blood-stained clothing were displayed.[144] Police also gave the college due recognition and, in mid-February 1936, staged a series of raids after Wang Cheng-t'ing reportedly had labeled a student government meeting Communist-run and turned over a list of campus leaders to the authorities. On March 12, Huang Ching sent a note to the Snows declaring that

<hr>

[143]Howard L. Boorman, ed., *Biographical Dictionary of Republican China* (New York: Columbia University Press, 1967–71), 1:221. For further information on this little-known institution, see Chang Ch'i-yun, *Ta-hsueh chih*, 2:407–409, and Hsin Ch'en pao, *Chuang-k'uang*, pp. 193–210.

[144]Shih Li-teh, "The Rapids," in *RON*, p. 15.

Sung Che-yuan had ordered the execution of six China College students (two-fifths of all students in jail at that time were from this school). When the head of the Public Safety Bureau refused to carry out this order, Sung allegedly removed him from office and put him in irons. The six were sent to a military prison prior to being transferred to Nanking. This is the last we hear of them.[145]

The unusually tense situation at China College is captured in two photographs depicting the Students' Self-Protection Corps guarding the school gates. One of these shows eight tight-lipped guards equipped with staves. In the other, three students challenge a would-be visitor during a secret Student Union Meeting. This time the guards are armed—not with clubs but with rifles—and one of them, finger on the trigger, is holding a suspect at bay.[146]

There are indications, however, that China College radicals carried on their activities within a student body that was either apathetic or terrorized by official intimidation. Even though the school was supposed to lead a column on December 16, fellow demonstrators arrived to find a crowd of students casually lounging around the gate. Only a few of these joined the march. "Perhaps they had not gotten organized," commented a Yenching participant.[147] A scant 13 percent of China College's 922 students are estimated to have marched on that day—the poorest showing of any college in Peiping.[148]

[145]*NCSM*, pp. 120, 124, 130, 143.

[146]The photos originally appeared in Nym Wales, "Students in Rebellion," p. 451, where the pickets with staves are incorrectly identified as Yenching guards. The same photograph, correctly designated as China College, was reprinted in Chung-hua ch'üan-kuo hsueh-sheng lien-ho-hui, ed., *Chung-kuo hsueh-sheng ti kuang-jung ch'uan-t'ung* [The glorious tradition of China's students] (Peking: Chung-kuo ch'ing-nien ch'u-pan she, 1956), p. 25.

[147]Chin (pseud.), "I-ko chin-ch'eng mai-fu ti chiu-ch'a tui-yuan ti pao-kao [Report of a scout who entered the city and lay low], *SECTK*, no. 3 (December 20, 1937), p. 10.

[148]"Shih-liu jih p'ing-shih hsueh-sheng shih-wei yu-hsing shih, ts'an-chia, pei-pu, shou-shang, shih-tsung jen-shu t'ung-chi piao" [Statistical chart of the

China College's faculty may have been more radical than its students. Party veterans included Huang Sung-ling, who participated in the movement to oust Chancellor Wang Cheng-t'ing, and Ch'i Yen-ming, a China College alumnus who went on from a teaching job at his alma mater to become dean of a political training institute in Yenan. The college, in fact, has been ranked with Peita and Peita's College of Law and Commerce as one of three hotbeds of faculty activism.[149] However, its ten or more faculty enthusiasts were natural targets for political reprisals; not all lived to serve in the post-1949 order. Sun Hsiang-chieh vanished after she was dragged off by detectives on December 21, 1935, and Wu Ch'eng-shih lost his life in occupied Peiping during the war.[150]

Most prominent among China College's surviving faculty Communists is Ch'en Po-ta, who emerged during the Cultural Revolution as Mao's left-hand man for ideological matters before suffering total eclipse in 1971. Under the pseudonym Ch'en Chih-mei, he had been teaching at China College since 1930. His presentation of Chou philosophy was laced with a strong measure of Marxism-Leninism.[151] At the time, Ch'en was a leader of the CCP's North China Bureau. KMT sources accuse him of instigating the December 9th movement,[152] but there is no evidence to support this contention. We cannot assume that Communist faculty members overexposed them-

---

numbers of participants captured, wounded, and missing during the Peiping student demonstration of the 16th], *ibid.*, p. 12.

[149]See Hsu Te-heng, note 117; URI, *Who's Who*, p. 278.

[150]United Press dispatch, in *NCSM*, p. 85; Shan Ch'eng, "I-erh i-liu hou i-chou-chien ti mien-mien kuan" [Perspectives on the week after December 16th], *PTCK*, no. 1 (December 30, 1935), p. 29. This source cites the *Ta-kung pao (l'Impartial);* (Tientsin) of December 22, 1935.

[151]Shih Li-teh, "The Rapids," in *RON*, p. 5.

[152]Fei-wei jen-shih tzu-liao tiao-ch'a yen-chiu-hui, ed., *Fei-wei jen-shih tzu-liao hui-pien* [Collection of materials on men and affairs of the bandit bogus regime], ([Taipei?]: n.p., 1956–58), entry no. 2634–20; Chung-yang tiao-ch'a t'ung-chi chü, ed., *Chung-kung tsu-chih shih-k'uang* [The actual state of Chinese Communist organization], [Nanking?] n.p. [1937?]. n.p.

selves through conspicuous recruitment and agitation among their students. More likely, they worked quietly behind the scenes and it may well have been through the efforts of men like Ch'en that Huang Ch'eng "with the help of the Party," was admitted to China College after his expulsion from Tsinghua.[153] Marked men like Ch'en were well-advised to exercise caution, for the career of leftist professors was a dangerous one. Ch'en's colleague Liu K'ai-yuan was arrested by police, and Ch'en himself was the target of attempted assassinations and a movement to expel him from the college.[154]

We find only a single post-1949 press mention of a China College student militant (Kao Yuan-kuei, named in 1958 to head the Peking College of Geology). How many of Kao's comrades fell victim to the perils of war and revolution is a matter for speculation, but we do know that the most promising of them, Student Union Chairman Tung Yü-hua, succumbed to disease while leading guerrillas in eastern Hopei.[155] Even without wartime casualties, however, it is unlikely that China College students would have risen very high on the basis of revolutionary activism; even under the new order they could not hope to compete with the Tsinghua-Peita elite.

China College's radical tradition and low academic standing were closely linked. Professional revolutionists joined its faculty *faute de mieux,* having had scant opportunity to accumulate the graduate degrees and lists of erudite publications that served as tickets of admission to Peita and Tsinghua. Nobody with the dubious scholarly credentials of a Ch'en Po-ta could have hoped to win a post at a first-rate university. Nonetheless, having established revolutionary records well before December 9, Ch'en and some of his colleagues rose to prominence while their former students remained obscure alumni of an undistinguished institution.

[153]Shih Li-teh, "A Tribute to Huang Cheng," in *RON,* p. 161.
[154]Shih Li-teh, "The Rapids," in *RON,* p. 5; *NCSM,* p. 142.
[155]See Hsu Te-heng, note 117.

FUJEN AND NORTHEASTERN

If China College—somewhat surprisingly—made the poorest showing on December 16, it was still more surprising that Fujen University, a Catholic missionary stronghold, made the best. With dormitories spread over a wide area, Fujen posed problems for student organizers but was not easily cordoned off by authorities. The night before the December 16th march, Yenching scouts found refuge in the Fujen dorms where pressure from Chancellor Ch'en Yuan had almost compelled students to cease patriotic agitation and resume classes.[156]

The next morning, some 550 Fujeners joined the march. They represented 76 percent of the student body—the highest proportion of any school in Peiping.[157] Certainly something more than the location of dormitories was responsible for the massive turnout. Nor does it seem likely that religious affiliation played a significant role since only 85 of the 674 students enrolled during the 1934–35 academic year were Catholic. More pertinent is the geographic distribution of Fujen's student body. Unlike Yenching and Tsinghua, which drew heavily from China's south and central coastal provinces, Fujen was predominantly a northern institution. Nearly half (321) of these 674 students hailed from Peiping's home province, Hopei. Adding those from the other four provinces that Japan had staked out for "autonomy," and the three Manchurian provinces plus Jehol already under Japanese occupation, one finds that two-thirds of Fujen's student body came from provinces already occupied or threatened with imminent takeover.[158] For them and their families, the enemy threat was no abstraction.

Aside from Wang Kuang-mei (Mme. Liu Shao-ch'i, class of 1943), who postdated December 9, Fujen's most distinguished graduate in the Communist elite is P'eng T'ao. Before his death in 1961, P'eng was the Minister of Chemical Industry and an

---

[156]Chin, "I-ko chin-ch'eng," p. 9.

[157]"Shih-liu jih p'ing-shih hsueh-sheng shih-wei yu-hsing," p. 12.

[158]*Fu Jen* 4 (February 1935): 19.

alternate member of the CCP's Central Committee. Except for Huang Ching, P'eng was the only December 9 student known to have been a Communist before the outbreak of the movement. When he entered Fujen in 1935, P'eng was a seasoned revolutionary having, by his own account, spent "nearly half" of his youth in jail.[159] He had joined the Communist Youth League in 1927 at the age of fourteen and became a Party member in 1932. P'eng T'ao was probably under Party orders when he enrolled at Fujen.

One school that played a very prominent role was Northeastern University (Tung-pei ta-hsueh or Tungta). Formerly located in Mukden, this institution was nominally under the chancellorship of the Sian-based Young Marshal Chang Hsueh-liang. Anti-Japanese sentiments were coterminous with the institution's history. Even before the school opened in 1923, the Japanese consul in Mukden politely suggested that the higher educational needs of Manchuria would be adequately served by existing Japanese-controlled medical and engineering colleges without the establishment of this new institution. When the Japanese occupied Mukden on September 18, 1931, a handful of diehard student patriots armed with pistols and clubs tried to expel enemy troops from the campus; the blood of these young martyrs flowed in Tungta's entryway, classrooms, and the factory attached to its engineering college. Shortly thereafter, the Japanese principal of the South Manchurian Academy visited the campus and assured school officials that all expenses would be provided if they would but carry on classes as usual. Rather than become a puppet university, outraged faculty and students moved en masse to Peiping and Tientsin.[160]

The years between the Mukden Incident and March 1937, when the school moved to Kaifeng, were difficult ones for the

[159]Chung-kuo ch'ing-nien ch'u-pan she, ed., *Hung-ch'i p'iao-p'iao* [Red flags waving] (Peking: Chung-kuo ch'ing-nien ch'u-pan she, 1959), 10:28.

[160]Tsang Ch'i-fang, "Kuo-li tung-pei ta-hsueh" [National Northeastern University] in Chang Ch'i-yun, *Ta-hsueh chih,* 2:291, 294; Chung-kuo hsueh-sheng she, *T'u-chien,* p. 83.

refugee university. Until a suitable campus was found, students attended other universities in Peiping and elsewhere. Then there was constant moving from one poorly-equipped facility to another, hand-to-mouth survival based upon subsidies from various government agencies, the added burden of student refugees from other Manchuria institutions, administrative upheavals, the closing of a number of colleges and departments, and the removal of others to Sian. But the college survived and with it a fierce revanchist patriotism. In April 1934, an inspector from Nanking ranked Tungta's military training program above those of all other Peiping institutions of higher education.[161] Northeastern's refugee students sent strong contingents to both December demonstrations and were chosen to lead one of the four divisions on December 16. Many joined the rural crusade of January 1936 from which the NLVC emerged. Nonetheless, very few Tungta alumni are prominent in the ranks of Peking's hierarchy.

Better known than these former students is Hsu Ping, a CCP underground operative who was a professor at Northeastern University in 1936. In the spring of 1937, he allegedly helped to transmit Liu Shao-ch'i's directive to the more than 70 CCP members imprisoned in Peiping, ordering them to secure their releases by signing confessions. Liu's "reactionary" act was widely criticized during the Cultural Revolution,[162] and Hsu lost his key post as director of the Party's United Front Work Department.

The importance of Tungta's students in the December 9th movement and their inconspicuousness since 1949 is an anomaly that invites speculation. Tungta, like China College, was not a prestigious university capable of attracting the cream of China's intelligentsia. It was a regional institution, lacking countrywide patronage, and a refugee institution as well.

[161] *Ibid.*, pp. 295–96 and p. 83, respectively.

[162] "A Chronicle of Events in the Life of Liu Shao-ch'i (1899–1967)," *Current Background*, no. 834 (August 17, 1967), p. 4.

Northeastern students were driven by what Communists later anathematized as "narrow nationalism," specifically a monomania to expel the foe from their homeland. They were less revolutionists than homesick patriots. As long as the Young Marshal was in Sian, their ties were to him, not to Mao in Yenan.

Already refugees, Northeasterners had no place to flee when war began. Disproportionate numbers, perhaps, elected to stand and fight, and many, no doubt, failed to live until V-J Day. We know that students of Northeastern University and its associated middle school constituted a third of the 300 student volunteers decimated with Sung Che-yuan's troops at the Nanyuan Barracks on July 27, 1937.[163] Furthermore, the lack of a solid CCP base in Manchuria prior to 1945 has limited the representation of Northeasterners in the Communist order. This may help to explain why Tungta alumni form such a small proportion of the December 9th generation.

[163]Edgar Snow, *Battle for Asia*, p. 20.

III

Students in the Streets

The saga of the December 9th movement has been told before. It is not our purpose to retell it. The subject of this chapter is not an anonymous mass but a particular group of future Communist leaders whom we have labeled "the December 9 generation." We shall discuss the movement simply to spotlight activities of these individuals. In so doing, we must emphasize certain features at the expense of others. Of particular interest is the role of the National Liberation Vanguards of China, for it was through this organization that so many December 9ers were channeled into the Chinese Communist Party.

DECEMBER DEMONSTRATIONS

The Peiping Student Union, defunct since early 1932, was reborn on November 18, 1935. A week later, a number of college chancellors and professors in Peiping and Tientsin, including such moderates as Chiang Monlin and Hu Shih, proclaimed support for the students' stand against the Japanese-instigated "autonomy" of North China. However, words failed to stem the tide of events. Two days later, the Japanese inaugurated an East Hopei Autonomous Council under puppet Chairman Yin Ju-keng. The capital of the new satrapy was but 13 miles east of Peiping. On November 29, Peiping strongman General Sung Che-yuan wired Nanking that he could no longer withstand the pressure for placing five northern provinces—Hopei, Shantung, Shansi, Chahar, and Suiyuan—under an "autonomous" regime.

On December 3, General Ho Ying-ch'in arrived in Peiping. Ho was the architect of the notorious agreement that had given the Japanese a toehold in North China. Convinced that the surrender of North China was at hand and that further procrastination on their part would be suicidal, students drafted a list of demands. They opposed North China's autonomy and demanded open conduct of foreign relations and restoration of civil liberties. The manifesto would be presented in a massive march to Ho's headquarters near Peiping's Hsinhua Gate. The demonstration was set for the following Monday—December 9, 1935.

The young marchers would face unknown dangers. Under tight police control, Peiping had seen no public demonstrations for nearly three years. Kuo Ming-ch'iu, the redoubtable young chairwoman of the December 6 meeting that decided upon the demonstration, put the question bluntly: how many students would dare participate? The Yenching and Tsinghua delegations estimated that each could turn out one or two hundred schoolmates, but the overall estimate totaled less than a thousand. Kuo thereupon declared with confidence that the First Girls' Middle School would provide 300. Finally a red-cheeked little delegate from the Chihch'eng Girls' Middle School piped up: "We have only four or five who are really enthusiastic. Chihch'eng Girls, unfortunately, will be unable to contribute very many. We few are all junior high students." However, inspired perhaps by Kuo's brave words, she pledged, "We certainly will not fall behind!"[1]

---

[1]X.A.N. (pseud.), "Shih-erh chiu hui-i-lu," [Reminiscences of December 9th] *SECCNCNTK*, p. 11.

The students had underestimated their own strength. At dawn on December 9, from the dormitories of Yenching and Tsinghua, some thousand students emerged and set out across frozen fields toward the city walls. En route they encountered a small cadre of police, and Chang Chao-lin was saved from arrest only by the heroic efforts of his faithful coed admirers. However, unable to enter the city, the group had to be content with oratorical protest outside the barred Hsichih Gate. Among the speakers was Lu Ts'ui, who urged students to carry their movement beyond the educated few to the common people in factories and villages.[2] While Lu was winning over hearts and minds, Huang Hua catered to students' stomachs, unappeased since a predawn breakfast. Huang returned to campus and secured dumplings from a cooperative cook, but, when he requested use of the school's buses to carry these to his hungry comrades, Acting Chancellor Lu Chih-wei refused. However, the future diplomat managed to win over the already sympathetic bus drivers, and the multitudes at the Hsichih Gate were fed.[3]

Inside the massive city walls, students were converging on Ho Ying-ch'in's headquarters. There, too, coeds acquitted themselves with honor. "I have never seen anything so serious as the way in which the middle-school girl students led by one midget in a Cinderella cloak [probably Kuo Ming-ch'iu] shouted 'Down with Japanese Imperialism!' " reported Helen Snow. "They ran up to the hundred and fifty or so gendarmes and police guarding the entrance to the Hsin-hua Gate and gave them handbills—which they hastily stuffed in their pockets."[4] But students who broke through police lines to gather in front of Ho Ying-ch'in's headquarters found that the crafty general had outwitted them. He was spending the day at a spa outside the

[2]*NCSM*, p. 111.

[3]Han Suyin, *A Mortal Flower* (New York: Putnam, 1965), p. 371.

[4]P.F.S. [Helen ("Peg") Foster Snow], "The Peiping Student Movement," *CWR*, December 28, 1935, p. 127.

city. The demonstrators, some 800 strong, then wound their way through the city until they finally neared the sensitive and heavily-guarded Legation Quarter, scene of the Boxer siege of 1900. There they were scattered by police who wielded broadswords, flailed leather belts, and sprayed jets of icy water from fire hoses. At that point, according to a demonstrator's recollections published in Peking a quarter of a century later, the seasoned Communist agitator Huang Ching rallied the students back to Peita, where he leaped to the top of a low wall and called for defiance:

The swords, whips and hoses of the pro-Japanese traitors can never cow us into submission. Let's go back to our schools and organize a general strike of the Peiping students, workers and tradesmen. Let's stage another parade on an even larger scale! We will never allow the pro-Japanese traitors to sell out the sacred territory of our motherland piece by piece.[5]

Allowing for the bias and exaggeration of a partisan eulogist, the Huang Ching portrayed here is consistent with the photograph of the real Huang delivering a speech from a streetcar during the December 16th demonstration. It seems improbable, however, that that massive protest was first proposed by this young Communist in the heat of battle on December 9.

Apart from these vignettes of Huang Ching, Chang Chao-lin, Lu Ts'ui, and Kuo Ming-ch'iu, the other members of the December 9th generation are lost in the masses. Many undoubtedly were among the 90 percent of Peiping's college and high school students who failed to participate on that historic day. It was, nonetheless, the demonstration and ensuing events that shaped the collective consciousness of these young Chinese.

Since late October, Yenching's student leaders had been on the outlook for people who could put them in touch with the Chinese Communist Party, the only significant political organization that seemed sympathetic to their goals. After the December 9th demonstration, they found their man—Huang

<hr>

[5]Wang Lin, "In Memory of Comrade Huang Ching," in *RON*, p. 131.

Ching. Huang had lost no time establishing contact with activists at Yenching and other schools. Introduced to the Snows by Huang Hua, he appeared to be the "advisor" to a five-man group that now held clandestine meetings at the Snows' home.[6] At a series of such gatherings, officers of the Peiping Student Union planned a second demonstration. According to Huang Ching's eulogist, Wang Lin, future Communist luminaries played a prominent role:

Two students, briefcases in hand, appeared at the Changan Hotel in the Western Changan Street at dusk on December 15. They said they had come from Tientsin and asked for accommodation overnight. They were ushered into a room and registered their names. Soon after their arrival three other student-like visitors called. Chatting and laughing they all sat down for a game of cards. As soon as the waiter left the room, they closed the door, and playing-cards in hands they discussed the detailed arrangements for the second demonstration, the time and starting place and how to resist and frustrate the reactionary authorities. The two who had reported that they had come from Tientsin were Yao I-lin, a student of . . . Tsinghua University, then secretary of the Peiping Students' [Union], and Kuo Ming-ch'iu, representative of the First Girls' High School and acting chairman of the Students' [Union]. The three visitors were Huang Ching, P'eng T'ao of . . . Catholic University and Tung Yü-hua of . . . China [College]. The discussion lasted through the night and ended at dawn.[7]

Thus, as the movement grew, the decision-making process became increasingly elitist. The proposal to hold the first demonstration had been argued at great length and voted upon by student assemblies in the constituent schools; the decision to hold the second was reached by the General Affairs Committee of the Student Union, and the details were worked out by little knots of activists. Secrecy was considered essential to maintain the element of surprise. Not until the evening of December 15 did the union's Communication Corps spread word to con-

[6]*NCSM*, p. 12.

[7]Wang Lin, "In Memory," pp. 134–35. The Chinese version (*IECHIL*, p. 169) calls Yao I-lin the "secretary of the Party cell in the student union" and refers to Huang and Tung as "comrades."

stituent schools of the next day's demonstration. At Peita, it was the following morning before the student Communications Corps alerted schoolmates, who rushed from beds, breakfast, and books to the point of assembly. (One student was listening to his radio and reading a novel when a friend burst in and dragged him from his earphones to join the march.) In an unsuccessful effort to keep authorities from learning of their plans, pickets invested Peita's main gate and guarded the school's telephones. Yenching students trying to phone home with news of the imminent activities had their calls cut off at the switchboard.[8]

The four divisions of the second demonstration were to be led by Peita, Northeastern, China College, and Tsinghua—all foci of radical activism in the months ahead. It was inconceivable that the students of Peita, China's most prestigious university and fountainhead of the May 4th Movement, would march anywhere but in the front ranks. The revanchist Manchurian refugees of Northeastern, a potent force on December 9, could be counted upon to provide momentum for anti-Japanese activities. China College, as noted, was a hotbed of underground Communists. Finally, to lead the contingent of schools from outside the city, leaders shrewdly chose Tsinghua. Yenching students had provided much of the initial thrust, but they could not compete with Tsinghua either in institutional prestige or in depth of political resources for a sustained, radically-oriented nationalist movement.

According to student statistics, 7,775 young men and women from 28 schools marched on December 16—nearly a 400 per-

<hr>

[8]Pei-p'ing-shih hsueh-sheng lien-ho-hui [Peiping Student Union], *Pao-kao-shu* [Report] (Peiping, January 28, 1936), pp. 17–18; Augusta Wagner to J. L. Stuart, December 17, 1935, cited in West, "Yenching University," p. 496; Hsieh Yen-hsiang, "I-erh i-liu chi-shih" [An account of December 16th], *PTCK*, no. 1 (December 30, 1935), p. 11; Yu Ch'en, " 'I-erh i-liu' wo tsai pei-ta ti tui-wu li" [In Peita's ranks on December 16th], *ibid.*, p. 15; Ho I-hsing, "I-ko pei-pu-che ti tzu-shu" [A personal account by one who was arrested], *ibid.*, p. 20.

cent increase over the 2,000-odd that paraded on December 9.[9] "Peita, Shihta [Pei-p'ing Shih-fan ta-hsueh—Peiping Normal University], and Tsinghua carried off the honors in strategy and those arrested and wounded in the field of battle," reported Helen Snow.[10] National Peking University, a late-comer to the December 9th march, was totally engaged from the outset. Blocked by a blast of icy water as they led their contingent down Nanchang Road, Peita stalwarts wrested the hose from firemen and used it to drive back attacking police and broadswordsmen. Among the heroes of the firehose confrontation was Chu Chung-lung, a foreign-language student from Shantung who became prominent in the NLVC and joined the guerrillas shortly after the outbreak of war.[11] By the time their assailants had rallied for a new assault, other Peita students had cut the hose with pen knives, allowing the marchers to continue on to the meeting place at Tienchiao outside the city walls.[12] There, once again, Huang Ching delivered an impromptu pep talk. A photograph shows the young revolutionist dressed in an open overcoat over a long gown, his head topped by a fedora, with one hand hanging onto the streetcar while he gesticulates with the other.[13]

Once the meeting was over, police prevented the column of students from reentering the city until they had agreed to split into three groups. The largest, led by Tsinghua, would follow the city wall westward to enter through the Shunchih Gate; a

---

[9]*NCSM*, p. 139; "Shih-liu-jih p'ing-shih hsueh-sheng shih-wei yu-hsing shih, ts'an-chia, pei-pu, shou-shang, shih-tsung jen-shu t'ung-chi-piao" [Statistical chart of numbers of participants arrested, wounded, and missing during the Peiping student demonstration of the 16th], *SECTK*, no. 3 (December 20, 1935), p. 12.

[10]H.F.S. [Helen Foster Snow], "Further Developments in the Peiping Student Movement," *CWR*, December 28, 1935, p. 130.

[11]John Israel, interview with Peita alumnus who wishes to remain anonymous, Hong Kong, December 11, 1973.

[12]For an eyewitness account of the firehose incident, see Yü Ch'en, "'I-erh i-liu,'" pp. 15–16.

[13]*RON*, frontispiece.

small contingent of several hundred, led by Peita, would enter the city and march on a parallel route to meet the first inside the Shunchih Gate; and the remainder would remain in place pending further developments. However, as the Peita contingent (allegedly led by Huang Ching)[14] made its way to the Shunchih Gate, it encountered police and sword-bearing soldiers in battle array. It was useless to try to break through, but, as the column turned to retreat, it was attacked once again. At that point Huang Ching is said to have appeared on the parapet of the city wall and shouted to comrades on the other side, "Look out; they're slaughtering our people inside the city!"[15] There was little they could do, however, for the treacherous authorities had closed and barred the Shunchih Gate. It was then that Lu Ts'ui dashed forward and thrust herself underneath the gate in her heroic but futile effort to break the impasse.

Huang Ching and Yao I-lin had agreed to meet at a friend's house after the demonstration, but Huang did not arrive until 11:00 P.M. Wang Lin depicts him as "excited and tired," clothes torn, and overcoat stained with blood. "In a triumphant mood," he showed these battle trophies to Kuo Ming-ch'iu. According to Wang, Huang had made his way out of the city to the Shunchih Gate, where "he made certain that every student left the place safely before he made his own way to the agreed meeting place."[16] But Huang was tragically deluded if he thought he had seen everybody safely on their way home, for the Normal University students were ambushed and ferociously attacked by police as they returned to their dormitories late that night. Sixty of the 500-strong contingent were wounded, 20 of them seriously. Peita wounded numbered 26, and the day's total for all schools reached 382. Eight students, including

[14]Wang Lin, "In Memory," p. 137.

[15]*Ibid.*, pp. 138–39. For an account of this incident by another Peita participant, see Hsieh Yen-hsiang, "'I-erh i-liu,'" pp. 13–14.

[16]Wang Lin, "In Memory," p. 139.

Huang Hua, were arrested, though all were released by the week's end.[17]

Meanwhile, press reports, telegrams, and personal envoys carried news of the December demonstrations to Shanghai, Nanking, Wuhan, Tientsin, Canton, and other university centers in northern and eastern China. By the end of the month, some 65 sympathy demonstrations had been staged in 32 different places. Yenching student newspaper editor Ch'en Han-po was a special delegate from Peiping to Shanghai, where he was gratified to see workers and merchants join students in the demonstration of December 20.[18] Socially, as well as geographically, defiant patriotism was spreading.

BIRTH OF THE VANGUARDS

In spite of the known activities of Huang Ching and his cohorts, the Communists were by no means in control at the end of December. First, communications with the Party leadership, recently emerged from their Long March and now ensconced in remote northern Shensi, must have been sporadic at best. Second, the handful of pro-CCP activists in Peiping simply had no means of exercising power over the 38,000 university and middle-school students in the city. Due to the representative structure of the Peiping Student Union, the sources of power remained decentralized in constituent student bodies. Nobody recognized this situation more clearly than Huang Ching, who reportedly told other leaders on the night of the December 16th demonstration that "The most critical problem facing us at this moment is that our organizational work does not keep pace with the swift upsurge of the movement." He urged them to "think up ways and means of uniting and organizing the strength of the students and help[ing] the activists among them to become leaders."[19]

---

[17]*NCSM*, p. 139; "Shih-liu-jih," p. 12.
[18]*NCSM*, p. 148.
[19]Wang Lin, "In Memory," pp. 139–40.

If the Communists wished to establish hegemony over the burgeoning movement, they would need three things: (1) A clear united-front policy that would appeal to the thousands of students whose most pressing concern was for resistance, not revolution. (As of December 1935, the CCP had yet to adopt an unequivocal stand on the question of priorities.) (2) A program of action that would keep the movement alive and students usefully occupied while maintaining the mass base developed through the December dernonstrations. (3) An organizational structure that would bridge gaps between the central leadership in Shensi and the handful of cadres and sympathizers in Peiping, and between these cadres and the student masses. In terms of organizational structure, the Party needed (1) a well-disciplined core of CCP and CYL members, (2) a broader front organization that would attract non-Party leftist activists and serve as a source of recruitment for the Party and League, and (3) a Peiping Student Union responsive to these elements and amenable to their guidance. Whether or not these needs were clearly recognized in the beginning, the Party moved toward their fulfillment.

The Paoan-based leadership in northern Shensi was unprepared for the patriotic upsurge in Peiping. The united front was mood rather than reality. Now, quite suddenly, the initiative had been seized by a distant group of urban students. How would the CCP respond?

The most immediate impact was on the Communist Youth League. According to post-1949 accounts, the reorganization of the CYL had begun in November 1935 with the CCP Central Committee's "Resolution on Youth Work." This resolved to turn the league into a broad mass-based national salvation group open to all anti-Japanese elements.[20] The first open

---

[20]"Ch'ing-nien-t'uan li-shih ts'an-k'ao tzu-liao" [Reference materials on the history of the Youth League], *Chung-kuo ch'ing-nien* [Chinese youth], whole no. 203 (March 16, 1957), p. 10. Also, Cheng Kuang, "Short History of the Youth League," *Chung-hsueh-sheng* [Middle school student], no. 2 (February 3,

appeal to the students, however, came 11 days after the December 9th demonstration in the League's "Declaration to Students and Other Young Countrymen on Resisting Japan and Saving the Nation." The CYL announced that henceforth its ranks would be open to "all patriotic youth, whether or not they believe in communism . . . with the sole stipulation that they be willing to resist Japan and save the nation."[21] This bold initiative could not be easily implemented. How could the CYL change from a loyal junior branch of the Party to a broad patriotic coalition? What would happen under such conditions to painstakingly developed organizational and ideological controls? It is not surprising that the transfiguration of the CYL required—in the words of an official historian—"more than a year of experiment and change."[22] In the course of that year, it became evident that Peiping's student patriots could be brought into the Communist orbit via an enlarged version of the Communist Youth League.

The National Liberation Vanguards of China, an effective, pro-Communist, student organization, developed during a student pilgrimage to spread the anti-Japanese movement to the countryside of North China. As early as December 9, leaders such as Lu Ts'ui had urged students to disseminate the word to the masses beyond their colleges' walls. Heeding the call, small propaganda teams had gone to win converts in nearby suburbs and factories. This was very much in keeping with the Communist view that no movement of petit bourgeois intellectuals could succeed without proletarian support. However, the notion

---

1957), trans. in *Extracts from China Mainland Magazines*, no. 77 (April 9, 1957), p. 12.

[21]Chung-kuo kung-ch'an chu-i ch'ing-nien t'uan chung-yang wei-yuan-hui [CYL Central Executive Committee], "Wei k'ang-jih chiu-kuo kao ch'üan-kuo ko-hsiao hsueh-sheng ho ko-chieh ch'ing-nien t'ung-pao hsuan-yen" [A proclamation to the entire nation's school students and various circles of young countrymen on resisting Japan and saving the nation], in *IECYT*, p. 138.

[22]"Ch'ing-nien t'uan li-shih," p.83.

that intellectuals had a responsibility to provide moral leadership for the masses also was a traditional Chinese idea antedating Marx by more than two millennia, and mass proselytization had been an essential element in every Chinese student movement since May 4, 1919. Hence, ancient precepts, modern precedents, and Communist preachings all converged on this one point: the movement must be carried to the people. When a student congress on December 18 resolved to "ally the oppressed masses to the student leadership in a struggle against imperialism,"[23] it drew strength from these traditions.

The decision to launch a rural crusade may have been precipitated by another, more immediate, impetus. Kuomintang authorities were anxious to break up the movement before it went any further. School administrators, therefore, were urged to advance dates for winter vacations so as to disperse the student mass. In addition, a nationwide representation of hand-picked students, teachers, educators, and KMT notables was to meet in Nanking. Thus the government would gain a forum for promulgating its position and an opportunity to consolidate an alliance to stem the leftward drift of the student movement.[24]

The rural crusade would meet these problems head on. It would move students away from campuses so they could not be affected by early vacations and would give them an opportunity to rally popular support. According to some versions, leaders hoped, ultimately, to reach Nanking and petition the government, though a Communist historian has recently asserted that a resolution to this effect was voted down.[25]

No more than a fraction of the nearly 8,000 students who had marched on December 16, could be enlisted in the rural crusade. It was one thing to join thousands of fellow students in a parade through familiar city streets where police brutality might be neutralized by the protection of comrades and the

[23]*NCSM*, p. 161.
[24]See *SNIC*, pp. 130–31; Wang Lin, "In Memory," pp. 140, 142.
[25]Wang Lin, "In Memory," p. 143.

presence of friendly foreign correspondents. It was quite another to sign up volunteers to march hundreds of miles through unknown territory in the dead of winter. Observers of recent American student protest are acutely aware that the level of personal commitment required for forcefully occupying a building is greater than that for attending a teach-in or marching in a nonviolent demonstration. In contemporary parlance, Peiping's students were being asked to "put their bodies on the line." The long, arduous, and lonely mission in the hinterland would require total commitment by each participant. Strung out along dreary stretches of primitive roads, marchers would be isolated and vulnerable. In crowded city streets, a demonstrator might emerge unscathed but, in a remote village, a group of young agitators could be ambushed and massacred or whisked off to prison in the bleak winter's silence.

In addition to physical danger, the pilgrims faced formidable social and intellectual obstacles. In Peiping, one could lose one's identity among the masses. In villages, each individual would have to be heard and few tasks were more demanding than this effort to penetrate cultural and linguistic barriers that separated young urban sophisticates from simple rural illiterates. For these reasons, the recruitment process weeded out all but the most dedicated. Of more than 15,000 students in Peiping and Tientsin institutions of higher learning, a scant 500 marched. On only a few campuses did as many as 5 percent show up for the first day of the excursion. Except for five institutions—Peita, Tsinghua, China College, Northeastern, and Yenching—none turned out as many as 50 marchers. Proportionally, the highest level of participation was at Northeastern where about 7 percent of the refugee student body showed up.[26] The Northeasterners were a valuable component. As victims of Japanese aggression,

---

[26]Statistics based upon figures in Haldore E. Hanson, "Stalking the Education Bugbear in Peiping," *CWR*, November 16, 1935, p. 386; *NCSM*, p. 150; Chang I-ku and Wang Hsiao-feng, "P'ing-chin hsueh-sheng lien-ho hui k'uo-ta hsuan-ch'uan-t'uan hsia-hsiang hsuan-ch'uan" [The Peiping-Tientsin Student Union Propaganda Corps Goes to the Countryside to

they could describe the trauma in immediate and personal terms. They spoke a dialect easily comprehended by Hopei's peasants. Moreover, in contrast to the overwhelmingly urban student bodies at Yenching and elsewhere, Northeastern's enrollment included a large rural component (41 percent in 1931).[27] This might have given them better rapport with fellow agriculturalists. A critical observer remarked that more than half of the 30 Yenching men and 20 women who participated were freshmen, "young, innocents . . . dupes of some cleverer leaders who stayed behind and are pulling the strings."[28] Some did, in fact, stay behind to provide communications, publicity, and logistic and financial support. Among those who remained in Peiping was Huang Ching, a victim of a heart disease, too ill to march. On the other hand, among the pilgrims was Huang Hua, certainly no "young innocent." Counting both those in the field and their support group in Peiping, no more than one out of 20 college students and a mere handful of middle school youngsters enlisted for this daring enterprise.[29]

The process of natural and ideological selection continued en route as the physically frail and the politically timid dropped out and returned to Peiping. The dominance of leftist elements intimidated the others. Wang Chueh, a Yenching student who later initiated the Endeavor Society to compete with radical groups, was appalled when leaders staged didactic street plays and struck up the chorus of "The Workers' Song," ending with the refrain, "The Soviet Union is a Communist country / With a new life of freedom and equality / With work for all, yo-ho-ho / With work for all."[30]

Disseminate Propaganda], in *IECYT*, p. 64; and "Pei-p'ing ko-hsiao hsiao-hsi" [News of Peiping's Schools], *SECTK*, no. 8 (January 9, 1936), pp. 6–8.

[27]*Ch'üan-kuo kao-teng*, Table 55, p. 88, reprinted in West, "Yenching University," p. 373.

[28]Margaret Speer to her father, January 5, 1936, quoted in West, "Yenching University," p. 396.

[29]Helen F. Snow to John Israel, April 19, 1971.

After the departure of a small group of anti-Communists, Huang Hua was able to report that the remainder was "pure."[31]

The march introduced students to political problems that would continue to plague advocates of a united front. After a week of haranguing the stolid northern villagers, it was evident that purely anti-Japanese propaganda was pointless. Except for a few rural teachers and schoolchildren, the local people were indifferent to what seemed a fanciful threat from the Japanese "dwarf slaves." Many had not even heard of the Mukden Incident. How were students to convince peasants barely aware of the next village that they were endangered by events in Manchuria? The solution was obvious: they must appeal to the masses' immediate needs. For some, among them Liang Ch'i-ch'ao's daughter, Liang Szu-i, the discovery that peasants cared about nothing but taxes was a rude awakening.[32] But others, especially those who had previous contact with Marxist ideas or prior experience in the Chinese countryside, knew full well that the peasants' most pressing concerns were economic and social. After heated debates, it was decided that slogans against exorbitant taxes, rents, and interest rates should accompany protests against the Japanese. These won an enthusiastic response from the peasants.

The students had no opportunity to make more than a superficial impact upon the peasants. Within three weeks after they had set forth, all the pilgrims were rounded up by police or the troops of Sung Che-yuan and shipped back to Peiping. The real impact had been on the students themselves. From this sojourn in the wilderness veterans returned physically and

[30]*NCSM*, p. 150; Li Ch'ang, "Recollections," Part I, *SCMM*, no. 296 (January 15, 1962), p. 29.

[31]*NCSM*, p. 150.

[32]Comment to one of her professors on her return. Former Yenching professor, letter to John Israel, August 24, 1970.

politically toughened. A conglomeration of individuals had become a cadre. This fact was of great importance in the difficult months and years ahead.

After returning to Peiping, the rural crusaders formed a permanent organization to continue the struggle—the National Liberation Vanguards of China. It soon became evident that the NLVC was to be a front organization for the Communist Youth League. It is unclear, however, to what extent the CYL (or the CCP) planned this in advance and to what extent Communists simply took advantage of the situation as it unfolded. Vanguard historians disagree on this point. In October 1938, an official NLVC account indignantly denied that the organization had been "established through the prior planning of some political party."[33] However, in 1961, former NLVC chieftain Li Ch'ang wrote that the organization "was made by the Party" and had "adopted the Party's political program as its program of struggle."[34] Both statements were politically inspired, the former to maintain a necessary fiction during the national united front against the Japanese, the latter to support the official post-1949 myth that the CCP was responsible for every important development in the Chinese revolution after 1919.

The manner in which the organization evolved suggests a high degree of coordination and at least some advanced planning, if not outright manipulation. The Third Corps, consisting mainly of Yenching and Tsinghua pilgrims, included such prominent radicals as Wu Ch'eng-ming, Li Ch'ang, and Hung T'ung. When they were surrounded by plainclothesmen at Kaopeitien, Li urged resistance, but they decided to capitulate when assailants threatened to burn down their place of refuge. They were then separated into four groups, each quartered at a separate inn, two students to a room, and with a guard at every door. The next morning (January 15) they were shipped back to Peiping by train. They immediately gathered at Yenching to form a permanent organization. Chiang Nan-hsiang, who

---

[33]*SNL*, p. 4.

[34]Li Ch'ang, "Recollections," Part I, p. 30.

attended the meeting though he had not been on the march, suggested that the Third Corps call itself the Chinese Youth Salvation Vanguard Corps. Chiang was widely respected for his analytic abilities, and his proposal was accepted.[35] The purpose of the corps was "to comprehend and grasp the correct theory for carrying out the antiimperialist, antifeudal national liberation movement."[36] Two days later, Li Min wrote Helen Snow that the group would "read books of social philosophy and economics in order to increase their understanding of the situation in China and the world. The advanced members will be selected for some other organizations (secret, don't publish this)."[37] This group evidently was to prepare and screen recruits for the CYL and CCP.

Five days later, after the First Corps and Second Corps had been surrounded by police and were waiting to be sent to Peiping, members decided to form a permanent organization to perpetuate their spirit of unity. They called themselves the National Liberation Vanguards.

On February 1, all three corps met at Normal University with the Tsinghua Bicycle Corps (just back from a frosty but fruitless ride to Nanking) and decided to merge into a National Liberation Vanguards of China.[38] The Vanguard was organized along Leninist lines. Its structure was based upon democratic centralist principles. The basic units were three- to five-man cells (*hsiao-tsu*). These would be secretly organized with no "horizontal" relations with one another but only "vertical" relations with the next-highest unit, the squad (*fen-tui*). One man in each squad would be in charge of general affairs, a

---

[35]John Israel, interview with Hung T'ung, Taipei, October 30, 1973.

[36]Chang I-ku and Wang Hsiao-feng, "P'ing-chin hsueh-sheng," in *IECYT*, p. 69.

[37]*NCSM*, p. 151.

[38]According to Li Ch'ang, the Bicycle Corpsmen had organized a "Salvation Corps" (*chiu-wang t'uan*) whose leader, Ch'en Yuan, currently is a KMT official on Taiwan. Li claims that this group was absorbed, with some difficulty, into the NLVC. See Li Ch'ang, "Recollections," Part II, p. 30.

second of organization, and a third of propaganda. Above the squad would be the regional headquarters *(ch'u-tui-pu)*, and above that the general headquarters.[39]

It is quite obvious that the NLVC was established under the general guidance of Leninist elements. Less clear is the precise relationship of this organization to the CCP and CYL leadership in Shensi. Participants in the rural pilgrimage included prominent leftists such as Li Ch'ang, Huang Hua, Ch'en Han-po, Yang Hsueh-ch'eng, Yü Kuang-yuan, and Tung Yü-hua.[40] However, except for Huang Ching, who probably remained in Peiping, none is known to have been a Party member at the time. Furthermore, when the CYL announced that its rosters would be opened to all anti-Japanese youths, it did not seem to envision the creation of a separate front organization. The uneasy relationship that developed between CYL and NLVC leaders (see below) strengthens the suspicion that the NLVC either lacked the blessing of certain key elements in Paoan or that it developed an unanticipated degree of independence. Communist youth policy was, after all, very much in flux, and frequent reorganizations and changes of officers in the NLVC may reflect Party efforts to control enthusiastic but still undisciplined young intellectuals. These qualifications notwithstanding, the organization of the NLVC was a milestone in the CCP's relationship with the December 9th generation.

COUNTERATTACK FROM THE RIGHT

If the formation of the Vanguard provided hegemony for the left, Chiang Kai-shek's conference in Nanking (January 15–17, 1936) expedited the consolidation of the right. The pro-KMT minority among the students gained encouragement and support, and school chancellors and professors returned to their

---

[39]"Chung-hua min-tsu chieh-fang hsien-feng tui wen-chien" [NLVC documents], *IECYT,* p. 75.

[40]Lutz, "December 9, 1935," p. 642.

campuses with a clear mandate to suppress radical activities. Following the conference, open warfare between right and left erupted on several campuses, especially at highly-polarized Tsinghua. There, the right-wing School Protection Corps locked horns with the leftist National Salvation Committee and published the *Tsinghua Critic,* an anti-Japanese, pro-Nanking newspaper. In response to this challenge, the Peiping Student Union retreated from some of the radical phraseology of its formative days, which had left the group with a pro-Communist and pro-Soviet image. Slogans switched from advocating domestic revolution to stressing the need for a broad anti-Japanese front.[41] On February 8, the union called off its strike and urged students to return to classes.

For a time, however, the initiative remained with the union's critics. Spearheading progovernment forces was Peita's Dean Hu Shih and Yang Li-k'uei, dean and chairman of the physics department at Peiping Normal University. Hu maintained the lofty mien befitting his reputation as China's most famous apostle of gradual rational reform. He prescribed uninterrupted study and the free, open exchange of ideas as proper cures for the nation's ills and warned students against blind obedience to charismatic agitators.[42] Yang's role was less glorious. According to a recent Chinese Communist source, he negotiated with a delegation from the Peiping Student Union consisting of Huang Ching, Yao I-lin, and P'eng T'ao, tried to convince them that Chiang was preparing to resist Japan, and finally offered the union KMT leadership and monetary subsidy. His arguments refuted and his offers rebuffed, Yang acrimoniously terminated the meeting, dubbing his antagonists Communists. A short time later Yang charged that the union was receiving funds from the Soviet Union.[43] Ten days after this, Nanking promulgated an

[41]Pei-p'ing-shih, *Pao-kao-shu,* p. 13.

[42]Hu Shih, "Wei hsueh-sheng yun-tung chin i-yen" [A word on the student movement], *Ta-kung pao (l'Impartial)* (Tientsin), December 15, 1935.

[43]Yang's charges are cited in Ssu-li pei-p'ing yen-ching ta-hsueh ch'uan-t'i hsueh-sheng [Yenching University student body], ed., *Wei yao-ch'iu chiu-kuo*

Emergency Law to Maintain Public Order. Next came a directive outlawing the Peiping-Tientsin Student Union, the regional body with which the Peiping Student Union was affiliated. In Peiping, the commander of the Bureau of Public Safety announced that he would use "whatever force is necessary" to destroy the union and other student political activities.[44]

During the last two weeks of February, police raided Peita, Tsinghua, Normal University, Northeastern, China College, and the Northeast Chungshan Middle School, arresting more than 100 students as well as several faculty members. Hapless youngsters caught with "dangerous" literature were hauled off to prison. Prominent on the lengthy list of fugitives still at large was Peiping Student Union President Tung Yü-hua, for whose capture a reward of 1,000 Chinese dollars was offered. Torture was freely employed to extract confessions, and a Tsinghua student was, at least temporarily, paralyzed. Key leaders, however, were alerted by a warning network and managed to evade police. Among these were Huang Hua and Huang Ching, who narrowly escaped from a boarding house where they had planned to spend the night. During a climactic military assault on Tsinghua, Chiang Nan-hsiang, Yao I-lin, Wu Ch'eng-ming, Huang Ch'eng, Yang Hsueh-ch'eng, and others slipped away. Lu Ts'ui hid at the Snows, who finally smuggled her off to Shanghai. Actually police raids netted only two known leftists.[45]

Nonetheless, cajoled by professorial blandishments and cowed by police terror, the student movement was silenced, radicalized, and deeply divided. In the face of armed invasions of college campuses, fair-weather activists became subdued. Many turned to apolitical forms of escapism. As Li Ch'ang recalled:

---

tzu-yu kao ch'uan-kuo t'ung-pao [A proclamation to countrymen of the entire nation in regard to demanding freedom to save the nation]; pamphlet, March 13, 1936.

[44]*North China Star,* February 22, 1936.

[45]*NCSM,* pp. 108, 131, 132, 179; *SNIC,* pp. 138–44.

During the crucial struggle against search and arrest, large numbers of leadership cores left their universities, and the Kuomintang-hired professors exercised some bad influence over a number of students and even a few NLVC members with their big talk of "national salvation through studies" and about peaceful college life. As a result, a number of people represented by Chang Chih-kuang, a responsible person of the NLVC battalion of Tsinghua University, began to lose heart. They became liberal and dissolute, advocated "love affairs first," and stopped [doing] their work. Thereupon, the NLVC organizations were demoralized, and the battalion and some platoons were unable to hold meetings. Quite obviously, this showed ideological disintegration inside the NLVC organizations.[46]

However, the repression that silenced some radicalized others. The defiant indignation of jailed young patriots was vividly portrayed somewhat later in this letter from Huang Hua to the Snows:

Prison is the school for [us] patriotic youths of [colonial] settlements. Imprisonment is not [an] honorable thing, but not shameful either. It is a lesson. It tells us the cruelty of the ruling class, who, in the shakiness of their control, can only use imprisonment and torture . . . What are waiting for us are more longer imprisonment and more cruel penalty and slaughter, but after receiving this lesson we are more persistently going on.[47]

Within the ranks of the left, the conciliatory line of the united front was temporarily forgotten. In the Tsinghua branch of the NLVC, a self-styled "young and vigorous sect" labeled a rival group the "senile sect." The former charged that the latter "attached greater importance to the work of liaison with the upper strata than it did with the arousing of the masses" and in its united front strategy "opposed the independence and self-determination of the proletariat." One of the "seniles" was Hsu Yun-shu (Hsu Kao-yuan), who died in 1969 on Taiwan. Hsu's group was crushed, and a new NLVC headquarters was elected, including Li Ch'ang, a student named Chung, and

[46]Li Ch'ang, "Recollections of the National Liberation Vanguard of China," Part I in *SCMM*, no. 296 (January 15, 1962), p. 32.

[47]*NCSM*, p. 114.

three who perished during the war—Yang Hsueh-ch'eng, Ling Sung-ju, and Chi Yü-hsiu.[48]

By mid-March 1936, the leftists had partially recovered from the February raids. Bruised, embittered, isolated from the majority of their fellow students, they became prone to what CCP historians have called "excessive leftism and reckless action."[49] Within a fortnight they staged two antigovernment demonstrations. On March 18, the tenth anniversary of Tuan Ch'i-jui's slaughter of antiimperialist demonstrators, an estimated two thousand youngsters gathered at the Summer Palace near Tsinghua, made invidious comparisons between the warlords and their present rulers, and denounced both for murdering student patriots. Emboldened by this success, they planned a demonstration inside the city walls to protest the death of an imprisoned middle school pupil. On March 31, following a memorial meeting at Peita, mourners marched down the avenue four abreast bearing a white-shrouded coffin. This time, however, armed motor cycle police were waiting. More than fifty demonstrators were arrested. Seven of these (three girls and four boys) were from Yenching. Margaret Speer (the anti-Communist acting dean of Yenching's Women's College) reported that only one of them (Huang Hua) had been on the left before the demonstration, but the other six joined the radical ranks thereafter.[50] However, the immediate impact of the incident was counterproductive. Four participants, including Han T'ien-shih, were expelled from Peita.[51] At least one arrested student found, after two months in prison, that the powers of academe could be no less hostile than those of the judicial system. Upon release, he was ordered to make up three monthly

<hr>

[48]Li Ch'ang, "Recollections," Part I, p. 32.

[49]Hsiao Wen-lan [Yang Shu], Hua shih-tai ti i-erh chiu [The epoch-making December 9th] (Hankow: n.p., 1937), p. 23.

[50]Speer to father, May 5, 1936, cited in West, "Yenching University," p. 295.

[51]*NCSM*, p. 101; John Israel, interview with a Peita student who wishes to remain anonymous, Hong Kong, December 11, 1973.

examinations in engineering dynamics within a week.[52] Others who escaped imprisonment were once again cowed into silence. The politics of confrontation had reached a dead end.

TOWARD A UNITED FRONT

From February 1936 on, the driving force of Peiping's student movement had shifted to the left while the CCP was moving toward the right. By spring, their paths had crossed. The students' December 9 petition to Ho Ying-ch'in had expressed hope that Nanking would provide leadership against Japan. The CCP was then adamantly opposed to Chiang's regime and regarded the united front as a coalition of anti-Japanese, anti-Chiang forces under the Party's hegemony. At the Wayaopao meeting later that month, Mao called for a coalition that would incorporate selected segments of the bourgeoisie, including the "petit bourgeois" student, but *not* "the big local tyrants and evil gentry, the big warlords and the big bureaucrats and compradors." As for Chiang, he was "chieftain" of a "camp of traitors" whose "interests are inseparable with imperialism."[53]

This formulation of Party policy was logically and politically unviable. Relentless hostility to Chiang implied further civil war, which would preclude a truly nationwide anti-Japanese alliance. In February and March, CCP leaders in Shensi wrestled with this problem while the student front in Peiping was crumbling under KMT attack. Finally, on March 14, Mao con-

---

[52]Ch'ien Wei-ch'ang, "Wo t'iao-ch'u-le ti-kuo chu-i ti hsien-ching" [I escaped from the imperialist trap], *Kuang-ming jih-pao*, ed., *Ssu-hsiang kai-tsao wen-hsien* [Selected documents on thought reform], Shanghai: *Kuang-ming jih-pao*, 1952), 4:85.

[53]"On Tactics Against Japanese Imperialism," *Selected Works of Mao Tse-tung* (Peking: Foreign Languages Press, 1964), 1:155. The language of this document may have been altered for political reasons as suggested by Stuart R. Schram, *The Political Thought of Mao Tse-tung*, rev. ed. (New York: Praeger, 1969), p. 204, and Lyman P. Van Slyke, *Enemies and Friends* (Stanford, Calif.: Stanford University Press, 1967), p. 59. However, both authors find this document substantively consistent with others of the Wayaopao meeting.

ceded the possibility of a truce with KMT armies.[54] A further shift to the right occurred on May 5 when the CCP telegraphed to the Nanking government its first public appeal to end the civil war. According to a Party historian, "This telegram marked another momentous change in the tactics of the Chinese Communist Party—from 'resisting Japanese aggression and opposing Chiang Kai-shek' to 'forcing Chiang Kai-shek to fight the Japanese.' "[55]

Although students had anticipated this position in December, the political realities within Peiping in February and March made it difficult to reach an understanding even with local authorities, to say nothing of the Nanking government. However, the disastrous finale to the March 31st demonstration made it abundantly clear, at least to the politically sophisticated, that the leftist leaders had embarked on a self-destructive course. Increasingly militant tactics had cut them off, not only from faculty members, administrators, and local authorities, but from the mass of students. Far from consolidating a national united front against Japan, they were promoting internecine warfare among Chinese.

By April 1936 both radical student leaders and the CCP were prepared to move in the same direction: toward a truly comprehensive united front. Additional support for this policy came from the National Salvation Movement, a loosely-knit coalition of professors, journalists, lawyers, bankers, businessmen, and military leaders that had emerged since December 9. The National Salvationists congregated in Shanghai where the International Settlement and French Concession offered hope of political refuge. From these sanctuaries they tried to establish lines of communication between the national government and the Communists. Always sympathetic, sometimes influential, these adults were a bastion of support for the student move-

---

[54]Van Slyke, *Enemies,* p. 60.

[55]Liu Ching-yu, "The Anti-Japanese National United Front, Part 2," *People's China,* no. 18/57 (September 16, 1957), p. 28.

ment; their single-minded agitation for resistance to Japan encouraged students to support the idea of a united front.

On March 28, Peiping student representatives, including Huang Ching and Lu Ts'ui, attended a preparatory meeting in Shanghai for a National Student Association. There they had opportunities to consult with leaders of the National Salvation Movement. By the summer of 1936, the difference between student patriots and National Salvationists had blurred as recent college graduates and drop-outs moved into the wider political world. At least one of these, Lu Ts'ui, became a National Salvationist of international renown.

In February 1936 a high-level Communist emissary from Shensi reached the Peiping area. His name was Liu Shao-ch'i.[56] In Tientsin, this experienced organizer established the CCP's North China Bureau, from which he disseminated the new spirit of moderation and conciliation. Liu kept in close touch with events in Peiping. According to Li Ch'ang, he:

transmitted to us the Party Center's policy of the national united front of resistance against Japan to "force Chiang to resist Japan" (and later to "unite with Chiang to resist Japan"), and the instructions concerning the directive, policy, method, and way of eliminating the remnants of "Leftist" isolationism in day-to-day work.[57]

According to Shih Li-te, Liu was responsible for calling attention to the "leftist" errors in the student movement. Among his articles on this theme was one entitled, "Wipe out Closed Doorism and Adventurism," in which he cautioned, "When the situation and circumstances are unfavorable to us, we must temporarily avoid a showdown with the enemy."[58] Subsequently Liu allegedly ordered jailed Communists to sign public confessions as the price of release. Liu's policies, though quite

[56]The month of Liu's arrival, heretofore a matter of conjecture, has been pinpointed by an anonymous December 9er. See above, Chapter 2, note 3.

[57]Li Ch'ang, "Recollections," Part I, p. 34.

[58]Shih Li-te, "Chi-liu" [The rapids], *IECHIL*. This passage does not appear in the English translation of Shih's article in *RON*.

consistent with the general line of the CCP in 1936, acquired a sinister meaning during the Cultural Revolution. In May 1968 a Maoist faction in the Communist Youth League charged that:

Like all revisionists in the international communist movement, China's Khrushchev always opposed participation of the young people in the actual class struggles of their time. As early as 1936, the year after the nation-shaking December 9th patriotic student movement broke out under the leadership of the Communist Party, he did his utmost to push a Right opportunist line in the student movement. He abused the students for "going to extremes" and "running risks" and tried to entice them to engage in "cultural activities and recreation" and "reading." All this was aimed to divorce the young people from the seething movement to resist Japan and save the nation. The following year, he went further to put forward a whole series of bourgeois reformist absurdities to lead the youth movement astray and openly avowed that he would fight for the "vital interest" of the young people including "time for practice," "subsidies" and "jobs."[59]

At times Liu traveled to Peiping; at others he relied upon liaison men. Peiping activists also traveled to Tientsin to supplement local leadership. Huang Ching, in particular, played an important role in organizing Tientsin's massive but peaceful demonstration of May 28.[60] P'eng Chen, according to a PLA publication of August 1967, was Liu's "sinister pawn" charged with drawing the student movement "into the orbit of struggle."[61]

Under Liu's guidance, the North China Bureau expanded rapidly. According to Li Ch'ang, the CCP "gave high priority to expansion and training of student movement leadership, recruitment of Party and CYL members, and attraction of a

[59]Proletarian Revolutionaries in the Chinese Communist Youth League's Central Committee Organization, "Repudiating China's Khrushchov: Be Successors to the Revolutionary Cause of the Proletariat," *Peking Review*, no. 22 (May 31, 1968), p. 27.

[60]*NCSM*, pp. 39–40.

[61]Ch'en Chieh, "Such an 'Exemplary Worker in the White Areas,'" *Chieh-fang-chün wen-i* [People's Liberation Army literature and art], no. 12 (August 10, 1967), quoted in *SCMM*, no. 604 (December 4, 1967), p. 24.

mass following."[62] In May 1936, CYL was "reorganized." The reason, explains Li, was that the proliferation of youth organizations made it "no longer necessary to preserve the then rather confined and completely illegal Communist Youth League." At that point, all League members, including Li, who had been in CYL for barely a month, automatically became Party members. This instantaneous promotion of fledgling understudies in the Party's youthful adjunct provided an infusion of fresh blood for the CCP's urban organization. No sooner had Li become a member than he was importuned by several classmates, including Yang Hsueh-ch'eng and Wu Chih-chou, who were eager to join. Recommended by Li, they, too, were brought into the Tsinghua Party branch. Even middle school members of the NLVC managed to join the CCP at this time.[63]

These recruits were a major source for the group of bureaucrats and specialists who would one day become mayors, university presidents, and bureau heads under Chairman Liu Shao-ch'i. Between 1936 and 1941, according to Red Guard accounts, Liu drew into the North China Bureau at least 29 young men and women who would later rise to official prominence and, during the Cultural Revolution, fall into disgrace. Among them were December 9 leaders Chiang Nan-hsiang, Li Ch'ang and Yang Shu (Hsiao Wen-lan).[64]

It would be unfair to accuse Liu of megalomania for his efforts to bring these talented youths into the Party. It would be equally misleading to portray him and his student subordinates as "subverting" an untainted movement to Communist ends. The process was rather, as Jessie Lutz suggests, one of convergence:

Those Peiping students in contact with the Communist Party undoubtedly used their influence to guide students toward a united front policy, and there is no question that some of the student leaders of the

<hr>

[62]Li Ch'ang, "Recollections," Part I, p. 33.
[63]*Ibid.*
[64]*Yomiuri*, April 5, 1967.

Peiping-Tientsin Student Union were associated with leftist organizations. It seems unlikely, however, that a few leftist leaders could have transformed a policy with little or no appeal into one which was both popular and accepted. It is not important to try to prove a causal relationship between Chinese Communist policy and the movement of youth leaders toward a united front program. The events of the winter and spring of 1936 amply demonstrated the logic of such a policy, if not indeed, the inevitability of such a policy. What *is* important is the fact that the Chinese Communist Party and many of the New Youth were on converging paths during the December 9th movement, and the result was a growing sense of rapport between the two.[65]

The addition of the words "National Salvation" to the names of existing student organizations testified to the spirit of the united front. On April 12, the Peiping-Tientsin Student Union became the Peiping-Tientsin Student National Salvation Union, and, on April 25, the Peiping Student Union followed suit:

The change in name signified a change in policy. Confessing past errors, the Peiping Student National Salvation Union [PSNSU] announced that it would now concentrate on publicity and on a boycott of Japanese goods. Outside support was assiduously courted. One delegate called on the president of the Peiping Chamber of Commerce; others visited newspaper offices. Appeals to school chancellors included guarantees that coercive methods would be shunned. A PSNSU spokesman assured the public that future actions would be "frank and open," and directed toward the single goal of national salvation. "All patriots" were invited to cooperate in this endeavor and to offer advice and criticism. There was no further mention of demonstrations against Sung Che-yuan's police brutality or against Chiang Kai-shek's appeasement of Japan.[66]

This appeal to reason, compromise, and patriotism was irresistible.

REVITALIZING THE NLVC

No longer at the extreme left wing of the student political spectrum, Communists moved easily into positions of leadership. By

[65]Lutz, "December 9, 1935," p. 647. Italics are hers.
[66]*SNIC*, p. 149, quoting *Voice of China* 1, no. 6 (June 1, 1936): 11.

May 1936 meetings of the PSNSU were being chaired by NLVC member Huang Ch'eng. He simultaneously directed propaganda for the local branch of the Communist Youth League.[67] The NLVC hastened to adjust to the new line. In an effort to broaden its appeal, the Vanguard discarded a key structural precept of Leninism by allowing "horizontal" relationships among its cells in different schools.[68]

Vanguard cadres developed new tactics suitable for an anti-Japanese united front. Guerrilla training was instituted to prepare students for resistance against the invader. On April 28 NLVC battalions from Tsinghua and Yenching conducted maneuvers, and on May 17 a larger exercise, sponsored by NLVC organizations inside the city, attracted some 200 stalwarts. Even in mid-July, after many students had dispersed for the summer, training camps in the Western Hills drew in excess of 160 participants the first week and 220 the next. During these exercises, NLVC recruitment was spurred by theatrical performances, including a popular propagandistic play by Jung Kao-t'ang.[69] The Vanguard grew from some 300 members at its inception to more than 1,300 by June.[70]

Implementation of the united front was not, however, a simple matter. On May 17, a wide-ranging debate broke out among more than thirty NLVC representatives assembled at a Peiping university. How many concessions dared they make to calm apprehensive school and city authorities? What tactics would maximize mass support without incurring official repression? Who were their true allies in the united front against Japan and who the false friends? These problems came to a head early in June with the outbreak of the "Southwest Rebellion"—the proclamation by Kwangtung and Kwangsi

---

[67]Shih Li-teh, "A Tribute to Huang Cheng," *RON,* p. 161; Li Ch'ang, "Recollection," Part I, p. 33.

[68]Li Ch'ang, "Recollections," Part II, p. 30.

[69]*Ibid.,* pp. 28–29.

[70]*WMTTW,* p. 14.

leaders of a northern expedition to fight Japan. Like the CCP's declaration of war in 1932, the announcement rang hollow since the nearest troops belonged not to Japan but to the Nanking government. Peiping students were faced with a conundrum, as was the CCP and the entire National Salvation movement. If students supported the southwest generals, they would be guilty of encouraging civil strife and abetting warlords. On the other hand, if they ignored or opposed the southwest initiative, they would appear to renege on their pledge to back all anti-Japanese forces. After much soul-searching, the PSNSU supported the renegade Southwest Political Council's anti-Japanese program with a demonstration on June 13. This event was most note-worthy for the unprecedented fraternization between students and 29th Army troops and local police. Few tears were shed among student leaders when, a fortnight later, the rebellion collapsed. Their agonizing dilemma had mercifully evanesced.

After the June 13th demonstration, students decided to strike, thereby creating further controversy in activist ranks. At some schools, notably Yenching, the strike proved exceedingly unpopular with graduating seniors. As the semester drew to a close, strike leaders found themselves isolated.[71] In the wake of the strike, some 200 Vanguards were expelled from Peiping schools.[72] In addition, professors sympathetic to the student movement were informed that their contracts would not be renewed. Though expulsion of so many cadres was a serious loss to the Vanguard in Peiping, it helped to disseminate the move-ment. While a few of the expelled, such as Huang Ch'eng, transferred to other schools in the city, and some returned to their homes, others carried the movement to China's northwest provinces where the CCP was expanding its sphere of influence.

Huang Hua, traveling as Edgar Snow's interpreter, became,

[71]John Israel, interview with a member of the Yenching class of 1936 who wishes to remain anonymous, Hong Kong, August 10, 1959.

[72]Chung-hua min-tsu, *WMTTW*, p. 17.

perhaps, the first December 9er to reach the Communist capital of Paoan in remote Shensi. Following him, dedicated young pioneers began to trickle into the soviet area. Larger numbers reached Shensi's more accessible capital city of Sian where revanchist northeastern troops of Chang Hsueh-liang were half-heartedly imposing a blockade of the Red areas. There, the Young Marshal and Northwest Army commander Yang Hu-ch'eng allowed their troops to be proselytized by Manchurian refugee students like Chang Chao-lin. To the east, in Shansi's capital of Taiyuan, the warlord governor Yen Hsi-shan was toying with various forms of mass organization to wean youthful support away from the Communists. By September 1936 these efforts had crystallized in a League for National Salvation through Sacrifice.[73] Peiping students, working through the "Sacrifice League," local student organizations, the Taiyuan branch of the NLVC, and other united front groups, helped to transform this sleepy provincial town into a hub of anti-Japanese activities.

The exodus of trained cadres had undesirable consequences for Vanguard headquarters in Peiping. After the second summer camp in the Western Hills was broken up by police, local leaders turned their attention to organizational problems. Their diagnosis pinpointed serious maladies. The NLVC suffered from incohesion. District and local units lacked initiative and creativity; general headquarters was isolated from the rank and file; cadres were of low quality; methods for choosing officers were undemocratic. During August, the organization was thoroughly overhauled. Elections were held at all levels. New general headquarters officials included Liu Tao-sheng, Yang Yü-min, (Miss) Yang K'o-ping, and Sun Ch'uan-wen; in the autumn Ku Te-huan was added. Secretary-general of the NLVC was Li Ch'ang. Huang Ching became official liaison

---

[73]Donald G. Gillin, *Warlord: Yen Hsi-shan in Shansi Province, 1911–1949* (Princeton, N.J.: Princeton University Press, 1967), pp. 230–32.

agent for transmitting directives from the Party's Peiping Committee.[74]

The assignment of Huang Ching as liaison agent seems indicative of an effort to strengthen Party direction and discipline in the NLVC by the use of seasoned cadres. Liu Tao-sheng, another member of the new leadership, had a record of revolutionary experience dating at least to the winter of 1929, when he joined the Anti-Imperialist Alliance. He was then a first-year student at Peiping Normal University's Associated Middle School and was still known by his prerevolutionary name, Liu Wen-cho. The following year he joined the Young Communist League and was arrested and imprisoned for 58 days for participating in an Alliance parade.[75] During his senior year Liu was an extremely active propagandist and organizer in the anti-Japanese student movement that followed the Mukden Incident. A close friend and fellow representative in the school's student union had initially considered him a pure patriot but became convinced by his radical behavior that he was at least a member of CYL if not of the CCP. Liu attempted to recruit this friend and others to join Esperanto classes taught by a Korean; Esperanto was then chic among student radicals. During the late spring or early summer of 1932, Liu became involved in a demonstration at the Tienchiao amusement quarter in the southern section of Peiping. Another friend, Huo Ju-t'ang (later known as Huo Fei) was arrested, and Liu narrowly escaped.[76] Liu was enrolled in Peita's history department in 1932. It is unclear whether he remained long enough to graduate with his class in 1936, but his membership in the reorganized NLVC undeniably brought an experienced revolutionary student leader into its upper ranks.

In light of this reorganization and the tightening of Party control, we venture an interpretation of an otherwise incomprehen-

[74]Li Ch'ang, "Recollections," Part II, p. 30.

[75]URI, *Who's Who*, p. 413.

[76]John Israel, interview with a classmate of Liu's, Hong Kong, December 18, 1973.

sible historical footnote in the *Selected Works of Mao Tse-tung*. The editors of this official collection tell us that the NLVC was "formed under the leadership of the Chinese Communist Party in September 1936"—seven months after its actual creation.[77] This probably simply means that the Vanguard was not considered a disciplined Party organization until the fall of 1936. Even this shakeup, as subsequent events would reveal, failed to completely integrate the NLVC into the CCP's youth apparatus.

GROPING FOR NEW DIRECTIONS

Summer recess traditionally is burial time for student movements. Experienced seniors leave in June; inexperienced freshmen arrive in September. Surviving leaders are unable to rekindle the fires of the previous semester. These problems plagued Peiping activists when schools reopened in the fall of 1936. Worse, the NLVC had come to monopolize the energies of young radicals. By the first anniversary of December 9, all leftist activists at Yenching were reportedly NLVC members.[78] This sapped the resources of other groups and left the city's Student Union moribund.

The NLVC itself was immobilized by disputes. These were especially severe at Tsinghua where only the skilled leadership of CCP Branch Secretary Yang Hsueh-ch'eng maintained a semblance of unity. Vanguardists were threatened, reports Li Ch'ang, by the "right capitulationism" of men such as Huang K'an. A delegate to Tsinghua's Student National Salvation Union, Huang was allegedly guilty of "attaching importance to connections with the upper strata and belittling the importance of the masses" and "talking about empty theories and neglecting practical work."[79]

<hr>

[77]*Selected Works of Mao Tse-tung*, 3:318.

[78]Yuan I, "Shih-erh chiu i-lai chih yen-yuan" [The Yenching campus since December 9], in *SECCNCNTK*, p. 18.

[79]Li Ch'ang, "Recollections," Part II, p. 33.

Nor was "right capitulationism" limited to Huang. Another activist who left the radical ranks was Hung T'ung. The Tsinghua sophomore's disillusionment with the Communists may be traced back to his relationship with a Hunanese coed in the junior class who had treated him with great solicitude since their association in the rural crusade of January. Hung's respect for this upper classman soon became tinged with feelings of love. His amorous dreams, however, were shattered one evening when she revealed that she was a CCP member and had been asked to invite him to join the Party. The abrupt intrusion of politics into a beautiful romance jolted the young man. That summer, when a Kuomintang official convinced him that the government was really preparing to resist Japan and was not going to sell out the country, Hung became a KMT supporter.[80]

Burdened by an excess of undirected energy, unchanneled idealism, and undisciplined ideology, NLVC cadres called a conference for October 4. Participants strove to eliminate the needless secrecy and excessive meetings that were destroying grass-roots spontaneity. In a tacit admission of failure to broaden the organization's social base, delegates resolved to consolidate the student foundation of the National Salvation movement.[81] Action centered in the NLVC's newly-established Military Department headed by Yang Yü-min and strengthened by instructors Yuan Yeh-lieh and Chu Ming who had been appointed by the CCP's Peiping Committee. Practice guerrilla maneuvers were held with increasing frequency, and interference by soldiers and police was foiled through skillful use of dispersion and regroupment tactics.[82]

---

[80]Hung T'ung, "Ts'ung-ts'ung san-shih nien" [A hectic thirty years], in Chü Hao-jan, ed., *Ch'ing-hua shih-chi pi-yeh san-shih nien chi-nien t'e-k'an* (Special thirtieth anniversary volume of Tsinghua's tenth graduating class), (Taipei, n.p., 1968) p. 60; John Israel, interview with Hung T'ung, Taipei, October 30, 1973.

[81]*WMTTW*, pp. 24–28; *SNL*, pp. 19–20; Li Ch'ang, "Recollections," Part II, p. 31.

[82]Li Ch'ang, "Recollections," Part II, p. 29.

Otherwise, the early fall months passed without incident. Students returned to their books, and the NLVC, in line with united front principles of nonprovocation, chose to react only where crises arose rather than to seize the initiative. Students were taken by surprise when armored columns of Japanese troops brazenly paraded through Peiping streets on November 3. The invasion of Suiyuan on November 15 prompted collections of money and clothing and the dispatch of small delegations to the front. But there were no mass demonstrations.

Kuomintang suppression finally produced what neither CCP organization nor Japanese aggression could accomplish: the rebirth of student militancy. The provocation was the intensified persecution of national salvation leaders in wake of the Suiyuan invasion. On November 23, six men and one woman prominent in the national salvation movement were arrested in Shanghai for alleged complicity with the Communists. Dubbed the "Seven Gentlemen" (after the "Six Gentlemen" martyred for protesting official misconduct during the Ming dynasty), they provided a stimulus for rallying patriotic indignation. The students were back where they had started a year earlier—challenging governmental intimidation of patriots. However, their protests failed to prevent further suppression. Student petitioners from Peiping were seized by secret police in Nanking and sent home under escort. Anti-Japanese strikes in Shanghai and Tsingtao were crushed.

The NLVC could ill afford to ignore this ominous turn of events. Though its mass base was narrower than that of the previous spring, its dedicated members, now 2,000 strong, inspired confidence. Bypassing the first anniversary of December 9 to avoid official countermeasures, a demonstration was set for December 12.

This event reflected the profound changes that had occurred in the student movement during the previous year. There was none of the naive antifascist rhetoric of the November 1, 1935, petition. Also lacking was the explosive spontaneity of December 9, 1935. The demonstration of December 12 was a professional production. Prominent in its planning were three leading Communists, all members of the NLVC. Huang Ching was commander-in-chief; Li Ch'ang was field marshal. From a hired limousine alternately leading and trailing the marchers, Yang Shu distributed pamphlets to onlookers.[83] Well-rehearsed dispersal and regrouping tactics were brought into play. Most remarkable was the positive response of local authorities. Moved by the spirit of the united front, seeing an opportunity to win student support, and hoping perhaps to steal a march on the central government in Nanking, Peiping's military rulers acted with unaccustomed permissiveness. The day culminated with a resounding speech by Peiping Mayor Ch'in Te-ch'un, deputy of Sung Che-yuan. Only months earlier Sung had been throwing demonstrators in jail. Now his deputy promised to fight shoulder-to-shoulder with students against enemy attack. Demonstrators were allowed to return to their campuses singing the "Marching Song of Volunteers."[84]

THE SIAN CRISIS

"Sian is gradually becoming a political and mass movement center."[85] The dateline was Sian, December 10, 1936, the author Chang Chao-lin. Twelve months before, as president of the Yenching student body, Chang had led schoolmates into the tumult of the December 9th movement. Now he was one of several hundred youths who had made their way to the Shensi capital since the beginning of the previous summer's vacation. James Bertram, an old friend from Peiping days, found Chang

[83]Li Ch'ang, "Recollections," Part I, p. 35.

[84]Bertram, *First Act*, pp. 8–16; Li Ch'ang, "Recollections," Part I, pp. 35–36; *WMTTW*, pp. 31–32; *China Weekly Chronicle* 8, no. 24 (December 10–16, 1936): 31; *NCSM*, pp. 68–70; A Student Correspondent, "Students March Again," *Voice of China* 2, no. 1 (January 1, 1937): 10, 16; Ch'in Te-ch'un, "Chi-ch'a cheng-wei-hui shih-ch'i ti hui-i," [Reminiscences of the period of the Hopei-Chahar Political Council], *Chuan-chi wen-hsueh* [Biographical literature] 2, no. 1 (January 1963): 21.

[85]*NCSM*, p. 66.

"in an office that shook with the furious thumping of underground presses . . . surrounded by a group of young assistants who had laid aside their blue student's gowns and were getting to work in shirtsleeves."[86] As editor of a local newspaper, Chang was doing his part to move Chang Hsueh-liang—and ultimately Chiang Kai-shek—into a united front with the Communists against the Japanese. He also managed a ratio station which broadcast in English, French, German, Russian, and Japanese.[87] Many students in the "Western Capital," like Chang, were from Northeast China. Those from Northeastern University were especially numerous. These veterans of the Peiping student front encouraged revanchist sentiments in the ranks of Chang Hsueh-liang's homesick soldiers.

On December 9, 1936, Sian students paraded to commemorate the first anniversary of the anti-Japanese crusade. Frustrated in attempts to see Sian officials, they marched toward Lintung, where Chang Hsueh-liang was reported visiting a distinguished guest—Chiang Kai-shek. Chiang was in Sian to persuade Chang Hsueh-liang to terminate his de facto truce with the Communists. In contrast, the students were demanding a total cessation of civil war and a nationwide united front against the foe. En route to Lintung, the procession was blocked by a contingent of cavalrymen with broadswords. At that point, Chang Hsueh-liang dramatically appeared and begged the marchers to avoid bloodshed by turning back. According to a recent Communist account, Chang, with tears in his eyes, declared:

Fellow students, I'm a patriot myself. Since the loss of the Northeastern provinces, many people throughout the country, men and women, young and old alike, have condemned me. I'm not afraid to fight the Japanese, but my superior won't permit me to do so. I'm deeply distressed about the situation, but there is nothing I can do about it. I do love my motherland. I will fight the Japanese. You can

[86]Bertram, *First Act,* p. 167.

[87]*Ibid.,* p. 175.

trust my word. Within a week I'll answer your demand with deeds. If I don't, you can take my life![88]

The Young Marshal was true to his word. The following night, he presented the students' petition to Chiang. He could scarcely have been prepared for Chiang's furious response: "I severely upbraided him for his acceptance of . . . the 'People's Front,' his enlistment of reactionary politicians, and his *laissez faire* attitude toward the activities of the so-called National Salvation Association," wrote Chiang in his diary.[89] We have no testimony from Chang Hsueh-liang as to how he received this tongue-lashing, but those who have witnessed Chiang's outbursts testify to their formidable impact. One thing that must have been evident to the Young Marshal was the futility of further argument. Chiang's allegation that Chang's resentment over this reprimand impelled him to accept Yang Hu-ch'eng's long-standing proposal of rebellion[90] must, however, be judged in context. The anti-Communist campaign was scheduled to resume on December 12. As Lyman P. Van Slyke notes, "This was the last possible moment for Chang to act. He risked losing the loyalty of his officers and men if he continued to follow Chiang Kai-shek's order."[91]

At dawn on December 12, the sound of gunfire at Lintung heralded the Sian mutiny. By breakfast time, Chiang Kai-shek was a prisoner of the Young Marshal.

Chiang's kidnapping severely strained the newly-laid foundation of a united front. The dilemma was similar to that posed by the Southwest Rebellion. The Communists had to choose between two tough alternatives: support the insurrectionists and destroy any chance of reconciliation with the central

[88]Li Lien-pi, "Flames of Wrath," in *RON*, pp. 95–96.

[89]Chiang Kai-shek, *A Fortnight in Sian: Extracts From A Diary* (Shanghai: The China Publishing Co., 1937), p. 91.

[90] *Ibid.*, p. 90; Earl Albert Selle, *Donald of China* (New York: Harper, 1948), pp. 323–24.

[91]Van Slyke, *Enemies*, p. 74.

government, or oppose them and lose allies far more reliable than the obdurate prisoner.

The CCP position was considerably more tenuous than it had been six months before. The June rebellion, after all, had occurred in a region remote from the forces of Mao Tse-tung, and its outcome was decided by factors quite beyond his control. The Sian Incident, on the other hand, occurred in Shensi on the very doorstep of the Communists' stronghold. If Chiang Kai-shek prevailed, it would mean the end of the secret truce between Communist and Nationalist units that had existed for the past eight months.

There was no *deus ex machina* to save the Communists from the agonizing choice. A public trial followed by Chiang's execution, as suggested by some extremists, had tremendous emotional appeal to men like Mao who had lost loved ones to Kuomintang vendettas. But such a move would expose Chang Hsueh-liang, Yang Hu-ch'eng, and the Communists to a powerful retaliatory thrust from Nanking that they were ill-prepared to meet. Moscow, moreover, had condemned the action of Chang and Yang as sheer treason; significant deviation from this position would disrupt the international Communist movement. Finally, there was the irrefutable fact that Chiang was somebody else's prisoner. Therefore, after one brief moment of unrestrained elation, a perplexing silence descended on Paoan.

Initial reports from Sian reached Peiping late on the night of December 12. Many students were sound asleep after a day of demonstrating. But in some of the dormitories there was all-night dancing and singing.[92] According to Li Ch'ang, the first reaction of left-wing students was "extreme excitement and joy. . . . How gladdening it was to learn [of] the arrest of the chief criminal and principal evil-doer who had rebelled against the great revolution and started the 10-year civil war!"[93] The

[92]*NCSM*, p. 160.

[93]Li Ch'ang, "Recollections," Part II, p. 31.

celebration was not restrained by imprisoned National Salvation leaders or dumbfounded Chinese Communist higher-ups. However, the first reports of Russian press reactions threw leftist ranks into confusion. As Helen Snow recalls:

The shock we received on December 12 was not greater than that received when Tass news carried an article in Izvestia . . . on December 14, 1936. This attacked Chang Hsueh-liang for staging a mutiny inspired by Wang Ching-wei, and the incident, an "entanglement of Japanese militarist intrigues," was called "danger not only for the Nanking government but for [all of] China as well." What could this possibly mean? It was incomprehensible to everyone, and especially to the young students. Some thought it was a lie to show they had no implication in it and wanted none. Others thought they had been deceived—but who could have thought up such a ridiculous idea? The fascists were amused and delighted—they laughed at the left-wing students who were simply non-plussed.[94]

Among those most rudely shocked was politically-sophisticated Huang Ching. "I saw him the day this [Izvestia] report appeared," writes Helen Snow, "and he was very disturbed and incredulous. He could not explain it, except that the Soviets had no information on China and were at sea. He did not think [Izvestia] was telling a lie to destroy the Sian position, but that they were not informed of the facts."[95]

Student perplexity was unsolved by the Chinese Communist statement of December 19, a full week after the incident. The declaration praised the "patriotic sincerity and zeal" of Sian's leaders and suggested that the "disposition of Mr. Chiang Kai-shek" be discussed by a broad spectrum of interested parties prior to the convention of a peace conference in Nanking.[96] The Communists obviously hoped to avoid a violent resolution of the problem that would intensify the civil war to their immediate

[94]*NCSM,* p. 72. For Soviet press reaction to the Sian Incident, see Charles B. McLane, *Soviet Policy and the Chinese Communists, 1931–1946* (New York: Columbia University Press, 1958), pp. 82–86.

[95]*NCSM,* p. 141.

[96]Mao Tse-tung and others, *China: The March Toward Unity* (New York: Workers' Library, 1937), pp. 122–23; Van Slyke, *Enemies,* p. 82.

disadvantage and end all hope for a united front. On the other hand, certain individuals in Nanking, including Ho Ying-ch'in, were more willing to launch a punitive expedition regardless of the personal consequences for their Generalissimo. To forestall such a move required the combined efforts of Mme. Chiang, T.V. Soong, Tai Chi-t'ao, and the Chiangs' trusted adviser, William Henry Donald. The idea of a punitive expedition received some support from Peiping's pro-Kuomintang students who, like their leftist opponents, were disinclined to temper emotion with reason. On December 16, fifty Peita students sent a telegram to Nanking advocating Chiang's release and endorsing a military crusade against the Young Marshal, apparently unaware that these were mutually exclusive alternatives.[97]

Less given to emotionalism was the self-confident CCP envoy, Chou En-lai. Chou was one of several CCP representatives who commuted back and forth between Nanking and Paoan. With the cooperation of Chiang's entourage (Mme. Chiang, T.V. Soong, and Donald), Chou helped Chang Hsueh-liang convince his prisoner that an agreement to form a united front was in the best interest of all. Though no explicit announcement was made, it appears that such an understanding was reached before the Generalissimo's liberation on Christmas Day.

RIGHTIST REVIVAL

Chiang's release placed Peiping's student radicals in a precarious position. In some quarters, nationwide rejoicing over the leader's safe return was combined with outrage against those who had delighted in his capture. The Left was caught flat-footed. "The situation changed too rapidly and abruptly for the [Vanguard] members to understand it immediately," reports Li Ch'ang. "Suddenly they became taciturn and felt disturbed at heart."[98] They were clearly in no position to resist the onslaught of their enemies.

[97]*NCSM*, p. 71.
[98]Li Ch'ang, "Recollections," Part II, p. 31.

Rightist revenge was unleashed on the night of December 25. After a torchlight parade, members of Tsinghua's School Protection Corps ransacked the office of the National Salvation Association and the rooms of NLVC members. Leftist books and newspapers were confiscated and thrown in a great heap on the athletic field. A counterattack was led by Yang Hsueh-ch'eng but not in time to save Vanguard literature from a giant bonfire.[99] Violent clashes also occurred in other places, including Northeastern University where a new chancellor replaced incumbent Chang Hsueh-liang, who had accompanied Chiang Kai-shek back to Nanking and was now his prisoner. At Normal University, Professors Yang Li-k'uei and Hsiung Meng-fei called for the expulsion of all NLVC members and pro-KMT students mauled Yen Shih-ts'un and a number of other Vanguards.[100]

Ever sensitive to vicissitudes in the political climate, Peiping's military commander Sung Che-yuan ordered censorship of newspapers, books, and magazines, a ban on student meetings, and the arrest of "progressive students."[101] Student unions in a number of universities and middle schools were forced to disband. On December 26, police arrested several prominent NLVC leaders, including Huang Ch'eng and Shih Li-teh.[102] Meanwhile, middle school students were granted a day's recess for a massive parade in support of a punitive expedition against Chang Hsueh-liang's now-leaderless troops.

Assailed by right-wing rivals and ignored by other schoolmates, NLVC members could derive scant satisfaction from the evolution of a Nationalist-Communist united front in the months following the Sian Incident. Chiang Kai-shek saw no inconsistency in settling scores with his non-Communist critics

[99] *Ibid.*, p. 32.

[100] *Ibid.*; *WMTTW*, p. 34; *NCSM*, p. 74; *China Weekly Chronicle* 9, no. 1 (January 6, 1937): 24; 9, no. 3 (January 20, 1937): 10; 9, no. 4 (January 27, 1937): 30; 9, no. 5 (February 3, 1937): 31.

[101] Shih Li-teh, "A Tribute to Huang Cheng," pp. 164–65.

[102] *Ibid.*, p. 165; Li Ch'ang, "Recollections," Part II, p. 32.

while negotiating a settlement with Mao. The "Seven Gentlemen" were held in prison. Chang Hsueh-liang also remained captive. Right-wing students in Peiping and Tientsin, heartened by new-found popularity, rebuffed leftist offers of a united front. Scores of young Sian activists left for Yenan as troops loyal to Nanking replaced those of Chang Hsueh-liang and Yang Hu-ch'eng. Student leaders who remained behind limited themselves to small-scale intramural activities.[103]

Thus, as Mao moved closer to Chiang, his student sympathizers became increasingly frustrated. They were hemmed in by the self-defeating policy of uniting with foes who pummeled and jailed their cohorts, burned their literature, and banned their organizations. For the first time since the outbreak of the movement, the right wing was more cohesive and effective than the left. While its heretofore feeble rival, the pro-KMT "New Student Union" gained confidence, the "Old Student Union" (PSNSU), which once had numbered its members by the tens of thousands, was reduced to a few thousand by the end of December.[104]

Apprehensive over indecision and internal strife among NLVC leaders, the CCP now placed Vanguard headquarters in direct contact with P'eng Chen of the North China Bureau. P'eng, a seasoned organizer recently emerged from six years in prison, was a trusted subordinate of Liu Shao-ch'i. On February 6, in Peiping, under P'eng's leadership, the NLVC convened its first nationwide congress. Officers were chosen, and Li Ch'ang was named general director. Hsu K'o-jen became secretary-general. Ting Fa-shan headed the Organization Department, Yü Chih-yuan the Training Department, and Ting Hao-ch'uan the Propaganda Department. About half of the 39-man Executive Committee (including these officers) survived the rigors of war and revolution to achieve high positions in the post-1949 period.[105]

---

[103]Bertram, *First Act,* p. 263; Li Lien-pi, "Flames of Wrath," p. 117.
[104]Hsiao Wen-lan [Yang Shu], *Hua shih-tai,* pp. 27–28.

The congress brought together twenty-four delegates from eighteen NLVC branches, as well as representatives of the Federation of National Salvation Associations and the North China National Salvation Association. The strongest components were those of Peiping, Sian, and Tientsin, with 2,300, 2,000, and 700 members, respectively. Nearly all were students except in Tientsin, where factory workers, members of the liberal professions, and policemen in the Peace Preservation Corps (!) constituted two-fifths of the roster.

In spite of these impressive statistics for the year-old organization, the congress took note of widespread despondency resulting from official repression since the Sian Incident. Delegates endorsed a proclamation urging their constituents to overcome a tendency to be "leftist in outlook, rightist in action."[106] This rather enigmatic formulation probably referred to the rank and file's outspoken, doctrinaire radicalism, which invited repression and in turn led to excessive caution. Yet, it may have been nothing more than a compromise formula worked out between factions. Either or both of these explanations is quite consistent with the facts as we know them, for there is no question that the NLVC was the victim of considerable bickering and confusion in the wake of the Sian fiasco.

This sad state of affairs was also reflected in a semiannual report of the NLVC's Tientsin headquarters issued on March 1, 1937.[107] Although students comprised 70 percent of the local unit and their union was the broadest "united-front" type student organization, noted the report, the Vanguard had at times "completely ignored" the union. This had greatly hampered the work of both organizations and obstructed communication with

---

[105]Li Ch'ang, "Recollections," Part II, p. 32; Klein and Clark, *Biographic Dictionary*, 1:474; and information provided by Roy Hofheinz, Jr.

[106]*WMTTW*, p. 57.

[107]T'ien-ching min-hsien tsung-tui-pu [Tientsin NLVC headquarters], Pan-nien-lai kung-tso chien-t'ao [Critical analysis of work during the past half year] (Tientsin: T'ien-ching min-hsien tsung-tui-pu, March 1, 1937).

the student masses. Vanguard members had not only ignored a headquarters directive to establish associations in various schools but had even allowed several existing associations to become inactive and dissolve. United front operations, bemoaned the writer, had been extremely clumsy. Vanguardists who had infiltrated student associations had transformed them into overpoliticized national salvation groups; those who won control of glee clubs refused to allow them to sing anything else but national salvation songs. In this way, the NLVC had isolated itself from "the relatively backward majority" and had raised the suspicion that it was a "manipulated group." Thus, most students had adopted an attitude, to paraphrase Confucius, of "respecting the spirits but keeping their distance."

During the spring semester, while Vanguards wrestled with these problems, the Old Student Union was floundering. Its leaders seemed unable to decide whether to attempt a united front with the New Student Union or to engage its rival in open competition.[108] While long-standing animosities obstructed ecumenical objectives, hesitation and self-doubt made it difficult to maintain tactical initiative. The NLVC's problems were likewise too complex for easy correction. Up to the outbreak of war the CCP continued to criticize vanguards for hewing to a narrow sectarian line, excluding youths of other factions and groups, and failing to develop into a mass organization.[109]

Unpromising as the situation may have been in North China, it seemed still gloomier elsewhere. Late in May, Edgar Snow encountered Yenching's former student body president Chang Chao-lin. "I never saw him so deeply in the doldrums," Snow wrote. "He has just returned from a long trip from the south, is very depressed, and sees little hope anywhere."[110]

---

[108]*SNIC*, pp. 177–78.

[109]Chung-kung chung-yang [CCP Central Committee], Kuan-yü tang yü ch'ün-chung kung-tso ti hsin ts'e-lueh [The new strategy regarding the Party's work with the masses] (n.p., 1937).

[110]Nym Wales [Helen F. Snow], *My Yenan Notebooks* (mimeographed, Madison, Conn., 1961), p. 24.

LEFTIST SURVIVAL

The survival of a vital Left in Peiping was due in no small measure to the renewed creativity and ingenuity of the NLVC. During spring vacation, the Vanguards conducted low-cost student excursions in the Western Hills. The first of these outings, at Hsiangshan, drew more than 3,000 participants, the following day's at Wenchuan more than 5,000. Mountain-climbing was followed by the performance of didactic songs and plays. At Hsiangshan, Chang Jui-fang and Ts'ui Wei, today leading actress and actor-director, respectively, in China, appeared in the popular street play, *Lay Down Your Whip.*

The Public Trial of the Seven Gentlemen, an improvised theatrical piece, was performed in a local confectionary. Among those later to win prominence in the Communist movement were production director Huang Ching, script writer Li Ch'ang, and Huang Ch'eng, who played the role of journalist Tsou T'ao-fen, one of the Seven Gentlemen. Huang Ching, who also assumed charge of make-up, showed considerable ingenuity by fashioning a beard for "Shen Chün-ju" (another of the Gentlemen) out of strands of horse hair. The judge's moustache was fashioned from a writing brush, and his briefcase was borrowed from Professor Ch'i Yen-ming. Even the police were cajoled into lending a hat and belt for their thespian counterparts.[111]

Verve and spontaneity compensated for the player's lack of professionalism. One of the "court policemen," refusing to confine his talents to his wordless role, insisted on forcing venerable Shen Chün-ju to bow before the judge. Several minutes passed while Shen stubbornly resisted and director Huang Ching nervously stamped his feet offstage. Shen concluded the scene with an impassioned speech on behalf of justice and human rights. The audience was spellbound. The performance inspired a collective telegram demanding the release of the Seven Gentlemen and all other political prisoners.[112]

---

[111]Shih Li-te, "Chi-liu," p. 61.

[112]*Ibid.,* pp. 61–62.

In May 1937, Communist student leaders were able to meet with high-level Party figures at a conference in Yenan. Leading the Peiping-Tientsin delegation was Liu Shao-ch'i; another delegate was P'eng Chen. Yang Hsueh-ch'eng of Tsinghua went as a Party representative of Peiping students. This was the young man who "had only a preliminary understanding of Marxism" during the early phases of the December 9th movement and who had joined the Party less than a year before.[113] Other student delegates included Huang Ching of Peita, Li Ch'ang of Tsinghua, and Lin I-shan of Normal University. Traveling in disguise, the group reached the soviet zone via the Sian office of the Eighth Route Army, arriving in Yenan in time for the May 1 celebration. Huang, accompanied by Helen Snow, took the train from Peiping to Sian. Prudently, he said nothing to her during the entire trip.[114] In speeches before the gathering, Yang and Li told veterans of the Long March about the sentiments and concerns of Peiping's revolutionary students.[115]

At the conference, Liu Shao-ch'i delivered a highly controversial report entitled "The Chinese Communist Party in the Past Decade." Liu blamed the "left opportunist" Party line for the CCP's disastrous record in the "white areas" and advocated the employment of open, legal united front tactics. The obvious implication of Liu's speech was that he, as head of the Party's North China Bureau, could succeed where others had failed. Since alleged perpetrators of self-destruction filled his audience, the speech caused an uproar and the conference was suspended while the impasse was resolved. The solution was to shelve Liu's address and replace it with a very different kind of statement by General Secretary Chang Wen-t'ien. After his formal report, which played down errors and accentuated the accomplish-

---

[113]Chiang Nan-hsiang, "In Memory of Comrade Yang Hsueh-cheng," in *RON*, pp. 150–51; *IECHIL*, pp. 179–80, varies slightly in wording.

[114]Helen F. Snow, letter to John Israel, April 19, 1971.

[115]Li Ch'ang, "Recollections," Part II, p. 35.

ments of the previous decade, Chang told the delegates that the imminence of Japanese invasion rendered it imperative that Party operations focus on the villages. Operatives in the city would have to go underground and prepare for guerrilla war. This would effectively reverse the direction of Liu's policies in Peiping and Tientsin. Liu was then relieved of command of the North China Bureau. Though his policies furnished ammunition for the assault on him thirty years later, he was saved from further humiliation at that time by his close association with Mao Tse-tung.[116]

One afternoon, Mao paid a visit to the delegates from the "white zone" and introduced them to Liu. According to Li Ch'ang, they now learned for the first time the true identity of "K.V.," who had transmitted Party policy in the mimeographed periodical *Huo Hsien* (Fire line). During the meetings, Liu called for widespread dissemination of the patriotic movement and the legalization of outlawed activities. He told students that war with Japan was imminent and that they would soon have to change scholars' gowns for the garb of guerrillas.[117] Mao's instructions to the conference made an especially profound impression on Huang Ching.[118] Mao evidently made good use of this opportunity to learn about the situation in North China's urban areas, for he was able to report to Western correspondents an overall rise in Communist influence in Peiping's schools in spite of a decline at Yenching.[119]

At the Yenan meetings, the delegation of young Peiping intellectuals also had an opportunity to fraternize with soldiers who had not been near a large city for a decade. Cordial relations developed. Li Ch'ang and Huang Ching were invited to move in with Kuan Hsiang-ying, commissar of the Second

---

[116]Warren Kuo, *Analytical History of the Chinese Communist Party* (Taipei: Institute of International Relations, 1970), 3:251–60.

[117]Li Ch'ang, "Recollections," Part II, p. 35.

[118]Helen F. Snow, letter to John Israel, April 19, 1971.

[119]Nym Wales, *My Yenan Notebooks*, p. 132.

Front Army, and the trio stayed up late into the nights discussing the situation in the "white zone." Under an invitation from Kuan and Second Front Army Commander Ho Lung, the two young men visited troops at Chuangli, Fuping, on their way home. There they told battle-hardened soldiers that the Red Army would be joined by NLVC members and other "patriotic students" on the front of resistance.[120]

However egalitarian the students might have considered themselves, they appeared otherwise to Helen Snow, who retraced her husband's footsteps to the Northwest. When Yenching students Fullsea Wang and Ch'en Han-po joined her on her travels, Mrs. Snow noted:

Wang and Ch'en insisted on bringing private property along—three big suitcases which filled the car. Strange how feeble the intellectuals are compared with the people. Ch'en cannot even carry his own suitcase and the Red Army man picked up his knapsack and suitcase and strode along.[121]

When she interviewed her old friends Huang Ching and Huang Hua, Mrs. Snow was shocked:

Both had taken on the airs of mandarins immediately and were completely engrossed in the Yenan scene. They were more attractive in the Peking days, when [Huang Ching] was starving and moving from one *kungyu* [apartment] to another for safety in his conspiratorial, romantic life. . . . After two weeks in Yenan, he had become healthy and fat and his heart condition seemed to be cured: "It's the first time I've been among friends and in safety," he told me. "I'm so happy here that I gain weight with everything I eat."[122]

Mrs. Snow's photograph of a beaming Huang Ching in army uniform bears witness to his happiness, while the 1958 obituary photographs of the then moon-faced official attest to his losing battle with a weight problem. Huang Hua was also very impressed with Yenan, wrote Mrs. Snow. "He said he had ex-

---

[120]Li Ch'ang, "Recollections," Part II, p. 35; Shih Li-teh, "A Tribute to Huang Cheng," pp. 169–70.

[121]Nym Wales, *My Yenan Notebooks*, p. 35.

[122]*NCSM*, p. 78.

pected poverty and was surprised by the discipline. He was amazed at the possibilities of the mass partisans and at the generosity of the Red Army and at the consciousness of the masses, also by the way they treat spies, etc. all by thought control."[123] Two years later, when Edgar Snow revisited the Communist area, he found that "Huang Hua had greatly matured and was now a man of quiet confidence, full of duties; he was secretary of a youth salvation association, and dean of a school somewhere farther north. Like all Christian-educated students I met in the Communist camp, . . . he somehow made me feel that he was more at peace with himself, psychologically, than Christian youths in other parts of China."[124] "Attractive" or not, Huang Hua had evidently found his milieu.

Upon returning to Peiping, Huang Ching and the other delegates to the Yenan conference began to prepare schoolmates for another summer of patriotic activities. Some attended a camp in the Western Hills at which Yang Hsiu-feng and other "progressive" professors provided ideological guidance. Propaganda groups also went into rural areas in the Western Hills and suburbs of Peiping.[125] Hoping to provide an alternative to left-wing leadership, Chiang Kai-shek ordered all second-year middle school and university students to enlist. Among those who shaved their heads and packed out to Sung Che-yuan's army camp in the Western Hills were Shih Li-teh and Huang Ch'eng.[126] Only three months before, these young men had been political prisoners in one of Sung's jails. The united front was becoming a reality as China prepared for war.

[123]Nym Wales, *My Yenan Notebooks,* p. 41. Based upon interview in Yenan, May 4, 1937.

[124]Edgar Snow, *The Battle for Asia* (New York: Random House, 1942), p. 282.

[125]Shih Li-teh, "The Rapids," pp. 32–33.

[126]Shih Li-teh, "A Tribute to Huang Cheng," p. 169.

IV

The War They Wanted

Although the Sino-Japanese War conventionally is dated from the Marco Polo Bridge Incident, China was not "plunged" into war on July 7, 1937. It was not apparent that this was anything more than another minor skirmish between Chinese and Japanese forces in North China. The next three weeks, punctuated by a series of related incidents, were also marked by negotiations at several levels. In the streets of Peiping, barricades were erected and torn down according to diplomatic needs and military prognoses. Even after the Japanese had occupied the city on the night of July 28, it was more than five weeks before the enemy launched its full-scale invasion of China.[1]

PEIPING BESIEGED

For Peiping students the weeks following the July 7th clash were uneasy ones. Though it was not immediately clear that Peiping was doomed, the time and manner of enemy occupation soon became subjects for daily speculation and rumor.

[1]Chalmers Johnson, *Peasant Nationalism and Communist Power* (Stanford, Calif.: Stanford University Press, 1962), p. 33.

137

Communications along the Peiping-Hankow Railroad were cut. Peiping-Tientsin service, first interrupted on July 9, was thereafter unpredictable. The crisis caught students unprepared. A few feverishly tried to get into Peiping while others scurried to leave. Yen T'ieh, a CCP member at the Northeast Chungshan Middle School, which had just been moved from Peiping to Nanking, headed back to Peiping en route to Shensi where he hoped to join the Red Army. When he reached Tientsin, he heard of the Marco Polo Bridge outburst but decided, nevertheless, to press onward. At Fengtai, just a few miles from Peiping's city walls, his train was halted by Japanese troops and ordered back to Tientsin. With several other intrepid passengers, Yen decided to proceed on foot. At the Tienchiao district, on the outskirts of town, Japanese guards were inspecting and tying up pedestrians who appeared "suspicious." After passing this inspection, Yen caught sight of an unnerving spectacle—more than ten Chinese corpses—before he finally reached his destination.[2]

Many students, including a sizable proportion of left-wing activists, had remained in Peiping for the summer. On July 10, as news of further clashes between Chinese and Japanese troops filtered into the city, the Peiping Student Union (and, according to some sources, the NLVC and the CCP Peiping Committee) established an auxiliary organization to aid the 29th Army. Students also joined other North China patriotic groups in conducting propagandistic, morale-boosting, and fund-raising activities on behalf of front-line troops.[3]

Sung Che-yuan's 29th Army, the principal force in the Peiping-Tientsin area, numbered about 40,000 men. Scattered at various points inside and outside the city and seriously underequipped, they were unprepared to confront the well-

<hr>

[2]Yen T'ieh, "Na-ch'i ch'iang-kan tou ko-ming" (Take up your guns and fight the revolution), *IECHIL*, pp. 156–57.

[3]*Ibid.*, p. 157; Li Ch'ang, "Recollections," Part II, p. 36; *SNL*, p. 23.

coordinated and highly mechanized Japanese force. For more than a year, students had been proselytizing and fraternizing with the 29th. Their efforts had produced results among the lower ranks of officers where anti-Japanese sentiments ran highest. Sung had reciprocated by accepting student volunteers. More than 300 had enlisted early that summer. One hundred of them, composed of Manchurian refugees from Northeastern University and its associated middle school, were organized into a special unit,[4] most of which was stationed at the Nanyuan barracks.

These ardent patriots translated the oft-repeated pledge to offer their lives for China's salvation into reality. On July 25, the Japanese North China Command issued an ultimatum to Sung Che-yuan: he had 48 hours to withdraw his troops from the Peiping region. The next day, Sung replied that Chinese troops had no alternative "but to defend the country to the best of their ability and resources." By this act of bravado, Sung signed a death warrant for the outnumbered, outpositioned, and out-gunned troops. For 24 hours the Japanese subjected the 3,000 men at Nanyuan to a steady barrage of shells and bombs. Two-thirds of the defenders were killed, including more than 200 of the students who had volunteered only a few weeks earlier.[5]

Sung's garrison evacuated Peiping and Tientsin during the night of July 28. On the 29th, students awoke to find Japanese sentinels patrolling the streets. Now it was too late to escape. "The ancient Tartar walls that had formerly given a false sense of security were now in grim reality a cage," wrote Edgar Snow. "The apocalypse had come; people felt like prisoners awaiting sentence."[6]

[4]Edgar Snow, *The Battle for Asia* (New York: Random House, 1942), p. 20. James Bertram, *Unconquered* (New York: John Day, 1939), p. 54, speaks of "nearly a thousand Peiping students quartered in the Nanyuan barracks," but the figure seems excessively high.

[5]Edgar Snow, *Battle for Asia*, p. 3.

[6]*Ibid.; SNL,* p. 24.

For about ten days, there was no communication with the outside world. With newspapers suppressed, rumors ran riot. In the student community demoralization prevailed. The Japanese were known to have drawn up a list of political suspects. Some of these, prewarned by sympathetic puppet police, moved from place to place to avoid capture. Other students, fearing to appear on the streets, remained in their rooms.[7]

Members of the CCP and NLVC were comparatively well prepared to cope with the emergency, but carefully drafted contingency plans were nullified by events. The CCP's Peiping Committee instructed its followers to organize guerrilla units or to join KMT armies whenever possible, otherwise to go underground. When Yen T'ieh established contact with comrades in the student association of the Northeast Chungshan Middle School, he found them hastening to obey these orders. Kan Chung-tou was getting ready to leave for Shensi, Hsu Mai-lun for northern Shensi, and several others to work in underground literary activities. Yen received orders to join the guerrilla movement. Through Hsu Mai-lun, Yen met Tung Hsueh-li of Northeastern University; in a Northeastern dormitory more than twenty students joined Yen, Tung, and Yen's middle school associate Hsu Ming, to lay the ground work for a military unit. But harsh facts separated dreams from reality. These zealots were totally unarmed and had no contact whatsoever with any armed force. Before they could solve this quandary, Peiping became an occupied city.

NLVC members reacted promptly to the enemy occupation. On July 29, Huang Ching called an emergency meeting in a tea house, which was attended by Huang Ch'eng, Wang Wen-pin, and Li Ch'ang. Plans were made for NLVC members to evacuate via various routes and to reassemble in Tsinan, Taiyuan, and Paoting. However, escape was no simple matter. Rail service east to Tsinan and west to Taiyuan had been suspended. A few Vanguards gathered at Tsinghua and tried to

[7]Yen T'ieh, "Na-ch'i," pp. 158–59.

sneak through enemy lines on foot toward Paoting, but Japanese troops prevented them from reaching a critical river crossing, and all but a few (among them Yü Kuang-yuan) were compelled to return to Peiping.[8]

Edgar Snow, a well-informed and trusted friend of struggling Chinese students and intellectuals, was besieged by inquiries and pleas for help. Desperation, he discovered, had given rise to some rather fanciful notions. A "distinguished" professor thought the British Embassy might "guarantee the safety of the anti-Japanese intellectuals." One of Snow's former Yenching students asked if it were true that U.S. Marines were about to garrison Peiping "in accordance with the Nine-Power Treaty." A Peita student asked if British and American authorities would provide military trucks to convoy anti-Japanese students to the hills. None of these wishful thoughts had any basis in reality. Snow did manage to smuggle out one prominent revolution-ist—Teng Ying-ch'ao (Mme. Chou En-lai)—who reached Tientsin disguised as his servant. In the final analysis, however, Chinese puppet police were much more helpful than British and American authorities when it came to getting students over the wall and on their way to guerrilla territory.[9]

By the opening of the fall semester, Peiping had been largely drained of intellectual resources. There remained but 1,700 of 13,000 college students, fewer than 500 of 2,200 professors, and only ten of 26 colleges and universities. Of these ten institutions, only three (Yenching, Fujen, and Sino-French universities) were bona fide institutions of higher learning, all of them with foreign connections.[10] Even though well-known anti-Japanese activists had fled, however, occupation authorities found remaining students uncooperative. When only seven students showed up for an organizational assembly of a pro-Japanese North China Student Union, a second meeting was called. To

[8]Li Ch'ang, "Recollections," Part II, p. 36.

[9]Edgar Snow, *Battle for Asia*, p. 4.

[10]T. A. Bisson, *Japan in China* (New York: Macmillan, 1938), pp. 313–14.

this came only six students plus some 38 primary and middle school principals; there was not a single college chancellor.[11] Some of the December 9th spirit seemed to have remained in Peiping even after the principal participants had departed.

VANGUARDS BECOME GUERRILLAS

Escaping from Peiping was one problem. Finding a guerrilla unit to join was something else—as Yen T'ieh and his friends discovered. One day a student heard a farmer mention 300 or 400 disbanded 29th Army troops who were said to be resting at the nearby settlement of Mentoukou. That night, two students lowered themselves over the city wall. They returned three days later after a fruitless search for these elusive allies. Another rumor sent Yen T'ieh scurrying off on an equally futile mission with a Peita student named T'ang, whose father was rumored to have a supply of hand grenades hidden in a storehouse.[12] Only with great difficulty did they finally locate still another man, Chao T'ung, who had gathered a score of men in the Western Hills. Disguised as vegetable peddlars, Yen and Hsu Ming left Peiping early one morning, located their contacts (two men from the Northeast—a former soldier and a former bandit), concealed their weapons in baskets of produce, and made their way to headquarters about 10 miles from Peiping.

The guerrilla squad was a rag-tag lot, thrown together from whatever human resources happened to be available. Chao T'ung was a KMT leader who later broke with his Communist comrades-in-arms and was killed in 1940.[13] Two other leaders, Northeastern University students Kao P'eng and Chi T'ing-hsieh, had previous guerrilla experience in Manchuria. Both were sympathetic to the CCP. The rank and file included soldiers from warlord armies and former bandits who saw

---

[11]U.S., Department of State, *Foreign Relations of the United States, 1937*, 3:512.

[12]Yen T'ieh, "Na-ch'i," pp. 158–59.

[13]*Ibid.;* Edgar Snow, *Battle for Asia*, p. 5.

guerrilla raids as opportunities for self-enrichment. The majority were patriotic peasant lads who had served in the 29th Army and the East Hopei Peace Preservation Corps, the latter veterans of an abortive uprising against the Japanese. In response to a report from Yen and Hsu, Peiping Party headquarters sent a contingent to work within this unit and bring it under Party discipline. The guerrillas rounded up an assortment of arms, added recruits, and won popular support. Since many of them wore student clothing, they were dubbed the "Student Army."[14]

Now numbering more than 50, the Student Army carried out a number of famous exploits in the late summer and early fall of 1937. Among its less illustrious ventures was the rifling of one of the western imperial tombs near Miaofengshan and the kidnapping of a number of priests.[15] Its most famous deed was the daring attack upon Peiping's Second Penitentiary, resulting in the liberation of some 1,000 prisoners. Having absorbed these men into its ranks, the unit later moved into the Shansi-Chahar-Hopei (Chin-Ch'a-Chi) Military District and was organized as the Fifth Brigade under Communist commander Nieh Jung-chen. Later it was reorganized as the Third Rangers under Nieh's subordinate Yang Ch'eng-wu and became a "model brigade" in the district. Eventually these men were moved to the Northwest to help guard Yenan. The unit later served in the Korean war.[16] The history of these students may not be atypical of similar groups who became absorbed into the Communist guerrilla apparatus.

Stories of student metamorphosis into guerrillas ranged from the spine-tingling to the bizarre. Chu Nan-hua, Chang Chao-lin's attractive and amiable successor as Yenching student body president, escaped from Peiping to the central Hopei guerrilla area in July 1938. Encouraged to follow in his footsteps, a group

[14]Yen T'ieh, "Na-ch'i," p. 160.
[15]Edgar Snow, *Battle for Asia*, pp. 5–6.
[16]Yen T'ieh, "Na-ch'i," pp. 161–65.

of schoolmates slipped out of Peiping disguised as village teachers and insurance salesmen. Though managing to pass frequent Japanese inspections on board the train, they were easily spotted as guerrilla-bound college students by a puppet commander who had just been mauled by the very same guerrillas. This officer not only allowed the astonished students to pass but showed up as a fellow recruit shortly after their arrival at guerrilla headquarters.[17]

Chu was one of the last of the December 9th generation to leave Peiping. Most who got out did so during the summer of 1937, generally via Tientsin. The dangers and uncertainties on this 70-mile train ride were at least as great as sneaking into the Western Hills. Rail service, resumed on August 7, was frequently cut by floods and sabotage or preempted for Japanese military and economic requirements.[18] Trains laden with refugees took 10 to 12 hours for the scheduled two-hour run. Japanese detained all suspicious-looking passengers. "Dozens of students," reported Edgar Snow, "had been robbed, arrested, and heard from no more."[19] Young intellectuals in peasant costumes that failed to conceal elitist origins could be seen marching off under armed guard at the Tientsin station.[20]

NLVC members once again enjoyed the advantage of organization. As soon as communications were restored, leaders met at Huang Ching's quarters and decided to travel disguised to Tientsin. Arrangements were made through resident members. After two days of feverish preparations, food and lodging were secured through a mining company and an elementary school. Most vanguards reached their destination without incident.[21]

[17]Claire and William Band, *Two Years with the Chinese Communists* (New Haven, Conn.: Yale University Press, 1948), pp. 80–81.

[18]See *New York Times*, August 9, 1937, p. 6; August 10, 1937, p. 12; August 24, 1937, p. 2.

[19]Edgar Snow, *Battle for Asia*, p. 7.

[20]Bertram, *Unconquered*, p. 68

[21]*SNL*, pp. 24–25.

However, problems did not end in Tientsin. Few planned to spend the war in the uncertain refuge of the city's international settlement. The problem was how to reach unoccupied China alive. By August 1937 Tientsin had become a bottleneck. James Bertram found hundreds of Peiping university and middle school students quartered in a warehouse, unable to afford the astronomical prices that scalpers were asking for deck passage to the South:

About half of them were making their way to the "emergency university" center in Changsha, or to new establishments set up in the interior, where they could continue their studies. . . . But many had already decided that they had had enough of their books, and were looking for ways to engage directly in war work. . . . Among this band was one thin and nervous youth I had known before as an active member of the old Students' Union in Peiping. Already he was twice an exile, for his home—before 1931—had been in Manchuria. His face was prematurely lined, and there was a fanatical look about his eyes, but his voice now was controlled and steady. I asked him where he was going.

"First to Shantung," he said. "I shall try to work in mass mobilization there. And then perhaps to Shensi . . . ."[22]

The massive movement of refugee intellectuals was restructuring the geography of China's academic world. According to George Taylor, 1,500 faculty members and 5,000 students from a dozen centers of higher education were on the move to temporary relocation centers in south-central Chinese cities such as Nanchang, Kuling, and Changsha.[23] In Kwangtung, more than 5,000 desperate applicants took entrance exams at Sun Yat-sen University (Chungshan) one of the few unrelocated public institutions on China's seaboard.[24] Others headed for Nanking or Shanghai to volunteer for military training or set out for Yenan

[22]Bertram, *Unconquered*, p. 69.

[23]George E. Taylor, *The Struggle for North China* (New York: Institute of Pacific Relations, 1940), p. 88.

[24]The Review's South China Correspondent, "South China Prepares for War against Japan—Japanese Trade Hard Hit," *CWR*, August 14, 1937, p. 403.

to enroll at Resistance University (K'angta). By July 1938, Helen Snow's young Yenching friends were scattered across the map. Li Min had reached Kweiyang via Hong Kong, Canton, and Changsha; Liang Szu-i was in Kiangsi working with Yenching sociology Professor Kitty Lei (Lei Kit-king, Lei Chieh-ch'iung). Ch'en Chien and Chang Chao-lin were in Wuhan, Kung P'u-sheng in Anhwei, Ch'en Han-po in Kiangsu, Huang Hua in Yenan, and Kao Ming-k'ai on a scholarship in France.[25]

For cadres of the NLVC, there could be no thought of continuing education during the war. Now was the time to make use of guerrilla training conducted so seriously in the Western Hills during spring and summer vacations. But where to go and how to get there were other questions. Vanguards who reached Tientsin held animated discussions over future plans. An official history written in 1938 reports that they had initially resolved to convene in Shanghai, but that when fighting broke out there on August 13 they decided instead to establish a student hostel in Tsinan, capital city of Shantung. An office was then established at Yentai to arrange for food, lodging, transportation, and shipment of baggage. After discussions en route between the Vanguard command and officers of the Peiping-Tientsin Refugee Students Association, Nanking, Tsinan, and Paoting were selected as staging areas.[26] Li Ch'ang's account differs in some details. As he recalls, two alternatives were debated in Tientsin: to go north and join the peasants in the fight against the Japanese or to "go south and arouse the masses there to urge on the Kuomintang government to resist Japan." Having agreed that both were necessary, some went to Tsinan via Yentai and Tsingtao, some to the front in other parts of North China, and some "to the rear to sow the seed of delivery from extinction."[27] In any case, Vanguards bade farewell and left

[25]*NCSM*, p. 198.

[26]*SLN*, p. 25.

[27]Li Ch'ang, "Recollections," Part II, p. 36.

Tientsin for prearranged points. For many, this would be the last meeting with their schoolmates and comrades.

While Japanese forces in North China struck northwest into Suiyuan and Shansi, the major portion of Shantung was temporarily spared. During the late summer and early fall, Tsinan was a hub of activity for radical activists from Peiping and Tientsin. By mid-August, more than 2,000 had gathered there and more were still filtering in.[28] Through the initiative of Yang Hsueh-ch'eng and others, a branch of the Peiping-Tientsin Student National Salvation Union was established.[29] Besides providing for the bodily needs of fellow refugees, young organizers carried on a variety of activities. More than 300 students joined a provincial government training class for young National Salvation cadres.[30] A theatrical troupe of Peiping and Tientsin students, including Jung Kao-t'ang, Yang I-ch'en, Ch'en Huang-mei, and Chang Jui-fang, performed patriotic plays. Tsinan was not, however, a secure center for operations. For most, it was simply a transit point to Nanking, Wuhan, or Yenan.

Early in October, Japanese troops moved into Shantung by the Tientsin-Pukow Railroad. The capital city was saved for the moment by the destruction of a key bridge by retreating Chinese forces. However, the half-hearted defense organized by Governor Han Fu-chü alarmed students. On December 25, the Japanese took Tsinan and continued their march south while Han beat a hasty retreat. Arrested on January 11 for dereliction of duty, he was executed 13 days later.

Han's alleged "sell-out" of the province and the country became a *cause célèbre* that brought many students and other patriotic elements into the resistance.[31] Popular mobilization

---

[28]*SNL*, p. 25.

[29]Chiang Nan-hsiang, "In Memory of Comrade Yang Hsueh-cheng," in *RON*, p. 152.

[30]*SNL*, pp. 31–32.

[31]Johnson, *Peasant Nationalism*, p. 110.

was facilitated by strong anti-Japanese sentiment dating most immediately to 1931—many Shantungese had relatives in Manchuria. By the time Tsinan fell, students from Peiping and Tientsin were able to take advantage of local connections they had established to create guerrilla units in the countryside.

The most famous Shantung guerrilla group was formed by Han Fu-chü's subordinate Fan Chu-hsien in the western part of the province. Instead of retreating as Han had ordered, Fan had withdrawn into the countryside to conduct partisan warfare. Some 1,600 NLVC cadres played a major part in organizing his unit. Working out of their office in Liaocheng, they visited the villages where they tried to win over local leadership and mobilize the masses. An NLVC newspaper, *Lao-hsiang jih-pao* (Rural daily news) proselytized and instructed the populace in guerrilla techniques.[32]

Students in Fan's outfit included Sun Ch'uan-wen, head of the Peiping NLVC Bureau, and Kao Yuan-kuei, Lu Shih-lung, Kuan Ta-t'ung, and Huang Ju-han, cadres from China College. By October 1938, many of them had become squad leaders. Some of their military techniques were borrowed from the Spanish Civil War. Among their exploits was the burning of several Japanese airplanes without losing a single Chinese. Their numbers, which had grown from three hundred to more than five thousand within two or three months, continued to increase rapidly.[33] Other NLVC leaders in Shantung were Liu Chü-ying, Lin I-shan, and Shih Wei (who was captured and executed by the Japanese). Vanguardists Wang Wen-pin, Wu Heng, and Chang Chen-huan played a major role in the defense of Süchow in the spring of 1938.[34]

In October 1938, an NLVC publication proudly claimed that NLVC guerrillas had kept the Chinese flag flying in western Shantung during the first year of the war.[35] A month later di-

---

[32]*Ibid.*, p. 111.

[33]*SNL*, pp. 32–33.

[34]Li Ch'ang, "Recollections," Part II, p. 37.

[35]*SNL*, p. 33.

saster struck. Japanese troops dealt the guerrillas a crushing blow and killed Commander Fan Chu-hsien. It was not until early in the following year that Ch'en Kuang, with reinforcements from the Eighth Route Army, was able to rearm and reorganize scattered remnants into the Fan Chu-hsien Column.[36]

LOSS OF URBAN BASES

In spite of the spectacular exploits of NLVC guerrillas in the North China countryside, the NLVC—in origin, composition, and predilection—was an urban group, accustomed to working among city-dwellers. Leading Vanguards, therefore, concentrated their efforts in cities, moving from one to another as the enemy occupied China's largest population centers.

After the outbreak of the war a number of prominent NLVC figures made their way south to spur mobilization in Nanking. Yang Hsueh-ch'eng helped to establish a branch of the Peiping-Tientsin Student National Salvation Union, as he had already done in Tsinan.[37] Fellow Tsinghua activist Chiang Nan-hsiang arrived with Tuan Chün-i, who was a delegate to the Peiping Student Union and an officer in the National Student Association.[38] Chiang and Tuan found no shortage of work, but official attitudes were discouraging. In the national capital, radical activities had long been suppressed and governmental efforts at mass mobilization effectively proscribed. Kuomintang authorities were sharply divided over what, if any, training program was appropriate for youths who wished to serve the war effort. For lack of alternatives, students were encouraged to move inland with their schools—a continued implementation of the widely-criticized formula, "Save the Nation through Study" (*tu-*

---

[36]Johnson, *Peasant Nationalism,* p. 113; based upon Liao Kuan-hsien, "Cavalry on the Western Plains," People's Republic of China, ed., *Saga of Resistance to Japanese Invasion* (Peking: Foreign Languages Press, 1959), pp. 39–40.

[37]Chiang Nan-hsiang, "In Memory," p. 152.

[38]Li Ch'ang, "Recollections," Part II, p. 37.

shu chiu-kuo). Under these circumstances, mass mobilization required outside stimuli.

In view of hostile official attitudes, there was more than a little irony to the NLVC's united-front motto: "Rally the Nation's Masses under the Government's Leadership."[39] Such conciliatory words failed to prevent police from closing and searching the branch office of the Peiping-Tientsin Student National Salvation Union and detaining its officers for three to four weeks. Tuan Chün-i and Chiang Nan-hsiang, newly arrived in the capital, were corralled into a military training class, which they found totally lacking in useful content.[40] An NLVC writer blamed official misunderstanding on the Vanguards' northern origins, their lack of experience working under governmental leadership, and the machinations of "traitors" who hoped to poison the minds of officials.[41]

Diligent efforts finally dispelled officials' hostility and enabled the Vanguards openly to carry on patriotic activities. Their endeavors to win friends were facilitated by the work of the NLVC chorus. With the cooperation of the Central Broadcasting Station, which carried their songs, they were able to explain their mission to listeners. As a result of this publicity, a number of groups, including the Air Force Academy, invited them to perform. They received governmental permission to broadcast a special commemorative program on the sixth anniversary of the Mukden Incident and were invited to hold two get-togethers between soldiers and civilians at the Gendarmes' Academy. Finally, they raised 1,000 Chinese dollars and consolidated the Vanguard's legal standing in a performance before high-ranking officials.[42]

Nanking's days, however, were numbered. Even as the Vanguards spread the message of resistance with speeches and

---

[39]*SNL*, p. 34.

[40]Li Ch'ang, "Recollections," Part II, pp. 37–38.

[41]*SNL*, p. 34.

[42]*Ibid.*, pp. 35–36.

songs, bureaus, schools, and factories were heading for temporary refuge in Wuhan and elsewhere in South-Central China and for more permanent quarters in the wartime capital of Chungking, 1500 miles up the Yangtze. By early November, the heroic defense of the Shanghai area had been shattered; by December 13, the enemy occupied Nanking.

In North China, NLVC headquarters moved from Peiping to Paoting, one of the three reconcentration points for NLVC members. There, they rallied to the support of Sun Ku-ying, Shih Yu-san, and other 29th Army commanders. However, the Japanese blitzkrieg made effective resistance impossible. On September 24, Paoting fell.

The next stop for retreating NLVC cadres was Taiyuan. Capital of Governor Yen Hsi-shan's "model province," the city boasted a tradition of radical student activity dating from the May 30th movement of 1925. During the post-Mukden outburst in 1931, Taiyuan students had clashed with local authorities; many young agitators had been jailed. Since the mid-1920s, several of the city's educational institutions, especially the Kuomin Normal School, had spawned a coterie of prominent Communist leaders only a few years older than the December 9ers. From September 1936 on, Kuomin graduates Po I-po, Jung Tzu-ho, and Lei Jen-min had been prominent in the League for National Salvation through Sacrifice, a Communist-dominated united front body that operated with the ambivalent blessings of Yen Hsi-shan. Since the 1930s, December 9ers have crossed paths with these men and other Shansi revolutionists such as Nan Han-ch'en and Sung Shao-wen.

Assisted en route by comrades, NLVC members reached the Shansi capital by all available means. General director Li Ch'ang traveled in an open railroad car via Shihkiachwang, where he was helped on his way by T'ao Hsi-chin and T'ao Lu-chia.[43] For a brief time, Taiyuan enjoyed prominence as the center of resistance in North China. Liu Shao-ch'i, P'eng Chen,

---

[43]*SNL*, p. 26; Li Ch'ang, "Recollections," Part II, p. 38.

and Chou En-lai were in the city. Patriotic groups, formed with the encouragement of Governor Yen Hsi-shan, had become foci for his cooperative-competitive relationship with the Communists. Yen had allowed the Sacrifice League's military arm, the Dare-to-Die Corps, to expand into a 15,000-man "New Army." Working through these organizations and the local branch of the Peiping-Tientsin Student National Salvation Union, the NLVC strengthened the position of the Left.[44]

Though mass mobilization and other national salvation work were not neglected, the unchecked Japanese drive across North China underscored the need for trained leadership in the guerrilla movement. Vanguard headquarters placed top priority on armed resistance.[45] Students who arrived were quickly dispatched to the front. Even members of the NLVC Executive Committee, such as Yang Yü-min and Yang K'o-ping, were sent off to work behind enemy lines, leaving a small staff (including Li Ch'ang and Yü Kuang-yuan) to manage affairs at headquarters. When the 120th Division of Ho Lung and Kuan Hsiang-ying passed through the city a number of students enlisted, including Vanguardists Jao Pin (from the Shanghai branch), Sung Ying, and K'ang Shih-en. In the Shansi-Chahar-Hopei Border Region Government, volunteers worked under Peita graduates Sung Shao-wen and Hu Jen-k'uei. Sung Shao-wen, named chairman of the border region's administrative committee in 1938, had been jailed for participating in the anti-Japanese movement of 1931 and had previously headed up the Propaganda Department of the Sacrifice League. Others went with Huang Ching to northeastern Shansi and central Hopei or to the Taihang mountains to fight under Yang Hsiu-feng, formerly of the Women's Normal Institute and the Normal University in Peiping. Professor Yang had rallied students at Paoting and masterminded the organization of a guerrilla base

[44]*SNL*, pp. 26–27; Li Ch'ang, "Recollections," Part II, p. 38; Donald G. Gillin, *Warlord: Yen Hsi-shan in Shansi Province, 1911–1949* (Princeton, N.J.: Princeton University Press, 1967), p. 262.

[45]*SNL*, pp. 26–27.

in southern Hopei before transferring operations to Shansi.

Other new resistance bases were established in southern Shansi with the help of vanguardist Li Che-jen.[46] Hence, as Japanese troops moved in on Taiyuan, Vanguardists were already at work in a number of areas harassing the enemy from the rear. In the course of the war, two of Li Ch'ang's early coleaders in the Tsinghua NLVC, Ling Sung-ju and Miss Chi Yü-hsiu, died in Shansi.[47]

With Taiyuan on the verge of collapse, many student refugees did not know where to turn. On November 9, as enemy units entered the city, a group of eighty Peiping students called the "Manchurian Volunteers" stumbled into the Eighth Route Army Headquarters near Mafang. Having heard that these headquarters were to be found somewhere near the Hopei border, they had left Taiyuan and wandered all over eastern Shansi before reaching their goal. Organized as partisans under Eighth Route Army leadership, the young northeasterners passed through enemy lines along the Cheng-tai Railroad and into western Hopei.[48]

Meanwhile, Li Ch'ang and others followed Yen Hsi-shan to his new headquarters at Linfen in southwestern Shansi. When they arrived they found a ghost town. Residents had fled, houses and shops were boarded up, and streets were empty aside from a few soldiers. Within weeks, however, the little city had become the hub of the National Salvation movement in North China. Hundreds of students from the Peiping Student Union wandered in and began training under the Eighth Route Army. Among them was NLVC member Li Wei, who later gained renown as an artist in the People's Liberation Army (PLA). Others joined the Student Army or the National Revolutionary University.[49] NLVC ranks were swelled by the

[46]Li Ch'ang, "Recollections," Part II, p. 38.

[47]Li Ch'ang, "Recollections," Part I, p. 32.

[48]Agnes Smedley, *China Fights Back* (New York: Vanguard Press, 1938), pp. 151, 153–54, 207.

[49]Li Ch'ang, "Recollections," Part II, p. 39.

arrival of comrades from Shantung. Even Vanguardist Wu Chih-mu, who had returned from France to join the war effort, showed up in Linfen.

Journalist James Bertram found Linfen humming with activity. Chou En-lai was making daily speeches in the city and its environs, organizers propagandized rural villages, and numerous groups worked for political mobilization. These included a War Zone People's Revolutionary Mobilization Committee, the Sacrifice League, the Dare-to-Die Corps, and the Shaonien Hsienfengtui or Youth Vanguard. Though they had been sanctioned by Yen Hsi-shan, all had Eighth Route Army advisers and instructors.[50]

Led by cadres Li Ch'ang, Lu P'ing, Ku Ta-ch'uan, Ting Hao-ch'uan, and Hsia Ying-che, the NLVC channeled youthful patriots into these activities. The NLVC continued to process students and send them to various parts of North China according to war needs. The NLVC was also instrumental in mass mobilization work, including the operation of a popular mobile theatrical troupe that toured rural areas. Representatives of the NLVC, the Shansi Branch of the Peiping-Tientsin Student National Salvation Union, and other organizations staged a massive "antitraitor" rally. Under the editorship of Chiang Nan-hsiang and with the backing of the local CCP organization, Peiping students edited a mimeographed daily newspaper, the only one in the city.[51]

Linfen fell on March 1, 1938. Under orders from Liu Shao-ch'i, the NLVC moved on to Sian. The old Western Capital was familiar territory. A Vanguard unit, established since June 1936 under the hospitable auspices of Chang Hsueh-liang, had continued activities during the difficult period following the settlement of the Sian Incident. After the outbreak of war, recalls local NLVC leader Li Lien-pi, the student movement had risen

[50]Smedley, *China Fights Back*, p. 297.

[51]*SNL*, pp. 27–28; Bertram, *Unconquered*, p. 153; Li Ch'ang, "Recollections," Part II, p. 38.

to "a new high tide." In June 1938, Vanguards numbered more than sixteen hundred.[52] However, they soon encountered difficulties. Unlike Taiyuan and Linfen, where the Communists could deal as equals with a cooperative warlord, Sian was Chiang Kai-shek's principal North China bastion, and the KMT would not permit a Communist front to organize the masses in this strategic outpost. To undercut leftist youth groups, the KMT attempted to organize anti-Japanese students through its Northwest China Vanguard of Youths for Resisting the Enemy.[53] Even the name, closely patterned after the Vanguards' own, suggested the competitive spirit.

Still under united front guidelines that bade them cooperate with Chiang, NLVC leaders were in an untenable position. On February 23, 1938, even before NLVC general headquarters had moved from Linfen, Sian newspapers announced that the KMT's provincial command had dissolved the NLVC's Sian branch. In a communiqué to members, Vanguard headquarters expressed agreement with the government's desire to unify all National Salvation organizations but took issue with the outlawing of nonofficial groups. Since the NLVC was an open, popular, law-abiding organization, the provincial government was asked to reconsider its decision. Chiang's personal help was solicited. Meanwhile, Vanguards were ordered to form an even closer united front with the government.[54]

Bleak though the situation was in Sian, there was no remaining urban center in North China to which the Vanguard could retreat. To move to Yenan would mean the end of the NLVC's unique mission as a united front-style mass organization able to operate in non-Communist territory. Therefore the NLVC desperately tried to consolidate its position and to reach an ac-

---

[52]Li Lien-pi, "Flames of Wrath," in *RON*, pp. 117, 119.

[53]Li Ch'ang, "Recollections," Part II, p. 39.

[54]Min-hsien hsi-an ti-fang tui-pu [NLVC Sian Headquarters], *Wei sheng-tang-pu ti-ling chieh-san "min-hsien" kao tui-yuan t'ung-chih shu* [A communication to fellow corpsmen concerning the provincial (KMT) party headquarters' order to dissolve the "NLVC"].

commodation with the KMT. In March Sian members elected a city headquarters group and laid the groundwork for a Northwest Bureau. The latter was formally established by an extraordinary congress of April 4, 1938, attended by NLVC representatives from as far away as Kansu.[55] A report by Fu Hsi-jung noted with pride that the Vanguards had expanded from a core of 10 or 20 to an organization of 5,000, from a single city to more than 30 countries (this was something of an exaggeration), and from a student organization to one that included workers, peasants, and shop clerks. Fu noted, however, that development had been "uneven" and lamented the failure to secure the "positive leadership and real assistance of the government."[56] The establishment of "an open and legal position," the delegates agreed, was "an essential task."[57]

At a dramatic meeting in May 1938, Li Ch'ang and several comrades attempted to induce Kuo Tzu-chün, secretary-general of Shensi KMT headquarters, to grant them legal status. After NLVC representatives had stated their case, according to Li's recollections, Kuo pounded his hand on the desk and bellowed, "Don't you give me that. I am not used to taking it. The Kuomintang has won political power through bloodshed. If you want to take over, just go ahead and try." The Vanguard emissaries rose and walked out.[58] The plea for a united front had failed.

WUHAN II

While NLVC leaders were fleeing across North China one jump ahead of the Japanese, the spiritual home of the united front had shifted to the Wuhan cities. Though some branches of the cen-

<hr>

[55]Li Lien-pi, "Flames of Wrath," in *RON,* pp. 117, 119.

[56]*SNL,* pp. 29–31.

[57]Pao Tsun-p'eng, *Chung-kuo kung-ch'an-tang ch'ing-nien yun-tung shih-lun* [A discussion of the history of the CCP youth movement] (Nanking: Pa-t'i shu-chü, 1947), p. 45.

[58]Li Ch'ang, "Recollections," Part II, p. 39.

tral government had moved to Changsha or Chungking after the fall of Nanking, China's de facto capital at least for the moment was this tri-city complex at the confluence of the Han and Yangtze rivers. Here were the agencies concerned with foreign relations, propaganda, and military affairs,[59] and it was here that the united front reached its zenith before it started to disintegrate.

"The ten months from December 12, 1937, to October 25, 1938 . . . were months as crowded as decades," wrote Agnes Smedley.[60] It was vaguely reminiscent of heady days in the winter of 1926–27, when in the same city the first united front had reached its culmination. Here, as before, gathered many of the literary luminaries of China—men such as Mao Tun, Kuo Mo-jo, Lao She, and Pa Chin. Here once again political organizations proliferated, manifestos were drafted, demonstrations, parades, and rallies were staged, conferences were convened—all to the delight of a steady stream of foreign writers and other sympathizers. Agnes Smedley, Freda Utley, Edgar Snow, W. H. Auden, and Christopher Isherwood, among others, provided the world with a series of glowing reports. "There in Hankow," wrote journalist Edna Lee Booker, "I came to realize that Japan was fighting a force more powerful than China's armies. It was a baffling, cogent force which Japan did not and does not understand. Her bombs cannot destroy it. It is a force motivated by a fire of Patriotism, Nationalism, New Life."[61] This euphoric effect of "Wuhan II" is vividly captured by journalist Israel Epstein:

The sober commercial city of Hankow began to wear a different aspect. In its crowded streets, one could meet active workers for China's liberation from Shanghai, from Nanking, and from the lost provinces of the North. On its walls were countless posters, wall

[59] Paul M. A. Linebarger, *The China of Chiang Kai-shek* (Boston: World Peace Foundation, 1941), p. 15.

[60] Agnes Smedley, *Battle Hymn of China* (New York: Knopf, 1943), p. 205.

[61] Edna Lee Booker, *News is My Job* (New York: Macmillan, 1940), pp. 328–29.

newspapers, and proclamations. Daily they changed, reflecting events in China and in the world. The walls of Hankow were the platform of the people. Whenever there were rumours of capitulation or betrayal, they bore a crop of slogans reaffirming the people's will to resist. When the Chinese air force won a victory vivid placards announced the fact. When Hitler spoke in favour of Japan, the walls bore his features in fierce caricature. When Australian dockers refused to load iron for Japan, proclamations signed by Hankow Seamen's Union shouted their thanks. China's best-known writers did not disdain to contribute to the wall of newspapers of the Cultural Workers' National Resistance Federation which were plastered all over the city. Changed every three days, they never failed to draw huge crowds of faithful readers. China's best artists drew the vigorous posters displayed on every street corner.[62]

To young Epstein, it was all very exhilarating. However, a Wuhan I veteran such as Rayna Prohme or Vincent Sheean would have found something missing. A dozen years earlier, the city had been a landmark for a triumphal Northern Expedition. Now it was a temporary stopover in a retreat before a relentless foe. With enemy bombers overhead, few entertained illusions that this place was destined to be a fountainhead for a new social order.

The shoes of famous Communists like M. N. Roy, Earl Browder, and Jacques Duclos could scarcely be filled by itinerant student leaders from England, Canada, and the United States. Gone were Michael Borodin and Eugene Ch'en. Gone was the phantasm of social transformation. Wang Ching-wei, the flamboyant and unpredictable "left" KMT leader of 1927, now represented the party's "right"—a faction that sought a compromise peace with Japan; his followers (though not Wang himself) were prominent in the tri-cities.[63] Kuo Mo-jo, who had played an important role in propaganda and other political work during Wuhan I, assumed similar responsibilities in Wuhan II. However, in Wuhan I, he had worked under the Communist agitator Teng Yen-ta (executed by the KMT in

---

[62]Israel Epstein, *The People's War* (London: Victor Gollancz, 1939), p. 154.

[63]Smedley, *Battle Hymn*, p. 205.

1931); in Wuhan II, he owed his appointment to KMT General Ch'en Ch'eng, veteran of the Communist extermination campaigns who headed the political department of the Military Affairs Commission. Wuhan now was Chiang Kai-shek's capital, and leftists enjoyed freedom at the sufferance of the Kuomintang. As Epstein observed, freedom of the press was a friable commodity:

On January 17 [1938] a band of strong-arm men wrecked the office of the [Communists'] *New China Daily*. . . . Newsboys who sold the paper returned, bruised and bloody, telling how they had been set upon and beaten and their papers taken away. On the following day, attacks on the Communists, their publications, and the Eighth Route Army, appeared once more in the Kuomintang Press. One editorial pointed to the German Nazis as China's best friends, and to the Third Reich as a model for her political party dictatorship and 'control of thought.' There is only one party in the Soviet Union, they argued, and the Press expresses its views only. How then, could the Chinese Communist [sic] be justified in their objection to the political monopoly of the Kuomintang in China? If the Chinese Communist Party wanted freedom for its Press, why did it not ask the Soviet Union to revise its Press laws?[64]

On February 10, the *New China Daily* [Hsin-hua jih-pao] published an interview in which Mao Tse-tung answered this argument by explaining that one-party rule in the Soviet Union reflected the fact that, following its revolution, only one class existed. In multiclass China, attempts to impose one-party rule had led to ten years of civil war.[65] These views may have convinced some but not P'eng Wen-k'ai, editor of the new KMT periodical, *Ch'ing-nien ch'ien-hsien* (Front line of youth). In an article, "Unify the Thought of Youth," P'eng called for strict control of all organizations and publications by governmental, military, and Party authorities. P'eng advocated an emergency law that would restrict freedom of publication, assembly, and association in the national interest, and proposed that central propaganda organs periodically specify the permissible limits of

---

[64]Epstein, *People's War*, p. 154.
[65]*Ibid.*, pp. 154–55.

speech and writing. Only such severe measures, he believed, might keep the thoughts of the young from going astray.[66]

Not until the spring of 1938 did Wuhan become a mecca for foreign reporters. Student refugees from the Nanking holocaust of December 1937 found the temporary capital wrapped in wintry gloom. Nanking had fallen after four months of heroic but exhausting resistance. Battle-hardened and vindictive Japanese troops had run wild in an orgy of looting, rape, and murder. With the cream of Chiang's army destroyed, no barrier stood between the enemy and Wuhan. It was generally recognized, talk of a second "defense of Madrid" notwithstanding, that this was but a way-station on the road of retreat. A writer in *Ch'ing-nien ch'ien-hsien* noted that the nation's "youth has fallen through exuberance, fury, excitement, pain, despair, and depression, culminating in the present state of silence."[67]

Homeless students, ill-clothed and undernourished, were continually frustrated in their quest for a meaningful way of contributing to China's defense. Eager to work with the masses, they had been allowed to perform only the most perfunctory duties. As one young man complained, "The cannon shells of the Japanese warlords are about to shatter our skulls, yet we are still shut up in the classroom discussing the marital system of ancient Rome."[68]

The government was widely criticized for failing to take the initiative to mobilize students. In some places local student groups tried to fill the vacuum. There was a Kwangsi Student Army, a Hupei Rural Cadres' Training Class, and a Student Army Group, but all lacked overall planning and guidance. Several hundred eager recruits at Hankow's National Military Training College soon were demoralized by indiscipline, riots, and poor training. "The boys used to sing songs of derision

[66]"T'ung-i ch'ing-nien ssu-hsiang," *CNCH*, no. 4 (February 15, 1938), pp. 6–8.

[67]P'eng Wen-k'ai, writing in "Ch'ing-nien t'an-tso" [Young people's roundtable] column, *CNCH*, nos. 2/3 (January 25, 1938), p. 34.

[68]"Ch'ing-nien t'an tso," *CNCH*, no. 4 (February 15, 1938), pp. 18–21.

about their teachers, and at the time the school authorities called the military to quell disturbances by means of machine guns," recalled a disillusioned trainee who later joined the Communists.[69] Entrenched Kuomintang bureaucrats resisted initiatives from below. In at least one instance, students had to overcome obstruction from a high-level educational administrator before they were able to organize a Battleground Service Corps.[70] In another, a girl trainee was threatened with a revolver when she refused to take an oath of fealty to Chiang Kai-shek, the Ch'en brothers, and her local superiors.[71] But young men and women were becoming accustomed to danger and often placed little stock in personal security. As Israel Epstein wrote:

Students from Peiping and Tientsin who had established a temporary university in Changsha were ordered to leave for Yunnan because of the imminent threat of bombing and invasion. Five hundred of them refused to go. 'Wartime education does not consist of constantly moving to the rear,' they said. 'Our duty is to remain and prepare for the enemy when he comes.' They continued to organize the people and conduct propaganda in Hunan . . .[72]

While students looked in vain for government leadership, educators squabbled over means of adapting the school system to wartime needs. On January 15 representatives of more than twenty educational groups established a Preparatory Committee for National Education during the War of Resistance. Their objective was "to work out a curriculum of wartime education to be recommended to all schools throughout the country."[73] The achievement of this goal, however, would require unified leadership from a sorely divided Kuomintang. Policies on education and mass movements, painstakingly

[69]Band, *Two Years*, pp. 92–93.

[70]*Ibid.*

[71]*Ibid.*, pp. 93–94. Ch'en Kuo-fu and Ch'en Li-fu were formidable leaders of the KMT "Organization Clique"—eds.

[72]Epstein, *People's War*, p. 151.

[73]*Ibid.*

developed during the prewar decade, were not readily abandoned.

There was a factional dichotomy in the Kuomintang on the issue of education and politics. The dominant group, voicing views of educators such as Hu Shih and Ts'ai Yuan-p'ei, opted for a wartime school system that adhered to the prewar goal—the long-term development of highly trained men and women who would master the advanced science and technology of the modern age. Another school of thought, championed by Central University Chancellor Lo Chia-lun, advocated an "emergency education" or "wartime education." This group included both moderates who sought only emphasis on scientific and technological subjects and their application to problems of wartime technology and radicals who called for a revitalized KMT youth movement. Among the men advocating sweeping curricular changes was *Ch'ing-nien ch'ien-hsien* editor P'eng Wenk'ai, who called for the replacement of regular schoolwork by propaganda, training, and organizing of the masses. P'eng also urged instruction in methods for increasing production, guerrilla warfare, espionage, first aid, fire fighting, and other subjects. He castigated those who stubbornly clung to traditional academic goals and continued to measure success by the report card.[74] However, even when China's leading eastern seaboard universities had been uprooted or bombed to rubble, few if any KMT leaders argued for a total suspension of the nation's school system.

The national crisis cut short the decision-making process. KMT activists were not prepared to postpone mobilization of youth until party unanimity had been achieved. Experience since December 9 had taught them that failure to seize the initiative would leave the field to left-wing rivals. Early in February a "Propaganda Week for the International Antiaggression Movement" provided occasion for action. A Youth Day rally at Chungshan Park attracted some 5,000 boys and girls.[75] The

---

[74]"Ch'ing-nien t'an-tso," *CNCH*, no. 4 (February 15, 1938), pp. 18–21.

meeting was chaired by P'eng Wen-k'ai, advocate of a broadly-based but tightly-regimented youth movement. This represented the high-tide of the KMT's effort to form a united front-style mass movement. Speakers included representatives of the city's KMT headquarters, the local Garrison Command, the Wuhan Young Women's Command, and the Shanghai Buddhist Priests' First Aid Team. On the podium were such disparate individuals as Wang Ching-wei, Chih T'i-chieh (identified by a KMT source as a "braintruster" of the National Student Union),[76] and Li Ch'ang, representing the Peiping NLVC. Li apparently came down from Sian for the meeting, since he did not move to Wuhan until late that spring. Li Ch'ang seems to have made a profound impression. A writer for P'eng Wen-k'ai's *Ch'ing-nien ch'ien-hsien* describes him as "young and strong" and exclaims that "each word from his mouth exploded like a bomb and reverberated about, piercing deeply the hearts of each and every youth."[77]

Interrupted by an air raid warning, the meeting reassembled in time to cheer Chinese Air Force planes passing overhead: "Down with Japanese Imperialism," "Long Live the Chinese Air Force," and (according to Epstein) "Fascist Aggression is the Enemy of World Youth."[78] At the conclusion of the meeting, participants marched from the stadium in military formation. As they passed before a statue of Chang Kai-shek, they broke into goosestep and cried, "Support the Leader to Fight to the End."[79] It was a stirring performance.

[75]Epstein, *People's War*, p. 152.

[76]Hsing-cheng-yuan she-chi wei-yuan-hui [Planning Committee of the Executive Yuan], ed., *Kung-fei ch'ing-nien yun-tung chih yen-pien yü p'ou-hsi* [The evolution of the Communist bandit youth movement and an analysis] (Taipei: n.p., 1953).

[77]Hsiao Kai, "Kuo-chi fan-ch'in-lueh yun-tung hsuan-ch'uan chou Chung-kuo ch'ing-nien k'ang-jih ta-hui su-hsieh" [Notes on the Chinese youth rally for the international anti-aggression movement propaganda week), *CNCH*, no. 4 (February 15, 1938), p. 23.

[78]*Ibid.*, p. 22; Epstein, *People's War*, p. 152.

As Epstein observed, "A strong mass movement was universally recognized as a necessity. But the question was still too often not 'how to develop it' but 'how to control it.' "[80] Determined not to lose the momentum of the Youth Day meeting, P'eng Wen-k'ai proposed the organization of a "National Youth Corps to Resist the Enemy" (Ch'üan-kuo ch'ing-nien k'ang-ti tsung-t'uan). This suggestion received the endorsement of the meeting's presidium.[81] Less than three months later a writer in P'eng's magazine announced that 120 student organizations from Hupei and other provinces had established a "Preparatory Office of the National Youth Council to Resist the Enemy" (Ch'üan-kuo ch'ing-nien k'ang-ti tsung-hui ch'ou-pei ch'u).[82]

While P'eng Wen-k'ai and his followers were trying to bring the youth movement under Kuomintang hegemony, a counter-movement was under way on the left. Radical organizers had to build from the bottom up, for the accomplishments of 1927 had been obliterated in the intervening years. During the December 9th period, Wuhan schools had been only moderately active. Tightly controlled by KMT authorities and divided by rivers, the Wuhan complex was not a promising place for unified and sustained student action. A Wuhan Student National Salvation Union established on December 16, 1935, was disbanded the following spring. At the time of the Sian Incident, the most noteworthy activity was the delegation of representatives from more than thirty Hupei schools to save the captive Generalissimo.[83] Only after the outbreak of war did a more permissive political climate in Wuhan make it possible for radical organizers to reestablish themselves.

[79]Hsiao Kai, "Kuo-chi fan-ch'in-lueh," pp. 22–23.

[80]Epstein, *People's War*, p. 153.

[81]P'eng Wen-k'ai, in "Ch'ing-nien t'an-tso," pp. 20–21.

[82]Mei Yin, "Hu-pei hsueh-yun ti kuo-ch'ü, hsien-tsai, yü chiang-lai" [The past, present, and future of the Hupei student movement], *CNCH*, no. 5 (May 4, 1938).

[83]*Ibid.*

During the fall of 1937, student refugees poured into Wuhan. Many Peita, Tsinghua, and Nankai University students attended Wuhan University while waiting for their temporary campus at Changsha to open. While there, they continued to conduct patriotic activities, most notably by caring for the growing numbers of wounded soldiers who made their way to the temporary capital as Japanese troops battered the defenders of Nanking. Peiping and Tientsin students also provided four or five hundred lower echelon cadres who worked in rural areas under the Hupei Bureau of Education.[84] Among those active in Wuhan were at least two Yenching December 9ers. Huang Hua headed the Wuhan office of the People's Volunteers (for the Eighth Route Army) and conducted youth work for the CCP's Yangtze Bureau. Chang Chao-lin worked under Kuo Mo-jo in the literary propaganda section in the political department of the Military Affairs Commission.[85]

Arrival of officers from the Nanking and Peiping-Tientsin student associations provided refugee youths with much needed leadership. In November 1937, a National Salvation Youth Corps led by NLVC cadres replaced an organization of north China students.[86] The new group spawned similar bodies in Honan, Anhwei, and elsewhere, and these groups in turn "instituted special schools, training groups, and lecture meetings to educate activists, of which many later came to the Communist areas."[87] On February 15 (one week after Li Ch'ang's oratorical *tour de force*), the Wuhan headquarters of the NLVC officially opened.[88]

Encouragement for the Communist youth movement came

[84]*SNL*, pp. 37–38.

[85]URI, *Who's Who*, p. 274; Li Min to Helen Snow, March 22, 1939, in *NCSM*, 199. This source also confirms Huang Hua's presence in Wuhan.

[86]*SNL*, p. 38.

[87]Klaus H. Pringsheim, "The Functions of the Chinese Communist Youth League (1920–1949)," *The China Quarterly*, no. 12 (October-December 1962), p. 85.

[88]*SNL*, p. 38.

from an unexpected source—the extraordinary congress of the Kuomintang, which met in Wuhan from March 29 to April 1. This very body elevated Chiang Kai-shek to the position of *tsung-ts'ai* (party leader), only a notch below *tsung-li* (director-general), a post reserved for Sun Yat-sen. This assembly also proclaimed the establishment of the *San-min chu-i ch'ing-nien t'uan* (Three People's Principles Youth Corps). However, as a concession to those apprehensive about these steps toward one-man and one-party dictatorship, the congress passed a sweeping declaration of civil liberties and decided to convene a People's Political Council (PPC).[89] The top-level Communist delegation to the council (which met from July 5 to 12) included Lin Po-ch'ü, Wu Yü-chang, Tung Pi-wu, Wang Ming (Ch'en Shao-yü), Po Ku (Ch'in Pang-hsien), and Teng Ying-ch'ao (Mme. Chou En-lai). These representatives and Chou En-lai constituted a formidable coterie of Communist luminaries in the Nationalist stronghold. Also present in Wuhan were some of the most able CYL and NLVC leaders.[90]

During the spring of 1938, youth groups proliferated and their activities multiplied. Though the NLVC claimed credit for promoting these developments,[91] the patriotic movement was too broad to be encompassed by any single organization. The National Salvation Youth Corps spread through Hupei, Honan, Anhwei, Hunan, Kiangsi, Szechwan, Kwangtung, and Kwangsi. Its membership in Wuhan reached five thousand and in Süchou approached ten thousand. Shanghai refugees formed an "Ant Society," which was also very active.[92] The April 15 issue of a youth magazine informed readers that the Fund-

[89]Lyman P. Van Slyke, ed., *The Chinese Communist Movement* (Stanford, Calif.: Stanford University Press, 1968), p. 63.

[90]Chiang Nan-hsiang, *RON,* p. 176.

[91]*SNL,* p. 38.

[92]Li Ch'ang, "Recollections," Part II, p. 40; *Wei t'uan-chieh chiao-yü ch'ing-nien i-tai erh tou-cheng: Chung-kuo hsin min-chu chu-i ch'ing-nien t'uan ti-i-ts'e ch'üan-kuo tai-piao ta-hui wen-hsien* [Struggle to unite the generation of educated youth: documents of the First National Congress of the Chinese New Democratic Youth League] (Peking: Ch'ing-nien ch'u-pan she, 1949), p. 101.

Raising Team of the Wuhan Young Women's Activities Corps was collecting money for front-line troops and war refugees; that a Wuhan Youth Groups' Antiaggression Propaganda drive had taken place; that a Youth Salvation Association (Ch'ing-nien chiu-wang hsieh-hui) had been founded at KMT party headquarters (presumably to compete with the leftist National Salvation Youth Corps), and that a Resist-Japan National Salvation Association of Shanghai Students was about to be founded.[93] A parade and antiaggression rally, which on April 29 allegedly attracted tens of thousands of people, was dubbed "unprecedented" by an NLVC writer.[94]

In late May or June, NLVC Secretary-General Li Ch'ang, disguised as an Eighth Route Army officer, arrived from Sian where KMT oppression had forced the Vanguards underground. In Wuhan he found a number of NLVC leaders already at work—Sung I-p'ing, Chiang Nan-hsiang, Yang Hsueh-ch'eng, Huang Hua, and Yü Kuang-yuan. Headquarters were in the home of Hsia Nung-t'ai, who only recently had arrived from France.[95] Also returned from France were two prominent student leaders, Ch'en Chu-t'ien of the National Student Association and Ts'ao Ch'eng-hsien of the NLVC, who had attended the congress of the International Federation of Students in Geneva in 1936. On March 27 Ch'en informed a national student congress that China's students had the support of their contemporaries around the world.[96] Both Ch'en and Ts'ao were killed in Japanese air raids.[97]

All these individuals had presumably been working under veteran CCP intellectual and united front organizer Wu Yü-chang, who had lived in Paris and Moscow since 1927. He

[93]"Youth World—News of the Month" column in *Ch'ing-nien yueh-k'an* [Youth monthly] 5, no. 5 (April 15, 1938).

[94]*SNL*, p. 38.

[95]Li Ch'ang, "Recollections," Part II, p. 40.

[96]*Hsin-hua jih-pao*, March 28, 1938.

[97]Li Ch'ang, "Recollections," Part II, p. 40.

returned to China in April 1938 after attending the London International Peace Conference. As we have noted, he was one of the six-man CCP delegation in Wuhan. Continued communications with NLVC offices in Paris and Lyon enhanced the cosmopolitan quality of Wuhan II. T. H. Wei of Lyon's Association des Étudiants de l'Institut Franco-Chinois reported on Chinese student activities in the Paris publication, *Student Voice*.[98]

Symbolic of Wuhan II's spirit of worldwide solidarity was the visit of the International Student Delegation, which arrived in the city on May 22. The group had been formed at the behest of the National Student Association at the World Student Association conference in Paris in August 1937. The delegates—James Klugmann, secretary of the World Student Association, Bernard Floud of the Student Committee of the British Youth Peace Assembly, Molly Yard, organization secretary of the American Student Union, representing the United Student Peace Committee, and Grant Lathe, representing the Canadian Student Christian Movement and the Canadian Student Assembly—were given an enthusiastic welcome by about a thousand student envoys at the Wuhan airport and by tens of thousands of people along the route into town. High Kuomintang officials received them, and approximately 700 people attended a reception in their honor organized by Chou En-lai, Wang Ming, and other prominent Communists. Following their visit to China, they went on to the World Youth Congress in New York where they expressed support for the struggle of China's youth against the Japanese aggressor.[99]

However, while Wuhan's student leaders were sharing the

[98]*See* T. H. Wei, "Chinese Students Work for Victory," *Student Voice* 4, nos. 3 and 4 (June 1938): 6–8.

[99]*See* "R.M.E. Delegation to China," *Student Voice* 4, nos. 3 and 4 (June 1938): 12–14; "Collaboration, Harmony, and Loyalty," *China Forum* 1, no. 14 (May 21, 1938): 375–76; Lu Ts'ui, "Shih-chieh ch'ing-nien tai-piao t'uan hsing-chiang lai-hua" [World youth delegation to visit China), *Ch'üan-min chou-k'an* [People's weekly] 1, no. 9 (April 16, 1938): 292–93.

limelight with these visiting dignitaries, new KMT policies were enunciated, with dire consequences for left-wing organizations. The ruling party's stricter attitude was, no doubt, coordinated with plans (announced in April) to establish the Three People's Principles Youth Corps. It was also a reaction to the growing strength and boldness of radical organizations. Following the Japanese capture of Süchow on May 19, 1938, the CCP promoted the slogan, "Defend Wuhan to the Death." This cry for a Chinese equivalent to the defense of Madrid had political as well as military implications that were unpalatable to the Kuomintang. The CCP urged the government to create an elite division of 5,000 to 10,000 youth "with the highest national revolutionary consciousness" to lead armed civilians. Prominent Communists Wang Ming, Chou En-lai, and Po Ku published a long article on the defense of Wuhan.[100] The CCP had, moreover, established a Wuhan Defense Committee, which Lyman Van Slyke calls "a kind of general directorate for some 16 mass organizations."[101]

Hugh Deane described the KMT's reaction: "In May 1938 all non-Kuomintang Youth organizations were destroyed by the simple expedient of compelling them to register with the government. Registrations proved difficult to secure. The three most powerful youth organizations were suppressed: the Youth Vanguards, the Northwest Youth National Salvation Federation, and the Wuhan Youth Salvation Corps."[102] On August 20 authorities disbanded the Wuhan Defense Committee and its constituent organizations.[103]

The anti-leftist assault was simply the more negative feature of the KMT's emerging youth policy. The creative aspect was the foundation of the Three People's Principles Youth Corps,

[100]Johnson, *Peasant Nationalism,* pp. 37–38.

[101]Van Slyke, *Enemies,* p. 162.

[102]Hugh Deane, "Political Reaction in Kuomintang China," *Amerasia* 5, no. 5 (July 1941): 210.

[103]*Ibid.,* pp. 201–202.

proclaimed by a KMT congress on April 1, 1938 and formally launched in July. On June 16, Chiang Kai-shek appealed to the youth of China to rally under the banner of the new corps. He made it quite clear that the period of a multilateral united front was about to give way to a more monolithic concept of order and discipline. "Situated as we are in the present critical times," he said, "our young people must not follow the example of youths in some countries where the existence and growth of several different political beliefs and movements are tolerated."[104]

Suppression moved most swiftly in Sian. There, where Kuomintang lines faced Communist territory, KMT-CCP relations had been deteriorating. In late spring or early summer, local authorities ordered the disbandment of 13 leftist patriotic organizations including the Northwest National Salvation Union, the NLVC's Northwest Bureau and its Sian headquarters, the Northwest Youth National Salvation Union's Sian office, the Sian Students National Salvation Union, and the Society for the Promotion of the New Script [Hsin-wen-tzu].[105] Three men prominent in these groups were arrested, including Sian NLVC leader Yü Chih-yuan. In addition, a warrant was circulated for Li Lien-pi, director of the NLVC Northwest Bureau, who happened to be out of town; he was picked up in Sanyuan County in July. With the apprehension of still another young man, the incarcerated leaders became known as the "Five Youths of Sian," and a movement was undertaken to secure their release. Well-organized groups from schools and other organizations staged daily demonstrations in front of the prison. The five were finally freed in September.[106] However,

---

[104]P. C. Kuo, "Youth in the War," *China Quarterly* 4, no. 1 (winter 1938–39): 44–46; also translated in *President Chiang Kai-shek's Selected Speeches and Messages, 1937–1945* (Taipei: China Cultural Service, n.d.), p. 28.

[105]Li Lien-pi, "Flames of Wrath," in *RON*, p. 121, places this event in May; Li Ch'ang, "Recollections," Part II, p. 40, says June or July.

[106]Li Lien-pi, "Flames of Wrath," in *RON*, p. 121.

repression had rendered it impossible for the Vanguards to operate openly in Kuomintang areas.

In Kweichow's provincial capital, Kweiyang, remote from international surveillance, repression was brutal. The nearly one hundred members of that city's NLVC branch were invited by KMT headquarters to hear a speech on August 13, the first anniversary of the Japanese attack on Shanghai. Upon arrival, they were arrested and sent to prison. Five leaders were shot, among them Chang I-shan, a graduate of Yenan's Resistance University, who had gone to Kweiyang to lead the local NLVC organization.[107] The CCP's response to these blows to the united front was ineffectual and short-lived. The *Hsin-hua jih-pao* protested the abolition of the Wuhan Defense Committee and was promptly suspended for three days.[108]

By now the CCP had all but written off the cities of KMT China. The united front, as Chalmers Johnson has observed, had yielded but one "concrete benefit": it had "permitted the recruitment, for a short period of time, of comparatively large numbers of students from urban areas."[109] By the summer of 1938, Communist organizers had enjoyed a year's grace in these KMT regions. The most receptive youngsters had already been won over. Thousands of volunteers had been processed and sent on to Yenan. Now, the political lines hardening, the gains to be realized by defending members of Wuhan's mass organizations from KMT harassment no longer seemed worth the risk. The Party's real strength lay in the countryside, in border regions. So long as the CCP enjoyed virtual autonomy in these vital areas, it was reluctant to antagonize the KMT. Hence, even sympathetic foreigners such as Freda Utley excoriated a Communist policy that "precluded any real struggle to improve the conditions of the wretchedly paid Chinese working class" and castigated the CCP for its attitude toward youth:

[107]Li Ch'ang, "Recollections," Part II, p. 41.
[108]Deane, "Political Reaction," pp. 201–202.
[109]Johnson, *Peasant Nationalism*, p. 14.

The same timidity and fear of splitting the "united front" was evidenced by the youth organizations. The young men and women I talked to were the leaders of the semi-Communist "Vanguards," A.N.T.S. [elsewhere called the Ant Society], which had just been suppressed (mid-August), but were carrying on in spite of the suppression in hope that they would in time "win the confidence" of the Government. The Government, they said, has suppressed them on account of a "misunderstanding." They believed, or professed to believe, that the Government "wants a mass movement to defend Wuhan."[110]

The same errors were later recognized by Party historian Hu Ch'iao-mu, who blamed Wang Ming (Ch'en Shao-yü), head of the United Front Department and one of the six-member Chinese Communist delegation in Wuhan, for carrying out a policy of "Right opportunism." Wang's followers, wrote Hu, had "demanded that the Communists make concessions to the anti-popular policy of the Kuomintang by confining their activities within the scope permitted by Chiang Kai-shek's Kuomintang."[111] Tetsuya Kataoka suggests a radically different interpretation: because Mao's bailiwick was the countryside, whereas Wang Ming was attempting to establish an urban base, "Mao was probably not unhappy to see Wuhan fall."[112] Whatever Mao's attitude, fall it did, and with it the hopes of Wang and others who had wanted to make Wuhan "China's Madrid."

Wuhan II, which had never promised as much as Wuhan I, disappeared, leaving even less of a trace. Thus ended the idea of an urban united front in KMT China. With the fall of Wuhan, many veterans of the city's defunct National Salvation Youth Corps fled to the nearby Tahung Mountains to carry on

---

[110]Freda Utley, *China at War* (London: Faber and Faber, 1939), p. 82.

[111]Hu Chiao-mu, *Thirty Years of the Communist Party of China* (Peking: Foreign Languages Press, 1959), pp. 60–61.

[112]*Shen-Kan-Ning pien-ch'ü chien-cheng shih-shih yao-kang* [Program for implementing the simplified government in the Shen-Kan-Ning Border Region] (Northwest Bureau of the CCP, December 1942), cited in Tetsuya Kataoka, "Communist Power in a War of National Liberation: The Case of China," *World Politics* 24, no. 3 (April 1972): 426.

guerrilla warfare, as brother groups were doing in the Süchow region of northern Kiangsu and adjacent Shantung and in the East River area of Kwangtung.[113] But the last urban rallying point in Kuomintang China was gone. For radical youth in search of refuge, only one town remained—Yenan.

[113] *Wei t'uan-chieh,* pp. 101–102.

V

Apprentices Under Fire,
1938–48

Yenan in 1938 was more than a name on a map. It was a mystique. Its magnetic appeal to the youth of China recalled Kuomintang Canton of the mid-1920s. In the history of Chinese Communism, Yenan had no precedent. The legions of Mao and Chu Te at Chingkangshan and Juichin had been separated from the academic centers of the major cities. During the Long March, isolation was still more complete. In the early months in northern Shensi, communication with the students of Peiping was mainly through publications in the "mosquito press" and "clandestine circulation" of the August 1 manifesto and other CCP declarations.[1] Now agents throughout unoccupied China proclaimed the promise of the new mecca.

The first sizable group of students to join the CCP since 1927 was recruited during the Red Army's foray into Shansi from February to April 1936. Anti-Japanese student demonstrations in Yen Hsi-shan's capital coincided with the invasion. "As the Red Army approached Taiyuan," reports Donald Gillin, "Yen arrested the demonstrators by the hundreds and shot at least a

---

[1] Edgar Snow, "Comment," *The China Quarterly*, no. 26 (April-June 1966), p. 172.

174

score of them for collaborating with the Communists."[2] Little wonder that hundreds of students joined the Communists in their withdrawal to Shensi.[3]

After the end of the school year in June 1936, college graduates, those expelled for political activities, and other student activists fanned out from Peiping and Tientsin to other cities of North China, especially to Taiyuan, where Yen Hsi-shan was developing a more lenient attitude toward anti-Japanese propagandists, and Sian where the sympathetic Young Marshal and his revanchist-minded troops provided a friendly milieu for patriotic activities. Initially, fewer students went to Paoan because of the remoteness of the Communist capital and the dangers of the journey. The CCP, moreover, lacked facilities for indoctrinating and training large numbers of student volunteers and was quite content to see them spreading the united front line in the realm of its regional rivals Yen and Chang.

THE LURE OF YENAN

During the Communists' last six months in Paoan, a handful of hardy pioneers made its way to this distant Red redoubt. The first December 9 veteran known to have gone there was Huang Hua, who journeyed from Peiping in the summer of 1936 to serve as Edgar Snow's interpreter. Huang subsequently helped to pave the way for other Peiping activists. As the idea of a united front against Japan gained acceptance in the Northwest and fighting between the Red Army and Chang Hsueh-liang's forces subsided, the hazards of getting to the Communist areas were somewhat lessened. Following settlement of the Sian Incident, Mao moved his capital to the more accessible city of Yenan. During Sian's ensuing interregnum, pending the

[2]Donald G. Gillin, *Warlord: Yen Hsi-shan in Shansi Province, 1911–1949* (Princeton, N. J.: Princeton University Press, 1967), p. 224.

[3]Samuel B. Griffith II, *The Chinese People's Liberation Army* (New York: McGraw–Hill, 1967), p. 58.

takeover by troops loyal to Nanking, many of the city's student activists were able to move northward to the new Red capital. By early 1937 the trickle of youngsters had become a steady stream. A Japanese observer spotted about a thousand youths heading for Yenan where they entered Resistance University in May 1937.[4]

Widespread confusion followed the Marco Polo Bridge Incident on July 7. Students were uncertain how far the war would spread and how long it would last. Many sought only to avoid interruptions in their education. As universities moved to temporary locations behind Nationalist lines, students moved with them. The CCP, at this time, was reluctant to compete openly with the KMT for student recruits. Communist leaders felt constrained to avoid activities that might antagonize Chiang during the consolidation of the united front. But confusion in Nationalist ranks presented a tempting opportunity to woo youthful converts. Hence, in August 1937, the Central Committee issued proclamations of support for a policy of "education for national defense" at a time when KMT educators and politicians were still hotly debating this issue. By this device, as Peter Seybolt has observed, they sought "to embarrass the National government and usurp leadership of the patriotic movement."[5]

By the fall of 1937 it was clear that Japan's ambitions were not limited to North China, and many students were beginning to look for ways to serve their country during what might be a protracted war. As Edgar Snow remarked:

Wherever I went after the war began young people would appear in the most unexpected places with a copy of *Red Star over China* (in the pirated Chinese edition) tucked under their arms, to ask me how they could enter one of the schools at Yenan. . . . If I had set up a recruiting

---

[4]Chalmers A. Johnson, *Peasant Nationalism and Communist Power* (Stanford, Calif.: Stanford University Press, 1962), p. 33 and note 5, p. 201, which gives the source as Kusano Fumio, *Shina henku no kenkyu* [The study of China's border region] (Tokyo, 1944), p. 79.

[5]Peter Seybolt, "The Yenan Revolution in Mass Education," *The China Quarterly*, no. 48 (October–December 1971), pp. 646–47.

station in Shanghai or Hankow or Chungking I could have enlisted several battalions. . . . [6]

The CCP quickly perceived the need for a recruitment network. At the zenith of the united front era in the spring of 1938, major cities in Kuomintang China had offices of the Eighth Route Army where young people could obtain passes for admission to Communist-held areas. The effectiveness of the CCP's recruitment system, even in far-off Canton, is attested to by Ma Fu-yao, a Cantonese newspaper reporter. After being heavily fined for printing a headline about the Eighth Route Army's resistance to Japan, the embittered journalist was approached by CCP agents and recruited into the NLVC. Ma's assignment was to register in a school for wartime education and select "progressive" students for the NLVC. He found 139 of these, all but two of whom agreed to continue their education in Yenan.[7]

Upon arrival in Yenan, new converts received a warm welcome. Their services were urgently needed. Tens of thousands of educated youngsters recruited between the May 4th Movement and the Northern Expedition had fallen during the antiwarlord battles of 1926–27, the KMT's Party Purification movement of 1927–28, the Canton Commune of December 1927, and the bloody civil war from 1928 to 1936. In June 1937, Lin Piao told Helen Snow that some 200 of the Whampoa cadets in the Red Army had been killed; only 30 had survived.[8]

If the Red Army was woefully short of educated leadership, the need for civilian administrators and teachers was still more acute. To rule and educate the illiterate masses over vast areas of North China, the CCP needed trained manpower. The job

---

[5]Edgar Snow, *The Battle for Asia* (New York: Random House, 1942), p. 259.

[7]Ma Fu-yao, *Wo yü kung-ch'ang-tang* [I and the Communist Party] (Hong Kong: Tzu-chi ch'u-pan she, 1952), pp. 1–9.

[8]Nym Wales [Helen F. Snow], *My Yenan Notebooks* (mimeographed, Madison, Conn., 1961), p. 117.

was quite beyond the capacity of the small number of intellectuals in the CCP's main force and on the local scene.[9]

The effective training and deployment of educated newcomers in the Shansi-Chahar-Hopei Border Region impressed even pro-KMT writer Paul M. A. Linebarger:

A very high degree of direct popular government has been achieved. Over wide areas, the average age of the *hsien* magistrates is in the twenties. Recruitment to the Region of numerous professors and students from Peiping has helped to fill the need for trained personnel, and has assisted in maintaining the areas as a genuine multigroup affair rather than a Communist front.[10]

Veterans of the December 9th movement, moreover, were highly experienced in propaganda and other forms of political agitation and organization. Having aroused the literate elite of China, they were eager to spread the message of national salvation to the masses. In fact, however, positions at the township and village levels were filled with locally-recruited cadres who, though often illiterate, generally had played instrumental roles in the land revolution and had a first-hand knowledge of the rural scene. Students and other exurbanites were employed almost exclusively at higher levels—in various branches of the county and regional governments.[11] December 9ers, moreover, provided a channel through which the CCP might hope to win at least tacit support from these youths' families, teachers, and former schoolmates in KMT and Japanese-occupied areas. Missionary school students in particular gave the Communists a previously unanticipated entree into the missions of North China. Here Communist civil and military personnel were able to find shelter and refuge.[12]

Each stage of the Japanese advance created new recruits for Yenan. The fall of the major cities—Peiping, Shanghai,

---

[9]Seybolt, "The Yenan Revolution," p. 644.

[10]Paul M. A. Linebarger, *The China of Chiang Kai-shek* (Boston: World Peace Foundation, 1943), p. 119.

[11]Ying-mao Kao, "Urban and Rural Strategies in the Chinese Communist Revolution," in John Wilson Lewis, ed., *Peasant Rebellion and Communist Revolu-*

Changsha, Wuhan—loosed successive waves. According to one source, after the temporary campus in Changsha closed, only 600 of its 2,000 students (Peita, Tsinghua, and Nankai refugees) showed up at the new campus in Kunming. Many of the others went to Yenan. Even Peita Chancellor Chiang Monlin, who estimates a much smaller drop in enrollment, calculates that "over three hundred and fifty students remained in Changsha to join the various war organizations."[13] As the evacuation of Wuhan became imminent, the stream of young migrants reached flood proportions. In the summer of 1938 a *New York Times* correspondent found a procession of students strung out along the rugged 300-mile road from Sian to Yenan. They had come from every province in China as well as Malaya, the Philippines, Java, and the United States. Fifty thousand, he wrote, were volunteering to enroll in educational, civil, and military institutions.[14] Writing in the January 1939 issue of *Asia*, Jack Chen reported "a waiting list of twenty thousand students."[15] Even a profoundly anti-Communist writer conceded that "around the time when Wuhan was abandoned,

---

tion in Asia (Stanford, Calif.: Stanford University Press, 1974), pp. 264-267. Also see Mark Selden, *The Yenan Way in Revolutionary China* (Cambridge, Mass.: Harvard University Press, 1971), *passim*.

[12]Fox Butterfield, "A Missionary View of the Chinese Communists, 1936–1939," in Kwang-Ching Liu, ed., *American Missionaries in China*, Harvard East Asian Monographs no. 21 (Cambridge, Mass.: East Asian Research Center, 1966), pp. 277–79; James Bertram, *Unconquered* (New York: John Day, 1939), pp. 165–69.

[13]"Wo-men ti tao-lu" [Our road], in Hsi-nan lien-ta ch'u-hsi fu-k'an, ed., *Lien-ta pa-nien* [Eight years of Southwest Associated University] (Kunming: Hsi-nan lien-ta hsueh-sheng ch'u-pan she, 1946), Preface, p. 1; Monlin Chiang, *Tides from the West* (New Haven, Conn.: Yale University Press, 1947), pp. 221–22. *Cf.* Israel Epstein's claim that 500 remained in Changsha, Chapter 4, note 72, above.

[14]"Red Army Trains the Youth of China," *New York Times*, August 14, 1938, Section 4, p. 5.

[15]Jack Chen, "Why They Go to Yenan," *Asia* 39, no. 1 (January 1939): 28.

thousands and tens of thousands of youths went to North Shensi to enter K'angta or the North Shensi Public School."[16]

The KMT's inability to hold cities and protect centers of higher education was but one factor that impelled students toward Yenan. Another was its procrastination in developing what James Bertram termed "a realistic approach to the problems of war mobilization."[17] Students whose radical proclivities had been given free rein during the December 9th movement were offered the unpalatable choice of continuing a conventional education (as much as wartime conditions would permit), or joining the regular army. There were some outlets in war service work through organizations such as the Boy Scouts, but this appealed mainly to the teenaged high school student and had scant political allure for the college radical. Authorities who tried to mobilize student volunteers were paralyzed by indecision. Typical is the story told to James Bertram by a graduate from a Christian college in North China (perhaps Yenching). When the Marco Polo Bridge Incident occurred, he said,

I was in Shanghai; and at once I went to Nanking to volunteer my services. But in Nanking there was nothing—only the old officials, the old bureaucrats. Always we were told to wait in an office, then come back the next day. Many were turned away like this. Such methods cannot help China: we all wanted to have practical training, to work among the people. Then my friend who is in the Party School in Yenan wrote to me, and told me of the new [North Shensi Public School], where many students have come since the United Front. I did not tell my family where I was going, but took the train for Sian [gateway to Communist areas in Shensi].[18]

Compared with the uncertainty, indifference, suspiciousness, and inefficiency of the KMT's urban establishment, the Communist leaders at Yenan were indeed attractive. Students iden-

---

[16]Wang Chien-min, "Yen-an ti k'u-men" [The agony of Yenan], *Chung-yang chou-k'an* [Central weekly] 3, no. 47 (June 26, 1941): 6.

[17]Bertram, *Unconquered*, p. 96.

[18]*Ibid.*

tified the almost legendary veterans of the Long March with China's heroic, long-suffering masses. Under the guidance of these men, they hoped to liberate themselves while liberating China. "Although some few went to recover faith in themselves," observed pilgrim-reporter Jack Chen, "the majority were going to Yenan confident that through that city they would find a broader, more direct way of using their talents and energies in the development of the country."[19]

At Yenan students felt they would find a wholeness, a sense of *communitas,* a style of life available nowhere else in China. "Why did you all leave home and go to Yenan in the first place?" George Hogg asked a group of students who had recently graduated from the western Hopei branch of K'angta:

Among a variety of answers, ranging from dissatisfaction with lives of comfort to having been driven out by Japanese bombs, the real reasons always seemed to have been the search for a place where comradeship and equality in a national cause were placed above everything else. It was as simple as that.[20]

The greatest appeal to students was the opportunity to continue education in a way that would prepare them for war work and allow them to identify with China's millions. "Before, our lives were much too sheltered," confided Bertram's informant. "We trained our minds, but not our bodies. Now in Yenan we will get another kind of training, and find some work that will be really useful for the war."[21]

Many NLVC cadres who arrived in Yenan from non-Communist areas were sent to the Youth Training School (*Ch'ing-nien hsun-lien pan*) at Wupao. Under the direction of youthful Chancellor Feng Wen-pin, this school prepared cadres for work in the youth movement.[22] The Communists' most

---

[19]Jack Chen, "Why They Go to Yenan," p. 26.

[20]George Hogg, *I See a New China* (Boston: Little, Brown, 1944), p. 19.

[21]Bertram, *Unconquered,* p. 96.

[22]Warren Kuo, *Analytical History of the Chinese Communist Party* (Taipei: Institute of International Relations, 1970), 3:234.

prestigious educational institution, however, was Resistance University. The school's name echoed student aspirations: to pursue higher education that would serve the war effort. The first call for student volunteers was issued in February 1936.[23] Soon, K'angta, a college whose *raison d'être* was the resistance, became the guiding star for a generation of young pilgrims.

From a curricular aspect K'angta was no ordinary university. It was, rather, a short-course army academy with a heavy political emphasis. The entire course of training took only six to eight months.[24] The program's orientation was military, the regimen spartan, the code of conduct severe. In addition to military subjects, matriculants studied political subjects ranging from techniques of revolution to economic and political problems. Eighty percent of K'angta's graduates went to the front. Many December 9th veterans from urban areas were put to work as lower-level political officers after commencement. An elite of each graduating class went on for further training at the Military Academy or political education at the Marx-Lenin Academy.[25]

The student influx left its mark upon the university. K'angta's progenitor, the Red Army Academy, had reopened at Wayaopao in June 1936 and shifted to Paoan in July. Its first class of some 240 students were Red Army veterans. Moving to Yenan after the Sian Incident, it changed its name to K'angta, expanded its enrollment, and changed the make-up of its student body. In the second class of about 1,200 students, which was graduated around the time of the Marco Polo Bridge Incident, approximately 200 were students from outside Yenan.[26] In June 1937, school President Lin Piao told Helen Snow that 30 percent of the 1,400-strong student body was drawn from the

[23]Stuart R. Schram, *Mao Tse-tung* (rev. ed., Baltimore: Penguin, 1967), p. 207.

[24]Warren Kuo, *Analytical History*, 3:233.

[25]"Red Army Trains," p. 5; Johnson, *Peasant Nationalism*, p. 14.

[26]Wang Chien-min, *Chung-kuo kung-ch'an-tang shih-kao* [History of the Chinese Communist Party] (Taipei: 1965), 3:278.

landlord, urban, petty bourgeois, and intelligentsia groups.[27] Forty percent of the class that attended K'angta between the Sian Incident and the beginning of the war were youngsters recruited from non-Communist territory.[28] During her visit, Mrs. Snow discovered that "Many of the best student leaders from all the big cities in China had come [to K'angta]. I met about a dozen that I had known in Peiping during the student movement of 1935, two of whom were from Yenching University. . . . Students [from Manchuria] numbered one hundred."[29]

K'angta was organized in 14 squads: squads 1 through 8 were for Red Army Cadres and 9 through 14 were for Party members and fellow-travelers from the "White areas." Squad 14 was exclusively women.[30] These, noted Helen Snow, numbered only 50 in a student body of 1,400 but "were all exceptional students, and made up what they lacked in numbers by superior ability."[31] K'angta's third class began in September 1937. Forty percent of the 1,800 enrolled were youths from other places. The fourth class, numbering 4,500, entered in April 1938 and was graduated in October. The fifth class, which began in October 1938, had about 10,000, of whom more than 80 percent were from KMT territory. In 1939, the school moved its main campus to Wuhsiang in southeastern Shansi.

One report gives a 1939 enrollment of 4,296, of whom 1,440 had completed high school, 145 professional school, 428 college, 11 graduate school, and 25 study abroad. By this time most cadres were said to be former students.[32]

In September 1937, North Shensi Public School (Shen-pei kung-hsueh) was established as a preparatory school for

[27]Nym Wales, *My Yenan Notebooks*, p. 117.

[28]Wang Chien-min, *Chung-kuo kung-ch'an-tang*, 3:278.

[29]Nym Wales [Helen F. Snow], *Inside Red China* (New York: Doubleday, 1939), p. 82.

[30]Warren Kuo, *Analytical History*, 3:173.

[31]Nym Wales, *Inside Red China*, p. 82.

[32]Hsin-pao Chang, "Data on Guerrilla War" (Notes of Ezra Vogel, file, Cambridge, Mass.: East Asian Research Center, Harvard University).

K'angta hopefuls. Unlike K'angta, Shenkung made no attempt to limit its enrollment to members of the CCP and other "progressive" organizations. There were no partisan or educational prerequisites. Only "traitors" and "Trotskyites" were excluded. Hence, even KMT agents found it possible to infiltrate the Shenkung student body.[33]

In spite of Shenkung's nonexclusive nature, its rigorous discipline and living conditions were much like K'angta's. The curricular emphasis, however, was not on military affairs but on politics and mass movements. According to Wang Chien-min, K'angta was 70 percent military and 30 percent political, Shenkung the reverse.[34] Shenkung's student body was smaller than K'ang-ta's and the course of study was even shorter. The first class (200 students) was graduated in November 1937, the second (400) in January 1938, the third (600) in March. By June 1938, some five classes had been graduated with a cumulative total of more than 3,000 students.[35]

CITY ELITISTS AND RURAL POPULISTS

The fantastic influx of students was a mixed blessing for the Communists. As early as June 1937, Helen Snow had reported that K'angta had enrolled 1,400 students but still "had so many applicants they could not take care of them." In September, James Bertram encountered some 50 K'angta hopefuls at a Sian army station. To reduce the numbers to manageable proportions, he discovered, "a system of elimination had been devised by which a stiff preliminary examination" selected the "most likely candidates." The students Bertram met were the finalists, serious young people who "filled in the hours of waiting, earnestly reading Lenin."[36] Bertram joined 20 of these youngsters in a truck bound for Yunyang, a dismal little town

[33]Warren Kuo, *Analytical History*, 3:173.

[34]Wang Chien-min, *Chung-kuo kung-ch'an tang*, 3:281.

[35]*Ibid*.

[36]Bertram, *Unconquered*, p. 82.

on the border of the Communist area, where a final examination was administered. Only survivors of this test were admitted to K'angta.[37] One purpose of the North Shensi Public School was to absorb at least some of the overflow.

These educated hordes brought with them a host of problems quite different from those that the Communists had faced in dealing with simple soldiers and peasants. According to Agnes Smedley, "Trotskyites" and political agents from the Blueshirts (a precursor of the Three People's Principles Youth Corps) infiltrated with ease.[38] Some students sought a more total "liberation" than even Yenan was prepared to offer. Ten such youngsters were arrested for forming a "Free Love Club."[39]

Other students found it difficult to shed urban elitist attitudes for rural populist orthodoxy. As Mark Selden notes, "Thousands who eventually made the arduous trip to Yenan had rarely experienced hardship, knew little of the previous land revolution, and were totally unfamiliar with the problems of the border area."[40] Few, perhaps, would have echoed the Peiping teacher's argument that "Sympathy with the people is utterly useless. There are too many of them,"[41] but there was an undeniable chasm between Peiping intellectuals and Shensi villagers. When refugees from the cities of East China tried to reproduce their idea of a good education in the rural northwestern schools, they failed miserably. They only succeeded in bringing down upon their heads criticism for accepting "the old traditions of foreign capitalist schools" and "the dogmatism of capitalist schools."[42] Chu Te, the tough Red Army chieftain, found his secretary, a former Yenching coed, too academic and

---

[37]*Ibid.*, p. 87.

[38]Agnes Smedley, *Battle Hymn of China* (New York: Knopf, 1943), p. 165.

[39]*Ibid.*

[40]Selden, *Yenan Way*, p. 146.

[41]Agnes Smedley, *China Fights Back* (New York: Vanguard Press, 1938), p. 30.

[42]Seybolt, "The Yenan Revolution," p. 656.

sent her to work with local village women.[43] After talking to two students from Manchuria who had trekked all over eastern Shansi to join the Eighth Route Army, Agnes Smedly expressed a caustic conclusion:

These students are rich men, they are smartly clad, but they are politically more backward than the peasants. I asked them what they intended to do, and one of them remarked that "some will join this army and some will go into politics!" The remark sounded exactly like some American politicians' speech. I asked the man where he had been educated, and he gave me the name of an American insitution. . . . I wonder how many of these rich men's sons will remain in the Eighth Route Army for more than a month.[44]

Many students arrived in the Northwest in a melodramatic mood. Typical of these was a young man named Liu who served as interpreter for James Bertram. Bertram described him as:

One of the young Peiping students who had come to Sian to do national salvation work under Sun Ming-chiu. He was a comical-looking youth, for he had cropped his head in an excess of patriotic zeal, and the style did not become him. Moreover, in his desire to "sacrifice himself," he wore nothing but a thin cotton uniform in mid-winter (because, he said, the heroic anti-Japanese fighters had only one blanket each, and he was not going to be more comfortable than they were). As a result, he usually had a cold, which he secretly rather enjoyed, as a sign of martyrdom.[45]

When Bertram set out in quest of the Red Army, he found Liu "almost frantic with impatience to visit the Red Camp. Like many young Chinese leftists, he had an overwhelming admiration for Chu Te and Mao Tse-tung and the Peasants' and Workers' Army . . . ."[46] When Liu suddenly spotted his first Communist troops in the field, he "nearly fell off his bicycle in excitement." And when offered a cigarette by an army commissar, "Liu, the complete hero-worshipper, put his cigarette

---

[43] Hogg, *I See a New China*, p. 33.

[44] Smedley, *China Fights Back*, p. 154.

[45] James Bertram, *First Act in China* (New York: Viking, 1938), p. 169.

[46] *Ibid.*, p. 237.

carefully away in his pocket. A gift from the Red Army was to be treasured."[47]

One may doubt whether students like Mr. Liu were suited for working with the tough survivors of the Long March and the shrewd, skeptical peasant of Shensi.

Communist spokesmen understandably entertained ambivalent feelings about the students. They welcomed them but they quite candidly voiced doubts about these young people's class background, motiviation, and adaptability. "In crisis students always waver," Li Wei-han, one of Yenan's leading Communists, told Helen Snow. "If capitalism cannot develop in China the intellectuals have no future, so they join the revolution. . . . Their motive is not only nationalistic but economic."[48] In an interview on July 4, 1937, Mrs. Snow heard similar words from Mao Tse-tung:

The students, intellectuals, and professionals come from the landlord, petty-bourgeois and bourgeois classes. They join the movement in opposing imperialists and in supporting democracy because their own [families are] bankrupt and [have] no future. Students are a very important [sector] of the social revolution but play no decisive role; only the proletariat and peasant play this role.[49]

Two years' experience with these new recruits did not change Mao's opinion. In December 1939, he wrote:

The revolutionary forces cannot be successfully organized and revolutionary work cannot be successfully conducted without the participation of revolutionary intellectuals. But the intellectuals often tend to be subjective and individualistic, impractical in their thinking and irresolute in action until they have thrown themselves heart and soul into mass revolutionary struggles, or made up their minds to serve the interests of the masses and become one with them. Hence although the mass of revolutionary intellectuals in China can play a vanguard role or serve as a link with the masses, not all of them will remain revolutionaries to the end. Some will drop out of the revolutionary

---

[47]*Ibid.,* p. 239.
[48]Nym Wales, *My Yenan Notebooks,* p. 104.
[49]*Ibid.,* p. 140.

ranks at critical moments and become passive, while a few may even become enemies of the revolution. The intellectuals can overcome their shortcomings only in mass struggles over a long period.[50]

Like other aspects of the CCP's wartime development, the influx of student pilgrims may be plotted on a contour: "expansion during the first couple of years of war; [retraction] until late in the war; a partial revival of activity in 1944 and 1945."[51] By 1939, the tide of student pilgrims was beginning to ebb. There are several reasons for this. First, the Nationalists had thrown up an effective blockade, especially around Sian, the main point of entry to the Communist zone. This effort was intended to hem in the Communists and to keep out new recruits. Students who were apprehended were sent to a special institution in Sian for thought reform. Second, as the Japanese tightened control over communications, it became increasingly difficult to penetrate enemy lines. Third, as the national government settled down for a long siege in Southwest China, émigré colleges and universities—and a new system of government-established high schools—were able to absorb youth who were seeking education. In spite of wartime thought control, many of the free spirits of China taught at such institutions as Southwest Associated University (Lienta) in Kunming, where Peita, Tsinghua, and Nankai finally settled. The amalgamation in 1939 of the North Shensi Public School and several other institutions into the North China Associated University was, perhaps, an imitation, at least in nomenclature, of Southwest Associated University—a tacit admission of how effective a competitor this school had become.

Students who managed to reach Southwest China were reluctant to undergo the added dangers and hardships of the long pilgrimage to Yenan. Furthermore, for young people in search of élan based upon shared hardships, the heavy Japanese

[50]"The Chinese Revolution and the Chinese Communist Party," *Selected Works of Mao Tse-tung* (Peking: Foreign Languages Press, 1965), 2:322.

[51]Lyman P. Van Slyke, *Enemies and Friends* (Stanford, Calif.: Stanford University Press, 1967), p. 160.

bombing of southwestern cities and campuses from 1939 to 1941 provided a wartime camaraderie. To flee to North China, no matter how difficult the route or how dangerous the conditions at the destination, would have seemed cowardly. It also is possible that news of the 1942–44 *Cheng-feng* (thought reform) movement, which trickled back to Nationalist areas and was exploited in KMT publications, had a deterrent effect on would-be pilgrims. Not until the final years of the war did demoralization prevalent in the Southwest and renewed reports of the good life in Yenan combine to produce a mini-migration, but this was nothing compared to the flood of 1938.

As the crest of the student influx receded, a small number of disillusioned youngsters began to leave Yenan and head back for Kuomintang territory. It took, perhaps, more courage to turn their backs on Yenan than to go there in the first place. Departees felt guilty for abandoning comrades in a revolutionary crusade. Switching sides was also dangerous. Those arriving in KMT territory were marked men, immediately suspect by authorities as possible secret agents. But for many young liberals, the social and intellectual conformity imposed by the Communists was simply impossible to endure.

A comprehensive list of complaints by a disillusioned former K'angta student is to be found in a collection entitled *The So-called "Border Regions."* The author of the article " 'Resist Japan University' and the Anguish of Youth," is one Wang Wen-hsiang. With the Japanese invasion of his native Soochow, he had fled and attempted to continue his studies in a middle school in the foreign concession of Shanghai. However, he found the school overcrowded and repressive. Having read about K'angta in a newspaper, he managed to contact a certain young woman who gave him a letter of introduction. He took a boat to Wenchow, continued to Sian via Nanchang, Changsha, and Hankow, and then hiked from Sian to Yenan.

The most depressing thing about K'angta, he wrote, was the nonexistence of the freedom he sought. Marxist-Leninist literature monopolized the library and the curriculum. It was impossible even to glance at a Sian newspaper without being criticized for reading propaganda from the "White" district. Contrary to united front propaganda, Sun Yat-sen's Three People's Principles were held in disrepute. One could not leave Yenan without a pass, a system that reminded him of the Japanese-occupied zones. Food, clothing, and shelter (he had to dig his own cave apartment) were uniformly wretched. Finally, there was practically no useful military training.[52] According to another author many independent-minded young Communists were impelled to leave the Party by the *Hsin-hua jih-pao's* endorsement of the Russo-Japanese pact of April 13, 1941. In a manifesto to the youth of the Northwest, more than a hundred K'angta graduates renounced loyalty to their alma mater.[53]

The antipathy of these young intellectuals for their Communist overlords was reciprocated by CCP cadres. In December 1939 the Party Central Committee criticized military, academic, and local Party units for hostility toward intellectuals. Some schools, it said, "still do not dare to enlist young students en masse." Party leaders conceded that intellectuals had to be steeled by struggle and trained to adopt a truly mass point of view and to get along harmoniously with veteran Party members and cadres, especially those of worker or peasant origin. However, proclaimed the Central Committee, all intellectuals who were loyal, willing to fight the Japanese, and capable of bearing hardship could be absorbed into the Party.[54] A majority, it seems, still met these standards.

However, the question of how to integrate independent intellectuals into an organization dominated by rustic Long March veterans was not easily resolved. This problem came to a

[52]Wang Wen-hsiang, "'K'ang-jih ta-hsueh' yü ch'ing-nien fan-men" (Resistance University and the sorrows of youth), in Ch'en Kuo-hsin and others, ed., *So-wei "pien-ch'ü"* [The so-called "border region"] ([Chungking?]), pp. 30–34.

[53]Wang Chien-min, "Yen-an ti k'u-men," p. 7.

[54]Conrad Brandt, Benjamin Schwartz, and John K. Fairbank, *A Documentary History of Chinese Communism* (Cambridge, Mass.: Harvard University Press, 1952), pp. 349–51.

head during the *Cheng-feng* movement of 1942–44. The first of the rectification campaigns that became trademarks of the Chinese Communists' operating style, *Cheng-feng* was a self-corrective device for maintaining unity, orthodoxy, and discipline in a growing and increasingly heterogeneous body. It was also an attempt to prepare the ground for a further stage of social transformation by decentralizing and debureaucratizing the governing apparatus of the Shensi-Kansu-Ningsia (Shen-Kan-Ning) Border Region. This involved a shift in emphasis away from the anti-Japanese united front that had attracted so many December 9ers and toward the rural revolution that had won mass support among the region's peasants. Outside intellectuals, whose scarce talents had enabled them to dominate the burgeoning bureaucracy, were "sent down" to work on local levels as village workers and teachers and as assistants to illiterate or semiliterate district magistrates.[55]

The *Cheng-feng* movement bore the imprint of Mao Tsetung's populism. In May 1942 at the Yenan Forum on Art and Literature, Mao voiced his profound antipathy for student elitism. This declaration revealed a fundamental part of his personality, an element deeply rooted in his youthful struggle against the old social order in which he had been raised. Mao made abundantly clear his scorn for students who failed to follow his own path of transformation and regeneration:

I began life as a student and at school acquired the ways of a student; I then used to feel it undignified to do even a little manual labor, such as carrying my own luggage in the presence of my fellow students, who were incapable of carrying anything, either on their shoulders or in their hands. At that time I felt that intellectuals were the only clean people in the world, while in comparison workers and peasants were dirty. . . . But after I became a revolutionary and lived with workers and peasants and with soldiers of the revolutionary army, . . . I came to feel that compared with the workers and peasants the unremolded intellectuals were not clean and that, in the last analysis, the workers and peasants were the cleanest people and, even though their hands were

[55]Selden, *Yenan Way,* pp. 188–207.

soiled and their feet smeared with cow-dung, they were really cleaner than the bourgeois and petty-bourgeois intellectuals.[56]

Though December 9ers in the audience might well have blushed at hearing these words, as individuals they were too young and too obscure to provide clear targets for *Cheng-feng* marksmen. More prominent were the literary intellectuals, dominated by Shanghai refugees, who had hoped to assume a role as independent critics in Yenan as they had (albeit in a more antagonistic manner) in Kuomintang territory. However, during March and April 1942, in a "barrage of critical essays,"[57] some of these writers sought support from disaffected youth including, presumably, members of the December 9th generation. Miss Tseng K'o, who participated in the literary debates of the period, recalls authors such as Hsiao Chün and Ting Ling urging youth and writers to "join hands in exposing the 'darkness' in the revolutionary ranks and satirizing the 'weaknesses' of the people."[58] Hsiao, a famous young novelist, gathered around him a coterie of writers and young people from his native Manchuria.[59] Most conspicuous of all in appealing to disaffected youths was another novelist, Wang Shih-wei. In one of his series of "Wild Lily" essays Wang wrote:

Youth are precious because they are simple, sensitive, enthusiastic, courageous, and full of the new strength of life. The evil which others have not perceived they perceive first, . . . the words others will not and dare not speak, they utter bravely.[60]

[56]*Selected Works,* 3:73.

[57]Merle Goldman, "Writers' Criticism of the Party in 1942," *The China Quarterly,* no. 17 (January-March 1964), p. 338.

[58]*Szechwan wen-i* [Szechwan literature], no. 3 (1962), pp. 87 ff., quoted in T. A. Hsia, "Twenty Years after the Yenan Forum," *The China Quarterly,* no. 13 (January-March 1963), p. 244.

[59]Merle Goldman, *Literary Dissent in Communist China* (Cambridge, Mass.: Harvard University Press, 1967), p. 28.

[60]Wang Shih-wei, "Yeh pai-ho-hua" [The wild lily], *Chieh-fang jih-pao* (Liberation daily), March 13, 1942, p. 4, cited in *Ibid.,* p. 26.

Wang's appeal struck a responsive chord and led to still bolder attacks. According to a CCP account of 1958:

Wang tried to stir up feelings among the "youngsters lower down." He said: "The great majority of them have come by devious ways and after painful struggle to Yenan. In the past they knew very little 'love and warmth,' but plenty of 'hate and coldness.' . . . Because they come to Yenan in search of warmth and beauty, they cannot help complaining when they see its ugliness and coldness. . . ." But according to him, although the young people complained, the men in power were too stubborn to change. . . .

Of course there were petty-bourgeois and bourgeois intellectuals who faltered in the face of difficulties or demanded absolute equality and "warmth." That was why Wang Shih-wei posed as their champion to stir up feeling against the Party among the rank and file of revolutionary workers and tried to turn young people into his tools. He argued that if certain older revolutionaries with heavy responsibilities had slightly better living conditions than the average, this was undemocratic and they were a privileged class. . . .[61]

The one December 9er singled out for criticism by the Party was Ho Ch'i-fang, whose membership in this group is situational, stemming from his presence at Peita in 1935–36 and not from any documented political activities. Ho's infatuation with the Communists was less ardent than that of the NLVC enthusiasts, and it was not until 1940 that he moved to Yenan for the duration of the war. He also stood apart from writers such as Ting Ling, Hsiao Chün, and Wang Shih-wei, the fearless critics of the Communist order prior to their humiliation under *Cheng-feng* criticism. Slightly younger and considerably more malleable than these veterans of leftist literary vendettas, Ho soon made the transition from guarded critic to orthodox inquisitor. Thus he stands midway between the loyal young bureaucrats from Peiping and the rebellious writers from Shanghai.

[61]"Re-examination—An Account of a Protracted Struggle in Contemporary Chinese Literature," *Chinese Literature*, no. 3 (May-June 1958), pp. 154–55, quoted in Frederick T. C. Yu, *Mass Persuasion in Communist China* (New York: Praeger, 1964), pp. 55–56.

Any hope of coalition between disgruntled writers and disaffected December 9ers died in the Party's counterattack after Mao's talks at the Yenan Forum. In appealing to these youths, the writers were seeking support from natural allies, also young urban intellectuals, against common antagonists: middle-aged top Party leaders and uneducated rural Party cadres. However, basic differences separated creative artists from college-trained careerists in a way that was reminiscent of the separate paths taken by literary and academic intellectuals in Nationalist China since the late 1920s. Both writers and students had come to Yenan voluntarily and enthusiastically and were prepared to contribute their talents to a common cause. Writers, even the young ones, came in mid-career, having already established credentials as independent creative artists. Students, on the other hand, were just embarking on a course that demanded adjustment to Party line vagaries. Though they had on occasion resisted Party pressures, their political experience since December 9, 1935, had meant working with and adjusting to Party leadership within the context of a mass movement. The *Cheng-feng* movement, however, compelled them radically to broaden the basis of their commitment—from nationalism to populism. As Mark Selden observes:

The success of the *cheng-feng* movement is attested by the fact that, in shifting its course to the intensification of rural revolution, the Party retained the support of large numbers of cadres from elite backgrounds who had initially rallied to affirm its anti-Japanese stance. *Cheng-feng* strengthened commitment to the Party and particularly to its revolutionary ideals which had been subordinated to united front considerations during the early years of the resistance.[62]

Both writers and students had been drawn to Yenan by ideology; the latter were attracted by organization as well. Thus, though both elitist groups remained at loggerheads with Party cadres over many issues, it was far easier for a December 9er to rectify his work style as an organizer, propagandist, or teacher than it was for a creative writer to endure the straight-

---

[62]Selden, *Yenan Way*, p. 196.

jacket of literary orthodoxy. Hence the saga of post-*Cheng-feng* creative writers is one of unmitigated frustration resulting in a depressing mediocrity of literary output in some cases, an ominous silence in others. The December 9th generation, on the other hand, overrode latent antagonism with other elements and wrote an impressive record of achievement in education, administration, youth work, and other fields where loyalty and organizational finesse were more important than inspiration and artistic creativity.

THE VANGUARDS' DEMISE

When Chou En-lai left Hankow for Yenan in August 1938 he was accompanied by a young Eighth Route Army officer. The young man was Li Ch'ang, disguised for self-protection as he fled the crumbling battlements of Hankow's united front.[63] In Yenan, Li worked to build a solid base for the NLVC. His efforts had, in fact, started early that year when Vanguard headquarters moved from Sian to the Communists' capital.[64] A national NLVC congress had convened in April and called for a general expansion of the organization culminating in a Vanguard-led "united front of youth."[65] On the heels of this had come a second congress convened by the NLVC's newly-established Northwest Bureau. Several notables of the December 9th generation had played leading roles. Li Ch'ang had provided a keynote address and concluding remarks. Ting Hao-ch'uan and Hsia Ying-che had delivered reports. Elected officers had included Li Lien-pi as bureau chief (tui-chang) and Hsia Ying-che as head of the Communications Department.[66]

[63]Li Ch'ang, "Recollections," Part II, p. 41.

[64]Pao Tsun-p'eng, *Chung-kuo kung-ch'an-tang ch'ing-nien yun-tung shih-lun* [A discussion of the history of the CCP youth movement] (Nanking: Pa-t'i shu-chü, 1947), p. 47.

[65]*Ibid.*, p. 45; *Chung-hua min-tsu chieh-fang hsien-feng tui lin-shih ch'üan-kuo tai-piao ta-hui hsuan-yen* [Proclamations of the Extraordinary National Congress of the NLVC] ([Yenan?], April 16, 1938). These sources differ slightly on the designation of the congress and its dates.

[66]Min-hsien-tui hsi-pei pu [Northwest Headquarters of the NLVC], *Min-hsien tsai hsi-pei* [The NLVC in the Northwest] ([Yenan?], n.d.).

The NLVC's Yenan municipal branch admitted anyone committed to the liberation of the Chinese people and willing to abide by the organization's regulations.[67] This policy underscored the oft-reaffirmed intention to broaden the Vanguards' social foundation beyond its student constituency. However, Li Ch'ang suggests that the Vanguards continued to be most successful among school youngsters. They had enlisted, he recalls, "the overwhelming majority of students" at Resistance University and the North Shensi Public School. Many of these joined the CCP shortly thereafter.[68]

The Vanguards' frantic effort to gain a foothold in Yenan was an outright struggle for survival. The crisis can be traced to the origins of the NLVC. The Communist Party's adjunctive youth organizations always had endured an uneasy relationship with the CCP. Given the degree of autonomy necessary to attract daring and independent-minded young radicals, these bodies tended to veer out of control. Briefly abolished in 1930, then revived in the soviet districts, the Communist Youth League had not held a major meeting since 1928. By 1935, it was said to be suffering from "vanguardism" and a tendency to become a "second party," rival to the mother organization.[69] The problem remained in limbo during the Long March but demanded resolution once the Communists had settled in Shensi.

The Party groped for an answer. On December 20, 1935, it announced that the Youth League would change its name to the Resist-Japan National Salvation Youth Corps and become a non-partisan organization open to all patriotic anti-Japanese

---

[67]*Yen-an shih ti-fang pu-tui chien-chang* [Summary bylaws of the Yenan Municipal Branch of the NLVC], (n.p., n.d.).

[68]Li Ch'ang, "Recollections" Part II, p. 42.

[69]"Ch'ing-nien-t'uan li-shih ts'an-k'ao tzu-liao" [Reference materials on the history of the Youth League], *Chung-kuo ch'ing-nien* [Chinese youth], whole no. 203 (March 16, 1957), p. 10.

youths.[70] The decision to use the NLVC as a front organization for students in "white areas" may have been an afterthought. Under the North China Bureau in Tientsin, run by urban-oriented leaders such as Liu Shao-ch'i and P'eng Chen, the NLVC became quite isolated from the Youth League in Yenan. The League, moreover, neither changed its name, broadened its ranks, nor dissolved, as some reports predicted it would. When Edgar Snow arrived in Paoan in July 1936, he was able to interview a newly-appointed League secretary, Feng Wen-pin. Feng's remarks to Snow indicated that this organization was absorbed with responsibilities in the soviet area, especially activities in support of the Red Army.[71] The League was divorced from the college scene in Peiping and Tientsin.

The emergence of Feng as Yenan's ranking youth leader carried long-range negative consequences for NLVC activities within the Communist-controlled area. Vast differences in background between this son of the proletariat and urban intellectual Li Ch'ang symbolized the split between the CYL and the NLVC. Aside from brief periods of political and technical training, Feng's formal education had been limited to a year or two of elementary school followed by some night school study. His youthful years had been spent as a worker in a match factory and a coal company. During his mid-teens, he had become a labor organizer for the Youth League and served as a member of a Red Guard unit in an armed uprising. Assigned more and

[70]Chung-kuo kung-ch'an chu-i ch'ing-nien t'uan chung-yang wei-yuan-hui [YCL Central Executive Committee], "Wei k'ang-jih chiu-kuo kao ch'üan-kuo ko-hsiao hsueh-sheng ho ko-chieh ch'ing-nien t'ung-pao hsuan-yen" [A proclamation to the entire nation's school students and various circles of young countrymen on resisting Japan and saving the nation], in *IECYT*, pp. 136–39.

[71]Edgar Snow, *Random Notes on Red China 1936–1945*, Harvard East Asian Monograph no. 5 (Cambridge, Mass.: East Asian Research Center, Harvard University, 1957), pp. 51–55. Among the members of the league's Central Committee at that time was a student, Huang Lien-i, but he was in prison. See p. 52.

more important political and military responsibilities in the
Kiangsi Soviet of the early 1930s, he had been appointed
political commissar for a special division of Youth League
members on the Long March.[72]

Under Feng, the Youth League spawned successor groups
with a stronger regional base and united front coloration. After
six months of preparation, 300 delegates (some from as far away
as Fukien, Kwangtung, and Korea) gathered in Yenan in April
1937 for the First Congress of Youths in the Northwest. At this
convention was organized the Northwest China Association of
Youths for National Salvation, with Feng as chairman.[73] The
membership was mostly young workers and peasants, veterans
of the Long March or fresh recruits from the villages of
Northwest China. At the national Party conference of May
1937, when Liu Shao-ch'i's urban-oriented united front policies
were pushed aside by Chang Wen-t'ien's rural guerrilla
strategy,[74] Li must have unavoidably been linked to Liu, and
Feng to Chang.

The arrival of Li Ch'ang and other members of NLVC during the first year of the war meant that Yenan now housed
headquarters of two youth organizations: one a federation of
battle-hardened Long March veterans and dirt farmers, the
other a band of experienced propagandists and neophyte
guerrillas drawn from the urban intellectual aristocracy. The
former had long enjoyed intimate ties with high-echelon Party
leaders; the latter had only recently begun to form such bonds.
Feng wore the magic mantle of a Long March leader,
something that no December 9 stalwart, no matter how prominent, could match. Instruction of the newly arrived NLVC
cadres in Feng's Youth Training School at Wupao served as an

---

[72]Klein and Clark, *Biographic Dictionary*, 1:282–83.

[73]Cheng Kuang, "Short History of the Youth League," *Chung-hsueh-sheng*
[Middle school student], no. 2 (February 3, 1957), trans. in *Extracts from China
Mainland Magazines*, no. 77 (April 9, 1957), p. 12. Also, Nym Wales, *My Yenan
Notebooks*, p. 91, and "Ch'ing-nien t'uan li-shih," p. 11.

[74]See above, Chapter 3, note 116.

interim device for bringing December 9 types into Feng's camp.[75] The ultimate outcome was never in doubt. If Li Ch'ang and his cohorts wished to continue activities in the youth movement, they would have to submit to the leadership of Feng Wen-pin.

In November 1938 the Northwest China Association of Youths for National Salvation convened a congress in Yenan. According to Li Ch'ang's account, delegates agreed that the basic task of the movement was to rouse and organize rural youths and declared:

The principal models of organization being the [National Salvation Youth Corps], the Vanguard of Youths for Resisting Japan, and the Children's Corps; and that in the Kuomintang areas, it was difficult for such organizations as the Northwest China Association of Youths for National Salvation, the NLVC, and the [National Salvation Youth Corps] to exist, and so it was necessary to preserve the force of the revolution by changing to more suitable forms of organization. All agreed to the Party Center's instructions concerning the adoption of all forms of organizations in rallying the broad masses of the youths. It was not necessary to expand the NLVC. The youth organizations set up a Joint Office of Chinese Youth Associations for National Salvation in Yenan as a liaison among all the former organizations of youths.[76]

This wordy account glosses over some irrefutable truths: (1) Though Feng's Northwest China Association, as well as the NLVC, was to be disbanded, the new Joint Office would be under Feng's control; (2) NLVC members in Yenan were political beggars, having lost their urban bases in the "white areas"; (3) The NLVC lacked the training and experience to be as effective as Feng's followers in the border regions; and (4) Any attempt to retain this organization would foster bitter rivalries and would leave conflicting lines of authority in youth organizations and guerrilla outfits where the NLVC had established a presence. Hence, it "was not necessary to expand the NLVC." In principle, the National Liberation Vanguards of China might

<hr>

[75]Warren Kuo, *Analytical History*, 3:174.
[76]Li Ch'ang, "Recollections," Part II, p. 42.

continue on paper but, as a functioning organization, it was all but dead.

Li Ch'ang's account, however, only hints at the struggle that must have occurred in the months preceding the conference. More substantial evidence is the publication *Three Years of the Vanguards* (October 1938), an account that stressed the accomplishments of the NLVC since its foundation. This history may be read as a brief for perpetuating the Vanguards. The authors conceded that there had been problems; for example, the reluctance of a majority of members to work in the countryside and the failure to establish a more broadly-based youth movement.[77] However, this exercise in self-criticism served only to underscore the efforts of Vanguard leaders to accommodate the expectations of the CCP.

"The Vanguards were born in struggle, only through struggle were they able to grow strong. In other words, at no time have the Vanguards failed to stand on the very front line of struggle, at no time have they failed to strive for the liberation of the Chinese nation [min-tsu]," boasted the report. "Should anyone ask once more what the Min hsien is all about, we would bluntly reply" [the following is paraphrased]:

In the Shansi-Chahar-Hopei (Wut'ai) Border Region, Vanguard members under Miss Sung Shih-to constitute the majority of some 150,000 to 160,000 guerrillas. In the Taihang Mountains, NLVC members provide the "basic cadres" for more than 5,000 troops under Professor Yang Hsiu-feng. Another 8,000 to 9,000 are at work under Northwest Vanguard headquarters in the Shensi-Kansu-Ninghsia-Tsinghai Border Region. In northern Shantung, there are 100,000 guerrillas, of whom 60,000 are NLVC members led by Peita's Sun Ch'uan-wen.

In southern Shantung, are upwards of 10,000 guerrillas, including more than 6,000 NLVC members led by Shihta's Wang Wen-pin. Moreoever, among about a dozen guerrilla county

[77] *SNL,* p. 49.

magistrates there, a majority are middle school and university students and, by implication, Vanguard members.

In southern and western Hopei's guerrilla army of 300,000, there are Vanguardists under Northeastern University students Chao T'ung and Yang Po-min. In eastern and northern Honan, Peita's Ko P'ei-ch'i leads a force of 50,000. In the unoccupied territory, directly under central NLVC headquarters, are more than 50,000 NLVC members, inspiring the nation's youth to join the war of resistance. In addition to these, there are overseas Vanguard groups, for example in Paris and Lyon, rousing peace-loving youth the world over to oppose aggression and demand that their governments render aid to China.

"In conclusion," boasted the report, "there are more than 600,000 guerrillas directly under NLVC leadership; more than 200,000 Vanguard members; and who knows how many hundreds of thousands of youth and masses who have been influenced by us."[78]

The Vanguards' figures were an exercise in *"ch'ui-niu"* (inflating the ox). Few of their estimates even approximate those of reliable sources. While Vanguards claimed 300,000 in southern and western Hopei, the Japanese estimated only 110,000 full-time guerrillas in Hopei, Shantung, Shansi, and Inner Mongolia together.[79] Vanguard figures of 60,000 NLVC members among 100,000 guerrillas in western Shantung compare with Chalmers Johnson's statistic of 1,600 Vanguards in a force of 70,000.[80] On December 27, 1939, the Japanese Army estimated the total number of Communist-affiliated military forces in North China at 800,000.[81] This included 500,000 to 600,000 villagers in the rural self-defense corps. If this is even ap-

---

[78]*Ibid.*, pp. 43–45. Some early wartime Japanese intelligence reports accepted these inflated figures. *See* Iwamura Michio, *Chugoku gakusei undō shi* [History of the Chinese student movement] (Tokyo: Sekai Hyoron Sha, 1949), p. 114.

[79]Johnson, *Peasant Nationalism*, p. 76.

[80]Iwamura, *Chūgoku*, pp. 111–12.

[81]*Ibid.*, p. 76.

proximately accurate, there could not possibly have been 600,000 guerrillas under NLVC leadership more than a year earlier. The Vanguards' claim of 200,000 members is exactly ten times the number generally ascribed to them.

Clearly, the Vanguards' assertion that "We are not boasting or making propaganda" cannot be taken at face value. The NLVC, in fact, was doing more than merely boasting or propagandizing. It was fighting for its life. The Vanguards' grossly inflated account of their exploits conveyed a message to Party leaders: "We are carrying out a vital role in rural guerrilla warfare, the very area where we are reputed to be weak. We have become virtually indispensable. You must let us continue." The NLVC was refusing to disband docilely. "Our propaganda," predicted its report, "will be manifest in all our work from now on." These scarcely were the words of men writing their own epitaph.

Even after the central apparatus of the NLVC had been absorbed into Feng Wen-pin's umbrella organization, local groups of Vanguards carried on a furtive existence in KMT areas. When the Party's order to "stop developing" reached Sian in the winter of 1938, some cadres remained in the city to carry on activities under other organizational structures.[82] In regard to those who remained in Wuhan after the government's withdrawal to Chungking, Li Ch'ang recalled that:

Many NLVC members joined the Party, and around the Party countless scattered, small mass organizations were formed. These youth organizations and some NLVC organizations were maintained for quite a few years [until] their merger in the Democratic Youth Alliance or the New Democratic Youth League after these new advanced youth organizations had been set up.[83]

Hence the Vanguards trickled on, like underground streamlets, briefly bubbling to the surface, and eventually becoming lost in the larger currents. According to Feng Wen-pin, the NLVC did

<hr>

[82]Li Lien-pi, "Flames of Wrath," in *RON*, pp. 121–22.
[83]Li Ch'ang, "Recollections," Part II, p. 41.

not officially disband until 1949, presumably upon the establishment of the New Democratic Youth League.[84]

In subsequent writings, the fate of the NLVC is veiled in evasion. A footnote in the *Selected Works of Mao Tse-tung* contrasts the KMT areas where NLVC organizations were "forcibly dissolved" to Liberated Areas where they "were later merged into the Association of Youth for National Salvation, an organization of even broader scope."[85] Like Li Ch'ang's euphemistic "It was not necessary to expand the NLVC," this account obfuscates rather than clarifies.

Li Ch'ang's reticence on the inner politics of the Communist youth movement arises in part from the strange case of Feng Wen-pin. Feng presided over a succession of wartime and postwar youth organizations and in April 1949 became secretary of the Central Committee of the New Democratic Youth League. After rising to the top of the League, he was ousted for unstated reasons in the early 1950s. In 1954, he disappeared from view. His fall from grace, one of the great mysteries of CCP history, has been attributed to his policy of expanding the League by lowering membership standards.[86] This explanation is consistent with the hypothesis that he represented a more populist organizational style than that championed by the relatively elitist Li Ch'ang. Li remained prominent first in youth and then in educational work until the Cultural Revolution, when he was labeled a revisionist. Whatever the reasons for Feng's downfall, his name has disappeared from Party annals. This famous revolutionist who, in 1950, was lauded for "twenty and more years of unceasing revolutionary work among the youths," a man said to be "well-known and respected by all young people in every part of China," became a non-person.[87]

[84]Feng Wen-pin, "The Communist Party of China is the Inspirer, Organizer, and Leader of Chinese Youth," New China News Agency, Peking, June 26, 1951, in *Current Background*, no. 100 (July 18, 1951), p. 38.

[85]*Selected Works*, 3:318.

[86]Union Research Service, no. 783, June 18, 1963.

HEROES IN OBSCURITY

Judging by the high-ranking positions that they attained after 1949, the December 9ers clearly must have proved themselves during the war. However, by the end of the 1930s most had disappeared from view. Throughout the 1939–49 decade, most of them were still too obscure to merit mention in print. From the sporadic glimpses we catch of a few dozen individuals during this largely undocumented period, we can only attempt to draw inferences concerning their less visible colleagues. On at least one occasion, however, December 9th veterans gathered in Yenan—to celebrate the fifth anniversary of their historic demonstration. Wang Ming (Ch'en Shao-yü) addressed the commemorative assembly and honored the December 9ers as the youngest generation of Party cadres. Present and singled out for mention were Li Ch'ang, Huang Hua, Chiang Nan-hsiang, Huang Ch'eng, Wang Wen-pin, Sun Ch'uan-wen, and Li Ming-i.[88] Four years later, Liu Shao-ch'i praised December 9ers who "became military commanders, political workers, and local administrators, directing the economic and cultural work" during seven years of war.[89] Recent findings by Tetsuya Kataoka suggest the indispensable role that the December 9ers and other urban intellectuals played in the CCP's wartime administrative apparatus:

In the Shen-Kan-Ning border region, more than 70 percent of the government personnel at the second tier (between the border region and the county governments) and above were intellectuals who had come from the outside after the war. Efforts were also made to attach some intellectuals to the lower-echelon governments since, for one

[87]*China's Youth March Forward* (Peking: Foreign Languages Press, 1950), p. 68.

[88]*Chung-kuo ch'ing-nien* 2, no. 3 (January 15, 1940): 1.

[89]*Survey of China Mainland Press*, no. 36 (December 22-24, 1950), pp. 26–27, cited in Jessie Gregory Lutz, *China and the Christian Colleges, 1850–1950* (Ithaca, N.Y.: Cornell University Press), 1971, p. 393.

thing, cadres of peasant origin could not read, write, or speak effectively in public.[90]

Some of the bravest and most promising December 9ers lost their lives in guerrilla operations or succumbed to disease while working in remote areas. Among these were three prominent Tsinghua students, Yang Hsueh-ch'eng (dead of tuberculosis at age twenty-nine), Huang Ch'eng (captured during the New Fourth Army Incident in January 1941 and martyred by the Kuomintang), and Ling Sung-ju (who joined the famed Dare-to-Die Corps and lost his life in battle in 1940 while serving as a regimental political commissar). Two other prominent Peiping Student Union leaders who perished in guerrilla areas were Tung Yü-hua and Wang Wen-pin. Northeast Shansi Party leader Li Kuang-han, a Vanguardist who had once served as secretary of the CCP's Peita and Peiping committees, died of illness in October 1941. Still others, such as Chang I-shan in Kweiyang, attempted to keep alive Vanguard activities in the KMT-held cities but were arrested and executed. Ts'ao Ch'eng-hsien, an NLVC member who had studied in France, was killed during a Japanese air raid on Wuhan, as was NLVC activitist Sun Shih-shih.

Among the survivors of guerrilla operations were the famous actor Ts'ui Wei, ex-Peita student Ko P'ei-ch'i, and Northeastern University alumni Kao P'eng and Chi T'ing-hsieh. A striking case of wartime service is found in the career of Tsinghua Engineering College student Li Wei. He fled to Changsha when the war broke out and later that year went to the Northwest to join an Eighth Route Army artillery regiment. Li was admitted to the Party in 1938 and was wounded a year later while fighting with his artillery unit in the Taihang Mountains of southeastern Shansi. He brought his engineering talents to bear in 1946 during the civil war when he helped blow up a bridge on the Sungari River in Manchuria, and in 1948 when he

---

[90]Tetsuya Kataoka, "Communist Power in a War of National Liberation: The Case of China," *World Politics* 24, no. 3 (April 1972): 426–27.

commanded a battalion in a railway column under Lin Piao's forces in Manchuria.

Another man with an impressive wartime record is the sometime playwright (and later prominent diplomat) Yao Chung-ming, a former Peking University student. When war erupted, Yao organized a student guerrilla unit in his native Shantung and later rose to be a brigade chief-of-staff and army group political commissar under the famed Ho Lung, whose mission was to protect the Communists' headquarters in Yenan.

Little is known of the December 9th movement in Canton, but one veteran of that city is Tseng Sheng, a former Chungshan University student. Early in the war, Tseng organized a "people's guerrilla column" in Huiyang and Paoan counties in Kwangtung, and later commanded the "East River Column." He continued his military career, and, when the Communists took Kwangtung in 1949, he was third deputy commander of the Kwangtung Military District.

Many December 9th veterans served in the important Shansi-Chahar-Hopei (Chin-Ch'a-Chi) Border Region, the closest of the wartime Communist zones to Peiping. Shortly after the war, prominent December 9 figure Yao I-lin wrote in the Yenan *Chieh-fang jih-pao* that there were "several hundred" December 9th youths in this area. The majority of them were not college students but recruits from middle and normal schools. Chin-Ch'a-Chi would soon become a strategic sector in the civil war with the Nationalists, and it was already the territory through which thousands of Communist troops and cadres were moving to Manchuria. Among the border region cadres were Huang Ching (Peita), Hu K'un (Northeastern University), Chou Huai-ch'iu (Normal University), Liu Chih (Normal University), Chao Chi-ch'ang (Tsinghua), and Chu Nan-hua (Yenching).[91]

[91]*Chieh-fang jih-pao*, December 13, 1945. Chu Nan-hua may be the same person as Chu Mu-chih, currently director of the New China News Agency. The importance of middle and normal school recruits is emphasized in a letter

Other December 9ers used their pens rather than their guns. The musician Lü Chi, for example, wrote a number of songs such as his "Song of Resistance University" exhorting fellow countrymen to continue the resistance against Japan. In 1948 in Shenyang (Mukden), he helped establish the Lu Hsun Institute of Literature and Art. Tsinghua's Yang Shu, who was to become the semiofficial historian of the movement, was gaining journalistic experience as a *Chieh-fang jih-pao* reporter.[92] Other accounts suggest the presence of a rather substantial Yenching contingent among the December 9ers in Communist zones. On January 14, 1939, Li Min wrote Edgar Snow that many mutual friends were in Shensi and Shansi, and, in September 1945, Mao Tse-tung told Yenching President J. Leighton Stuart that many of his former students were in Yenan.[93]

Two December 9 veterans whose career patterns for this period are known in considerable detail are Huang Ching and P'eng T'ao. This is not surprising, for both men were already seasoned Communist organizers by 1935 and were prepared to assume positions of considerable responsibility during the war while others were undergoing apprenticeships in less prominent posts. Huang was one of the featured speakers at the January 1938 conference that brought the important Shansi-Chahar-Hopei Border Region Government into existence. For a time he directed political education in a military academy and in subsequent years was the senior secretary for the Party's Shansi-Chahar-Hopei Committee and its Central Hopei Committee, and Hopei-Shantung-Honan Committee. In the period immediately following V-J Day, he was mayor of Kalgan, then

---

from Carl E. Dorris to John Israel, January 4, 1975. In addition to individuals mentioned above, writes Dorris, December 9ers active in the Chin-Ch'a-Chi region included Lü Chi, Hsu Ming, Shih Li-te, Wang Nien-chi, Kao P'eng, Ts'ui Wei, Li Kuang-han, Lu P'ing, and Yang Shu.

[92]*Chieh-fang jih-pao*, February 1, 1946.

[93]*NCSM,* p. 199; John Leighton Stuart, *Fifty Years in China* (New York: Random House, 1954), p. 199.

capital of Chahar Province, and deputy secretary of the Shansi-Chahar-Hopei Committee. In the months just prior to the inauguration of the People's Republic of China (P.R.C.) in 1949, Huang held top administrative posts within the North China People's Government (NCPG).

P'eng T'ao's vita for this period is also impressive. In the late 1930s and early 1940s, he directed Party organizations subordinate to the CCP Taihang Committee and headed the Committee's "Popular Movements" *(min-yun)* and Propaganda departments. In the later war years, he worked at the Natural Sciences Institute *(Tzu-jan k'o-hsueh yuan)* in Yenan. Returning to the Taihang area after Japan's defeat, P'eng served as political commissar for the Third Column, a unit under famed Communist general Liu Po-ch'eng.

IN THE CAMP OF THE ENEMY

Hazardous conditions were not confined to the front lines. Formidable dangers also confronted December 9th veterans engaged in underground activities in KMT areas. A Kuomintang intelligence report on Communist activities during the early war years lists among CCP front organizations a Peiping-Tientsin Alumni Association *(P'ing-Chin t'ung-hsueh hui)* and a North China Alumni Association *(Hua-pei t'ung-hsueh hui)*. Other groups in which December 9 leaders may have been involved in an organizational capacity are the Students' National Salvation Union *(Hsueh-sheng chiu-kuo lien-ho hui)* and the Student Branch of the Resistance Auxiliary Association. *(K'ang-ti hou-huan hui hsueh-sheng fen-hui)*. By 1939, however, the government had uncovered these activities and new Party directives were issued instructing operatives in educational institutions to redirect their efforts toward intramural endeavors and to conserve their strength.[94] At least one famous CCP underground worker,

---

[94]Ssu-fa hsing-cheng pu tiao-ch'a chü [Bureau of Investigation, Ministry of Justice), ed. and publ., *Kung-fei hsueh-yun kung-tso ti p'ou-shih* [The Communist bandits' student movement work exposed] ([Taipei?], 1961), p. 28.

Chiang Nan-hsiang, reportedly returned to Yenan after being exposed. More successful in hiding his Communist identity was Peita graduate Ch'en Chung-ching. After joining Hu Tsung-nan's Hunan Youth Field Service Corps in 1938, Ch'en rose to its Central Committee by 1945 and the following year was an executive member of the Shensi KMT Headquarters. Two of Ch'en's close friends also worked under Hu Tsung-nan during the war years. One, Shen Chien, had been a student at Normal University, and the other, Hsiung Hsiang-hui, had studied at Tsinghua. However, most December 9 men were too clearly identified with the left to play such a double role.

For others, it was possible to work in the open as members of Communist political and propaganda organs whose presence in Chungking was guaranteed by the united front. Most famous of these was Chou En-lai's attractive public relations agent, Kung P'eng (Mme. Ch'iao Kuan-hua). One of Kung's classmates, Li Min (Mme. Yeh Teh-kuang), responded to a *Hsin-hua jih-pao* advertisement for a position in international work for the CCP Propaganda Department, but she applied too late and as of January 1939 was teaching in a "very liberal middle school" in Kweiyang. Such a position was not without risks, however, for, as Li noted, the KMT headquarters was "very conservative and suppressing [the] youth movement by every method."[95] Kweiyang, it will be recalled, is the city where five months earlier the KMT had arrested and shot NLVC leaders. Kung P'eng's sister, P'u-sheng, and her Yenching schoolmate, Chang Shu-i, were supporters of Indusco, the Chinese Industrial and Cooperatives movement which had been inspired by New Zealander Rewi Alley, promoted by Edgar and Helen Snow, and harassed by Kuomintang officialdom. P'u-sheng also traveled to the United States both during the war in connection with international YWCA activities and after the war to work for United China Relief and the United Nations Human Rights Commission.

[95]*NCSM*, p. 199.

Others likewise spent some time in the United States. Among these were Lu Ts'ui, whose husband Jao Shu-shih apparently edited a newspaper in New York during the late 1930s; Liang Szu-i and her husband, Chang Wei-hsun, who served his residency as a pediatrician at Bellevue Hospital in New York City, and Chang Shu-i, who arrived sometime in the mid-1940s. Other U.S. sojourners included the above-mentioned friends— Ch'en Chung-ching, Shen Chien, and Hsiung Hsiang-hui. All of them were students, Ch'en in Columbia University's Economics Department and the other two at Western Reserve University in Cleveland.

At least one December 9er, Han Ming, spent the war years working not for the CCP but the KMT. We earlier encountered Han as the *bête noire* of Tsinghua's student left. He was suspected of turning traitor, serving as a pawn for Chancellor Mei I-ch'i, and feeding information on student leaders to the police. Han was by no means the only December 9th veteran identified with the KMT, but he may have been unique in his determination to switch directions and remain on the mainland after 1949. Han was something of an enigma even to those who knew him rather well. According to John S. Service, a wartime American diplomat who relied upon him for information and contacts, Han worked for the government's Central News Agency and had extensive contacts with such diverse KMT figures as Dr. Weng Wen-hao, the Belgian-educated minister in the Ministry of Economic Affairs, and Tai Li, the mysterious chief of Chiang Kai-shek's intelligence service. Han also had friends on the CCP's newspaper, the *Hsin-min wan-pao* (New people's evening news). Service was pleased to have so well-connected a source, but he was also a bit puzzled for, unlike so many informants, Han went out of his way to develop the friendship without apparent ulterior motives.[96]

Like Weng Wen-hao, who also cast his lot with the new order after 1949, Han Ming became progressively disillusioned with

[96]John S. Service, letter to the authors, November 15, 1972.

the corrupt postwar KMT regime. In 1947, a friend found him still in Chungking, but working for the outspoken anti-KMT daily, the *Hsin-min pao*, a small but highly respected newspaper that editorialized for democratization.[97] Another December 9 veteran who wrote for an anti-KMT newspaper after V-J Day was Ch'en Han-po, who helped edit a prominent Shanghai publication. In an article written in the autumn of 1945, Ch'en asked why, now that the war was over, U.S. troops had been landed in the Tientsin-Peiping area and Japanese troops in China remained armed. On the other hand, he expressed gratitude toward Soviet forces which, he noted, were in the process of withdrawing from the territory they had liberated. The article, though nonpolemical and cogently argued, concluded with a demand for the immediate withdrawal of American forces.[98]

Ch'en's schoolmates, Li Min and her husband Yeh Te-kuang, remained in the Southwest after the war. On June 1, 1947, during a nationwide anti-Communist vendetta against government critics, they were among hundreds of students, professors, journalists, and other intellectuals and workers arrested in Chungking.[99]

Two other prominent December 9th leaders, the omnipresent Chiang Nan-hsiang and Sung I-p'ing, were working in Yenan in the summer of 1945 when they were sent to Manchuria as leaders of a ninety-member youth team. The following year, they founded the Northeast Democratic Youth League. Earlier, from 1941 to 1945, Chiang had been a delegate

[97]John Israel, interview with Jack Huang, Hong Kong, August 13, 1959. For a description of the *Hsin-min pao*, see Chao Wang, "Sheng-li hou ti ch'ung-ch'ing hsin-wen chieh" [The Chungking news world since V-J Day], *Shang-hai wen-hua* [Shanghai culture], no. 3 (March 30, 1946), p. 14.

[98]Ch'en Han-po, "Ch'ing yu-chun t'ui-ch'u Chung-kuo" [Would our friends' armies kindly leave China], *Wen-ts'ui* [The digest], no. 7 (November 20, 1945), pp. 13–14, reprinted from the combined supplement of *Chung-hua lun-t'an* [The China tribune], and *Tung-fang tsa-chih* [Eastern miscellany], published in Szechwan.

[99]*NCSM*, p. 4; *New York Times*, June 2, 1947, p. 3.

to the legislative assembly of the Shensi-Kansu-Ningsia Border Region Government. Traveling across Communist-occupied sectors of the North China plains in 1947, correspondent Mark Gayn found other December 9ers "serving as mayors, police chiefs, or Party secretaries in small towns, as propagandists and junior army commissars."[100]

Perhaps the most striking example of a clustering of December 9ers after V-J Day was in connection with the Marshall Mission. In an attempt to mediate the civil war between the Nationalists and Communists, General Marshall arranged for a tripartite organization of Nationalists, Communists, and Americans. Marshall himself spent most of his time in Chungking, and later in Nanking and Shanghai, as did Chou En-lai. December 9er Kung P'eng, who had worked so closely with Chou during the war years, remained with him during this period.

But the major operative arm of the Marshall Mission was in Peiping, the locale of the Executive Headquarters, where each of the three sides had scores of personnel. Here, a heavy concentration of Yenching and Tsinghua students was valuable for their bilingualism and experience in dealing with Americans. Hsu Ping was deputy to the CCP's chief-of-staff. A professor at Northeastern University during the December 9th movement, Hsu, in collaboration with Liu Shao-ch'i and K'o Ch'ing-shih, had been instrumental in getting Edgar Snow to Yenan in 1936. Huang Hua worked as the personal aide to General Yeh Chien-ying, the head of the Communist unit at the Executive Headquarters, and also doubled as chief of the Communists' press unit.[101] Former Tsinghua basketball star Jung Kao-t'ang represented the Communists in both the Personnel Section and the

---

[100]Mark Gayn, "Mao Tse-tung Reassessed," in Franz Schurmann and Orville Schell, *The China Reader* (New York: Random House, 1966), 3:98–99.

[101]Huang's wife, Ho Li-liang, also worked for the Communists at Executive Headquarters. A quarter of a century later, she was in New York with her husband as counselor of the Mission of the People's Republic of China to the United Nations.

Administrative Department of the Marshall Mission's Executive Headquarters. Lu Ts'ui served as one of the Communists' four secretaries.

Still others, like T'ao Hsi-chin and Kan Chung-tou, served with "field teams" in various parts of North China. Kan was the Northeast Chungshan Middle School student last encountered trying to leave Peiping after July 7, 1937. Yao Chung-ming was with the Military Mediation Department of the Tsingtao Armistice Team.

On the surface, Nationalist-Communist-American relations at the Peiping Executive Headquarters were harmonious but numerous incidents marred the work of the field teams. For example, Kan Chung-tou, who represented the Communists at a town in southern Shantung, was involved in a fracas with the KMT in May 1946. Kan allegedly suffered three broken ribs and "was disabled for life."[102] In view of Kan's post-1949 activities, the charge may have been exaggerated, but it aroused Chou En-lai to make a direct protest to General Marshall.

The labors of the elaborately structured organization that Marshall had set up failed to prevent renewal of civil war. In late January 1947, the United States announced the withdrawal of the mission, and a month later Lu Ts'ui, Jung Kao-t'ang, and presumably others returned to Yenan. They were not long there, for the Communist capital was abandoned to the Nationalists the following month. Yenan's leaders, including Mao and Chou En-lai, fled, and for a number of months the Communist movement lacked a nerve center. By late 1947, however, the tide had turned decisively and during the next summer administrative steps were taken to consolidate the ever-growing areas under Communist control. One important measure was the merger of two key Communist zones—the Shansi-Hopei-Shantung-Honan and Shansi-Chahar-Hopei border regions. This resulted in the establishment, in mid-1948,

---

[102]U.S., Department of State, *Foreign Relations of the United States, 1946,* (Government Printing Office, 1972), 9:1102.

of the North China People's Government. The NCPG capital was located near Shihkiachwang, a key rail junction in southwestern Hopei, but soon after the fall of Peiping in early 1949 the NCPG moved there. A persuasive case can be made that the NCPG was the approximate equivalent of the central government, if one recalls the fact that the Communists did not establish a national administration until the P.R.C. was inaugurated on October 1.

The clustering of December 9th figures in the NCPG was akin to that found in the Marshall Mission. Yang Hsiu-feng, the professor-turned-guerrilla leader, was one of three vice-chairmen of the government. Yang and Huang Sung-ling, another "sympathetic" Peiping professor from the December 9th period, were chairman and vice-chairman, respectively, of the People's Supervision Committee. The key post of secretary-general of the North China government fell to T'ao Hsi-chin; Liu Ai-feng was deputy-director of the Education Department. The largest number of December 9ers worked in the economic sector. Huang Ching directed the State-Operated Enterprises Department and Yao I-lin headed the Industry and Commerce Department. Moreover, Huang was a vice-chairman and Yao a member of the Finance and Economics Committee, the most important economic body under the NCPG. Chiang Ming, who would become a central figure in post-1949 foreign trade circles, was deputy-director of the Trade Administrative Bureau, while Kuo Ta headed the Saltpeter Administrative Bureau.

This brief survey of the late 1930s and 1940s has touched upon the lives of a small group of men and women often highlighted by dramatic circumstances, such as martyrdom on the field of battle. Yet, with hindsight, it can be assumed that the events of this period made an intense and lasting impact upon all December 9ers. Until the war, most of this elite group viewed the peasantry as an abstraction. They knew China's cities. Now they knew the countryside as well. They had seen at first hand triumphs against the Japanese and then the Nationalists—victories achieved by a predominantly peasant army.

They had learned, or should have learned, the wisdom of Mao's credo: lead the masses but, more important, learn from them.

More concretely there is little doubt that December 9ers gained a wealth of administrative experience during these 12 years of war and civil war. This experience was predominantly within a civil government milieu rather than in the army or Party apparatus. Helping to govern vast Communist zones that were, for all practical purposes, states within states, these talented young officials were well prepared to assume still greater responsibilities in a reunified China.

VI

A Time to Rule

The phrase "New China" was already achieving popularity when the first People's Liberation Army troops moved into Peiping early in February 1949. More than a year's fighting still lay ahead, but the fall of Peiping coincided with the collapse of the Nationalists north of the Yangtze. It was imperative for Communist inner councils to take the "long view"—total victory was now virtually assured. Mao and his colleagues needed to ponder the implications and specifics of ruling a vast land of some 600 million people. Mao delineated these preoccupations in a message of March 1949, even before he left for Peiping from his humble village headquarters in southwestern Hopei.

Mao's words were directed to the backbone of Communist power—the People's Liberation Army. The army, he said, must switch from fighting and ruling peasants in the countryside to garrisoning the huge coastal and Yangtze River Valley cities. He conceded his soldiers were short on experience, and he counseled them to be modest and mentally attuned to cooperation with officials (mainly non-Communists) who still ran the cities. The most urgent task was restoration of the shattered economy. Elaborating on these themes a few months later, Mao asserted the now familiar theme that peasants and urban workers must join with the urban petty and national bourgeoisie as the four groups constituting the "people's democratic dictatorship." Communist ties with both elements were marginal at best. Yet, because of their administrative and technical skills, they were vital to Mao during the transition to socialism and communism. He summarized his case with compelling candor: "We must learn to do economic work from all who know how, no matter who they are. We must esteem them as teachers, learning from them respectfully and conscientiously."[1]

One might surmise that such thoughts were welcomed by the December 9th generation, which was now coming of age. Unlike most leaders in Mao's generation, who had long severed connections with non-"proletarian" pasts, the December 9ers were still young enough to have links with the bourgeois elements of the four-class coalition and, more important from the viewpoint of the CCP hierarchy, they were trusted, tested, and experienced members of the Party.

THE YOUTH LEAGUE

In the early post-1949 years, as we shall see, the December 9ers would hold a variety of posts across the breadth of China. But nowhere in this period is the concentration of December 9 talent more apparent than in the Youth League. Indeed, in retrospect, it appears that a basic decision was made to test them in the League, which was then undergoing rejuvenation. The initial setting for this was the convocation of the first congress of the New Democratic Youth League (known from 1957 on as the Communist Youth League).

The congress was held in the spring of 1949, just as the army was crossing the Yangtze and a half-year before the national government was inaugurated. The week-long meetings received front-page coverage and were attended by the top leadership. Jen Pi-shih, the "father" of the Youth League and one of the few

---

[1] *Selected Works of Mao Tse-tung* (Peking: Foreign Languages Press, 1961), 4:423.

survivors of its stormy days in the 1920s, fittingly gave the all-important political report. Equally appropriate, Feng Wen-pin, the key youth leader of the Yenan era, gave another major report on the responsibilities of League members. The third most important talk was by December 9th veteran Chiang Nan-hsiang, who spoke on the newly adopted Youth League constitution.

Prior to the election of the Youth League's Central Committee and the appointment of the top organization officials, there was little promise that the December 9th group would play a significant role in League affairs in the formative years of the People's Republic. But the Central Committee elections quickly altered this view. More than one-fifth (10 of 45) of the Central Committee's members were drawn from December 9 ranks. The "old school tie" theory may or may not apply to this feature, but it is striking that former Tsinghua, Peita, and Yenching students constituted eight of these 10 December 9ers. Even more impressive than the Central Committee ratio is the fact that six out of nine Standing Committee members were drawn from December 9 ranks. And at the very apex of authority, one of the two deputy secretaries (Chiang Nan-hsiang) under Youth League Secretary Feng Wen-pin was a December 9th man.

The predominance of December 9ers in the highest Youth League echelons is well illustrated by Table 1 (the names of December 9 men are italicized and university affiliations are provided).

The particularly strong hold of December 9 men within the propaganda and publishing fields is well demonstrated in Table 2. This trend seems to have continued to the spring of 1953 when China Youth Publishers merged with another publisher (Kaiming Book Store) to form Chinese Youth Publishing House. In the new structure, Yang Shu continued as director, and his December 9 colleague Li Keng was one of the three deputy-directors. Moreover, Li concurrently served as chief editor. The board of directors was headed by three executive

TABLE 1

YOUTH LEAGUE HIERARCHY, 1949

Standing Committee Members	University
Feng Wen-pin (concurrently Secretary)	
Liao Ch'eng-chih (concurrently Deputy Secretary)	
Chiang Nan-hsiang (concurrently Deputy Secretary)	Tsinghua
Ch'ien Chün-jui	
Jung Kao-t'ang	Tsinghua
Li Ch'ang	Tsinghua
Sung I-p'ing	(unknown)
Lu P'ing	Peita
Han T'ien-shih	Peita

Note: The pervasiveness of December 9 veterans is still more striking in the departments at Youth League headquarters. This is illustrated in Table 2, in which the names of December 9th leaders appear in italics.

TABLE 2

ORGANS SUBORDINATE TO THE YOUTH LEAGUE, 1949–51

Secretary-General:	*Jung Kao-t'ang*
Dpty Secretary-General:	Ma I
Staff Office	
Director:	*Jung Kao-t'ang*
Dpty Directors:	Shih Lo-wen
	Ma I
	Wang Chao-hua
Organization Department	
Directors:	*Chiang Nan-hsiang*
	Kao Yang-wen
Dpty Directors:	Kao Yang-wen
	Shih Lo-wen
Propaganda Department	
Director:	*Yang Shu*
Dpty Director:	*Hsu Li-ch'ün*

(Cont.)

(TABLE 2 — Cont.)

International Liaison Department
    Directors: Liao Ch'eng-chih
                                          Ou T'ang-liang
    Dpty Directors: Ch'en Chia-k'ang
                                          Wu Hsueh-ch'ien

Research Office
    Director: *Chiang Nan-hsiang*
    Dpty Director: Yang Ti-sheng
Culture and Education Department
    Director: Ch'ien Chün-jui
    Dpty Director: Ho Li
Railway Work Committee
    Secretary: *Lu P'ing*

Students Department
    Directors: *Jung Kao-t'ang*
                                          Ho Li
    Dpty Director: *Yang Ch'eng*
Young Workers Department
    Director: *Lu P'ing*
    Dpty Directors: Tung Hsin
                                          Huang Jo-t'un

Young Peasants Department
    Director: Hsu Shih-p'ing
Young Pioneers Department
    Director: Ho Li
    Dpty Director: Tso Lin
Social Services Department
    Director: *Jung Kao-t'ang*
    Dpty Director: Li Tao
Editorial Committee
    Director: *Li Keng*
    Dpty Director: Yang Chün
Youth Fine Arts and Drama Academy
    Director: Liao Ch'eng-chih
    Dpty Directors: Wu Hsueh
                                        Chin Shan

(*TABLE 2 — Cont.*)

China Youth Publishers
    Director: *Yang Shu*
    Editor: *Wei Chün-i*
Central League School
    Presidents: *Chiang Nan-hsiang*
                              Feng Wen-pin

SOURCES: This table is a composite of information drawn mainly from *Jen-min jih-pao*, June 8, 1949, and the editions of the *Jen-min shou-ts'e* (People's handbook) for 1950 and 1951. The listing of more than one director means that the second man replaced the first during the 1949–51 period.

members, one of whom was December 9er Liu Tao-sheng. The same news item that reported this reorganization also listed publishing statistics that indicated the enormous volume of youth materials. It claimed that between them China Youth Publishers and Kaiming had published almost 41 million copies of 1,600 books between 1950 and 1952 and that the new house planned to publish 471 volumes in 1953, of which 240 would be new books totaling 27 million copies.[2]

The December 9 veterans were not, with some exceptions, journalists or authors, but they were rather prolific contributors to the press during the first decade after 1949. We have uncovered 255 articles written by them in the post-1949 period, and it is striking that nearly half (121) appeared in the League's journal, *Chung-kuo ch'ing-nien*.[3] Many of these articles were exhortatory, stressing such themes as the need to increase production, study diligently, or care for one's health, and many others were popularizations of Marxism-Leninism-Maoism.

[2]New China News Agency, April 15, 1953, in *Survey of China Mainland Press*, no. 553 (April 17, 1953), pp. 11-12.

[3]Aside from *Chung-kuo ch'ing-nien*, December 9ers contributed most frequently to *Hsueh-hsi* (Study), 45 articles; *Hung-ch'i* (Red flag), 28; and *Jen-min jih-pao* (People's daily), 22. Yü Kuang-yuan is by a wide margin the most prolific December 9th writer, contributing no less than a quarter of the 255 articles noted above.

The greatest concentration of December 9 men was in League headquarters, but many others held posts at regional, provincial, and municipal levels. For example, Propaganda Department Deputy Director Hsu Li-ch'ün doubled as head of the Peking branch, and Standing Committee member Han T'ien-shih was director of the entire Northeast (Manchuria) apparatus. The most impressive cluster was in the East China region, where Li Ch'ang was the secretary and Liu Tao-sheng his deputy. Li concurrently headed the important Shanghai chapter. When he left his various East China assignments in 1952, Liu Tao-sheng succeeded Li as secretary, and still another man of this generation, Shih P'ing, became Liu's deputy. Also, by 1951 (and possibly earlier), Huang Huan-ch'iu held the top spot for the South China branch (covering both Kwangtung and Kwangsi provinces), and Li Lien-pi and Li Ming headed the Shensi and Kirin committees, respectively.

From the fragmentary data on the Youth League training apparatus, it appears that December 9th figures were also in the commanding posts. Chiang Nan-hsiang, as noted in Table 2, headed the Central League School, while his Tsinghua classmate Li Ch'ang presided over the East China League School. The ubiquitous Yang Shu, prolific chronicler of the December 9th movement and already director of both the Propaganda Department and China Youth Publishers, also headed the Youth League branch within the New China News Agency. At the international level, the League was affiliated with the then Moscow-dominated World Federation of Democratic Youth (WFDY). In 1949, Lu Ts'ui, yet another Tsinghua alumna and the wife of Central Committee member Jao Shu-shih, became a vice-president of the World Federation, and Manchurian League branch chief Han T'ien-shih was a member of the WFDY's Council. In the next year, Yang Ch'eng, the number two man in the League's Students Department, became a vice-president of the International Union of Students.

The League was without doubt the premier organization for

China's youth and would soon be organically linked to the CCP.[4] At the same time, the League was ostensibly only one among equal member organizations under the All-China Federation of Democratic Youth (ACFDY). The Federation, set up in May 1949, was a united front-type umbrella body covering subordinate bodies as disparate as the Youth League and the YMCA. Several key Youth League members served concurrently as ACFDY National Committee members (e.g., Chiang Nan-hsiang, Li Ch'ang, Lu P'ing, and Liu Tao-sheng), and from 1953 to 1956, Liu Tao-sheng was one of several Federation vice-chairmen. But the preponderant evidence is that the major youth leaders (of the December 9 era or not) minded the League store and left lesser figures to deal with the Federation.

In the fall of 1951 the League hierarchy was reorganized. The former structure—a secretary and two deputy-secretaries—was succeeded by a six-man Secretariat. Direct evidence is lacking, but the change might be interpreted as a pruning of Feng Wen-pin's authority. Such an interpretation is plausible when we recall Feng's apparent hostility toward the NLVC during the late 1930s. Under the new arrangement, Feng was no longer the sole secretary. Rather, he was merely one among six secretaries, four of whom—Chiang Nan-hsiang, Li Ch'ang, Jung Kao-t'ang, and Sung I-p'ing—not only were in the more broadly based December 9th movement but had also been key Liberation Vanguard leaders. This may be a fanciful interpretation, and indeed there were no hints in late 1951 and the first half of 1952 that Feng was headed for a political downfall. However, he abruptly left the Youth League in mid-1952 and was relegated to a lesser post prior to his total disappearance from the political scene in 1954. Feng was replaced by Hu Yao-pang in the autumn of 1952 as the senior League secretary.

---

[4]Article 55 of the CCP Constitution adopted in 1956 stated that the League "shall function under the direction of the Communist Party" and that the League Central Committee "shall be directed by the Central Committee of the Party."

Hu Yao-pang was himself a seasoned youth leader, though he had not engaged in youth work since the 1930s. We have no way of judging his relations with the hard core of December 9 men around him. In any case, the question soon became largely irrelevant when, at the League's second congress in mid-1953, the dominance of the December 9 men ended. With a few exceptions, most of them were phased out of the League at that time. During the previous four years, the organization had undergone a staggering growth and moved past the Party in membership. The comparable figures are:[5]

Membership

	Party	Youth League
1949	4,490,000	190,000
1953	6,610,000	9,000,000

The December 9ers had ignited a youth movement in the mid-1930s, turned to other tasks for a decade and a half, and then returned for a four-year stint to guide a youth movement operating in a dramatically new atmosphere. As we shall see, their exit from the League did not signify a diminution of their influence but rather signaled an advance to other, more important work.

THE NATIONAL GOVERNMENT

Under the direct guidance of Mao Tse-tung, the Chinese People's Political Consultative Conference (CPPCC) convened in September 1949. The conference, which was the counterpart of a constitutional convention in the West, organized the national government, formally proclaimed as the People's

[5]Party membership figures are rounded from John Wilson Lewis, *Leadership in Communist China* (Ithaca, New York: Cornell University Press, 1963), p. 110; Youth League figures are from Klaus H. Pringsheim, "Chinese Communist Youth Leagues (1920–1949)," *The China Quarterly*, no. 10 (October-December 1962), pp. 90–91.

Republic of China on October 1. Participation in the CPPCC was based upon geography or organization. Their key posts in the inner councils of the two youth organizations enabled several December 9th veterans to attend the CPPCC. Six of them were delegates from either the Youth League or the Federation of Democratic Youth, and another four representatives and two alternates were from the National Women's Federation, the Peking-Tientsin area, and three "Liberated Areas" in Northeast, Central, and South China.

One can imagine the mood at these impressive meetings. Fourteen years earlier, when some of the delegates were still in their teens, they had huddled together in dormitory rooms and tea shops in Peking seeking ways to express their profoundly nationalistic sentiments. Now, in this same majestic city, the revolution had succeeded, and those who had survived were able to stand at Mao's elbow to witness and participate in this epochal event. In the presence of such figures as Mao Tse-tung, Chu Te, Chou En-lai, Lui Shao-ch'i, and Mme. Sun Yat-sen, the December 9th veterans were dwarfed. Not surprisingly, they made no speeches, but their talents were utilized by four of the *ad hoc* committees that performed many of the basic tasks of establishing a new state and government. Lu P'ing and Yang Shu, for example, served on the committee to draft the organic law of the CPPCC, and four others sat on the committee that selected the national flag, the national symbol, the national capital, and National Day.

At the September 1949 meetings and in the ensuing weeks and months, the national government structure was created and staffed. Given the strong Peking orientation of the December 9th movement, it is not surprising that many of the participants received central government assignments. On the other hand, an average age of about thirty-five meant that the December 9th generation was simply too young to fill the highest-echelon cabinet posts. These, of course, went to the senior Party personalities or to various "third force" politicians who had joined the Communist cause at the eleventh hour. Tsinghua alumnus

Yao I-lin, one of the central actors in the December 9th movement, was awarded the highest level post: a vice-ministership in the Ministry of Trade, then responsible for both foreign and domestic commerce. In a figurative if not literal sense, Yao had to do little more than change the sign on his office door because, during the previous year, he had been director of the Industry and Commerce Department of the North China People's Government. And at the very moment when the People's Republic was being established, the NCPG was directed to cease operations and relinquish its responsibilities to the new national government.

But if Yao was the only December 9th vice-minister when the P.R.C. was formed, his colleagues received a host of positions only a notch or two below this level. With a few exceptions noted below, the pattern of appointments did not show a heavy concentration of December 9th men in a single ministry. Rather, they were spread through the various ministries, commissions, administrations, and bureaus. In the Ministry of Fuel Industry, for example, Kuo Ta directed the Staff Office, and Kan Chung-tou was deputy director for the same office in the Ministry of the Interior. Staff offices, intimately involved in day-to-day administration and personnel management, are regarded as pivotal, even though the office holders are seldom in the news.[6] A particularly noteworthy staff office directorship went to Liu Ai-feng in the Ministry of Education, then headed by Ma Hsu-lun, one of the professors in Peiping in the mid-1930s who had been particularly helpful to student dissenters.

Other important central government posts given to December 9th veterans in the early P.R.C. years included the chairmanship of the Yangtze River Water Conservancy Committee and membership on a counterpart committee for harnessing the Huai River, two positions held concurrently by Lin I-shan, and the secretary-generalship of the Government

---

[6]A. Doak Barnett, *Cadres, Bureaucracy, and Political Power in Communist China* (New York: Columbia University Press, 1967), pp. 13–14, discusses the importance of ministerial staff offices.

Administration Council (GAC) i.e., the cabinet, a position delegated to T'ao Hsi-chin. In the same year, T'ao also became the second man to become a vice-minister when he assumed this post in the newly established Ministry of North China Affairs. Within the same ministry, T'ao also headed the Political and Legal Division, while his December 9th colleagues Chiang Ming and Li Che-jen directed the Industry and Commerce Division's Staff Office, and the Agriculture Division, respectively.

In the Foreign Ministry Kung P'eng was placed in charge of the Information Department, and her sister, Kung P'u-sheng, became deputy-director of the International Affairs Department. Kung P'u-sheng's post, her fluency in English, and familiarity with the United States were presumably the reasons for her assignment to the small delegation led by Wu Hsiu-ch'üan, which went to New York in late 1950 to present China's case for its entry into the Korean War a few weeks earlier. In retrospect, Wu's mission was historic in terms of Sino-American relations, for he and his colleagues were the first P.R.C. officials to visit the United States in the post-1949 period. Twenty-one years passed before another Chinese group set foot on U.S. soil and this was the celebrated delegation to the United Nations that arrived in New York a few weeks after Peking was admitted to the world organization in October 1971. China's chief delegate to the Security Council was Huang Hua, a stellar figure among December 9th men.

In the subministerial Press Administration, former Yenching student Ch'en Han-po was deputy-director of the Peking Press School. For Ch'en, this was familiar territory. He had majored in journalism at Yenching, and, at the time of his 1949 appointment, it was noted that he was head of a Press Training Class under the New China News Agency.

One of the more noteworthy, but not easily explained, concentrations of December 9th figures occurred within the Ministry of Railways. Ch'ien Ying-lin headed the ministry's Planning Bureau and a decade later became a vice-minister. In

Manchuria, Liu Chü-ying was vice-manager of the Changchun Railway Administration. The Changchun Administration was then jointly run by the Chinese and Russians. Because the terms for the management of the rail line provided for alternate directorships by Chinese and Soviet administrators, Liu succeeded to the managerial post in 1951 after serving for a year under a Russian manager. In Hunan, Ma Tsai was political commissar of the Hengyang Railway Control Bureau. But the man most involved in the ministry was Youth League stalwart Lu P'ing, who would gain lasting fame years later when he was deposed as president of Peking University during the early phases of the Cultural Revolution. From 1950 to 1952, Lu headed the ministry's Political Department; from 1952 to 1954, he was director of the Harbin Railway Administration, and then in 1954 he was called to Peking to become a vice-minister of the Ministry of Railways, a post he held until transferring to Peking University in 1957.

Two men who later became central figures in the foreign trade field got their start in this work in 1950. Chang Hua-tung headed the Northeast Customs Control Bureau and Chiang Ming was in charge of trade planning for the GAC's Finance and Economics Committee. Chang's involvement in Manchurian affairs must account for his presence with Mao Tse-tung and Chou En-lai in Moscow in early 1950 for the talks that led to the historic Sino-Soviet Treaty of Friendship, Alliance, and Mutual Assistance (signed February 14, 1950). On the same day, and during the ensuing weeks (after Mao and Chou returned home), the Chinese negotiated a number of economic agreements, several of which involved Manchuria. Teng Li-ch'ün, another December 9th veteran, also attended the Mao-Stalin talks. Teng's presence clearly derived from his positions as a Party and government leader in Sinkiang, which figured prominently in the Moscow agreements. For example, it was then that joint Sino-Soviet stock companies were established to mine nonferrous and rare metals and to drill for oil in Sinkiang.

One can surmise that these December 9ers in the cabinet

found themselves in compatible surroundings, because many top cabinet posts were held by men of similar backgrounds. Yao I-lin, a vice-minister of trade, is a case in point. The minister, Yeh Chi-chuang, and the other vice-minister, Sha Ch'ien-li, came from well-to-do families and had studied law. Moreover, Sha was one of the celebrated "seven gentlemen" arrested in 1936 for persistent advocacy of military resistance to Japan and it is very likely that Yao, recalling his student days, regarded Sha the way an American student activist of the late 1960s might regard Daniel Berrigan.

To cite but one more among many other examples, Kan Chung-tou was deputy-director of the Staff Office under the Ministry of the Interior. His immediate superior, Staff Office Director Lei Jen-min, was a member of a student generation only slightly ahead of Kan, and had joined the Party while studying at the Kuomin Normal School in Taiyuan. Lei and Kan reported directly (as of 1949) to Minister Hsieh Chueh-tsai and Vice-Ministers Wu Hsin-yü and Ch'en Ch'i-yuan. Minister Hsieh, one of the "five elders" (*wu-lao*) of the Party, received a classical education and was a journalist and educator in the early years of the Communist movement. Vice-Minister Wu was trained at the Peiping Normal University and in Japan, and was teaching in Peiping at about the time of the December 9th movement. The other Vice-Minister, Ch'en Ch'i-yuan, was a Peita graduate, an educator, and a confidant of Sun Fo (Sun Yat-sen's son) when Sun was major of Canton in the early 1920s.

The early appointees to the cabinet, in short, reflect only a partial adherence to the four-class coalition of workers, peasants, and the two elements of the bourgeoisie. Senior Party leaders were mixed with substantial numbers of industrialists, sympathetic (but still bourgeois) professors, and the December 9ers. One searches in vain for either peasants or workers, who were not even given token representation in the cabinet.

In sum, during the early years of the People's Republic, the cream of the December 9th generation was in Peking, working principally in the Youth League, the cabinet, or both. They were in one of China's most cultivated cities, and whatever their allegiance and devotion to the generalized goals of a peasant- and worker-dominated political system, their everyday tasks kept them in close association with one another in the League and with many men in the cabinet whose social and class backgrounds were similar to theirs.

THE REGIONS, PROVINCES, AND CITIES

We have underscored the many December 9th leaders working in Peking during the early years of the People's Republic. There was clearly a greater concentration in the national capital than anywhere else, but many were assigned to Party and government tasks in the multiprovincial "great administrative regions," the provinces, or the cities. It should be understood that work "out in the regions" does not connote a rural setting. So far as we know, the regionally-based December 9ers worked in an urban environment. Indeed, some of the cities—Shanghai and Canton, for example—were metropolitan centers the equal of Peking and often the administrative hub for areas and populations far bigger than those of any Western European country.

Party and government hierarchies were established in three tiers of administration: regions, provinces, and cities. First, the Party apparatus in the six regions essentially paralleled the Party Center: under the secretary and several deputy secretaries were such familiar organs as the Organization and Propaganda departments. For the most part, this structure was duplicated in the provinces and, below that, in the cities. The government apparatus was more complex, though it is a complexity of detail and not of essence. Each region had a "military and administrative committee"[7] (and later simply an "administrative

---

[7]We have taken liberties in stating that all regions had "military and administrative committees." Neither the Northeast nor the North had such a body, but the difference seems to have been more nominal than real. For the exact nomenclature, see Klein and Clark, *Biographic Dictionary*, 2:1116–19.

committee") which consisted of a chairman, several vice-chairmen, and about 40 to 50 committee members. Below this structure, the various functional departments (e.g., Finance, Agriculture) were virtually identical to the cabinet in Peking. The apparatus in the provinces and cities approximated that of the great administrative regions.

Generally, regional posts were the most important, the provinces next, and the cities last. Common sense, of course, tells us that a key Shanghai position was far more important than many provincial posts in sparsely populated Tsinghai or even some positions in the entire Northwest Region. Many Communist leaders held posts at all three levels, as the following hypothetical career illustrates. Wang Wang was director of the Swatow Municipal Education Department and head of the Swatow Party Propaganda Department. At the next higher echelon, he was deputy director of the Kwangtung Education Department. Wang was too junior to be a director or deputy director at the regional level but was still important enough to be a member of the Culture and Education Committee subordinate to the Central-South Military and Administrative Committee. Most of the time, to continue our theoretical career, he worked in Swatow, but once a month he went to Canton to attend provincial-level meetings, and twice a year he journeyed to Wuhan for meetings of the regional body.

Turning again to the December 9ers, it is clear that in 1949 they lacked the stature to fill the regional secretaryships within the Party apparatus or chairmanships or vice-chairmanships in the government. Such posts went exclusively to Party stalwarts P'eng Te-huai, Lin Piao, Kao Kang, and others of similar repute. The December 9th veterans had, however, held various posts prior to 1949 in multiprovincial administrative units in the Shensi-Kansu-Ningsia and other border region governments and Party bureaus. Although they did not attain any top regional offices in 1949, they did win, as we shall see, many second- and third-echelon regional posts and a significant number of top jobs in the provinces and cities.

Some generalizations can be made about the dozens of December 9th veterans who were not based in Peking. First, like virtually all Communist leaders, they tended to hold multiple positions in both the Party and government hierarchies, but with a clear edge for the latter. Secondly, they were assigned principally to North China or Manchuria and least often to the Northwest and Southwest. Third, in terms of "systems" *(hsi-t'ung),*[8] i.e., fields of work, the predominant ones were (1) propaganda, education, and culture; (2) finance, economics, and trade; and (3) industry and commerce. In addition, a large number were "generalists," a point to which we shall return later. Finally, to a striking degree, they tended to gravitate to Peking in the post-1954 period.

We can refine these generalizations in several ways. First, Table 3 presents regional distribution figures. The strong

TABLE 3

REGIONAL DISTRIBUTION OF DECEMBER 9TH GENERATION, 1949–54

	Persons	*Posts*
North	22	64
Northeast	19	51
Central-South	11	47
East	9	28
Southwest	5	17
Northwest	4	10
Total		217

Because a small handful of men worked in more than one region, numbers in this column do not total in the ordinary sense. Moreover, still other persons worked in the regions but did *not* work in either the Party or government hierarchy.

representation of December 9ers in the North is, presumably, a reflection of their familiarity with the area from their college

[8]See Barnett, *Cadres,* pp. 6–9 and 456–57.

days, and the similarly high number in the Northeast may result from the fact that significant numbers of "Manchurian refugees" were among the most active members of this generation. Table 3 provides a rough guide to the holding of concurrent posts—in general, about three per man. Table 4 demonstrates the predominance of government over Party posts by a 3:1 ratio.

TABLE 4

GOVERNMENT AND PARTY POSTS OF DECEMBER 9ERS, 1949–54

| | *Government* | | *Party* | |
	Persons	*Posts*	*Persons*	*Posts*
North	20	42	11	22
Northeast	16	37	7	14
Central-South	9	29	6	18
East	8	24	2	4
Southwest	5	12	2	5
Northwest	3	9	1	1
Totals		153		64

For the reasons given in Table 3, totals for numbers of persons have been omitted.

Another refinement probes beyond the Party-government breakdown to unearth the system in which the December 9 men worked. But first, some words of caution and explanation. There is a very high number of "generalists" or "general administrators." For example, we have placed the post of provincial Party secretary or governor in this category. In our data, however, only eight generalists had no other more specialized post. Secondly, in the institutions now under consideration—the government and Party—there is little or no reflection of some important systems. No government bodies, for example, had "youth departments." Yet, the previous discussion of the Youth League demonstrated beyond reasonable doubt the critical role played by December 9ers in national and regional youth affairs. With these caveats, Table 5, which details the systems, can be readily understood.

TABLE 5

POSTS OF DECEMBER 9TH GENERATION IN THE MAJOR SYSTEMS,
1949-54

System	Number of Posts
General	112
Propaganda, Culture, Education	31
Finance, Economics, Trade	26
Industry, Commerce	18
Political, Legal, Internal Affairs	10
Agriculture, Forestry	7
Organization, Personnel	6
Military	3
Foreign Affairs	3
United Front	3
Women	1
Youth	1
Total	221

Those unfamiliar with Chinese Communist terminology or institutions might argue that the "Finance, Economics, Trade" and the "Industry, Commerce" systems cited on Table 5 should be combined. The point is well taken because there is, in fact, a large amount of data demonstrating considerable lateral movement between these two systems, in striking contrast to the general lack of such movement between any other two systems. In this sense (i.e., ignoring Chinese Communist terminology), it is clear that the broad category of "economic affairs" becomes the major field of December 9 veterans at the subnational level.

Finally, as a last generalization, we have noted the tendency of the December 9ers to gravitate to Peking after 1954—a year that was clearly a watershed in China. In that and the following year, both Party and government *regional* organs were dissolved,[9] eliminating, of course, a number of positions. At the same time, the "constitutional era" opened in Peking with the convocation of the First National People's Congress, which in turn opened up scores of rather high-level posts in Peking. Coinciding with these institutional changes, the First Five-Year Plan was moving into high gear and thus the national civil bureaucracy was expanding rapidly—especially in the economic sphere. We have no way of knowing if regionally based December 9th veterans sought jobs in Peking, or if their already numerous colleagues there maneuvered to have them reassigned to the capital. But the end result, as Table 6 shows, was the assignment of large numbers of economic specialists to Peking. This table pertains to transfers in all hierarchies—Party, government, military, and mass organizations.

TABLE 6

1954–55 TRANSFERS TO PEKING OF DECEMBER 9TH GENERATION

| | *Number of Peking Posts* | |
System *(marginal categories omitted)*	*1954–55*	*Post–1955*
General	73	35
Propaganda, culture, education	25	8
Finance, economics, trade	26	1
Industry, commerce	16	2
Political, legal, internal affairs	10	1
Agriculture and forestry	5	4
Organization, personnel	6	1

[9]For the dates when the regional Party and government organs were dissolved, see Klein and Clark, *Biographic Dictionary,* 2:1093–95 and 1116–19.

The description of each officeholder in every region, province, and city would be a useless burden on the reader. Some examples of outstanding individual careers, area clusterings, and posts of critical importance do lend substance to the preceding generalizations, however.

Few careers are more noteworthy than that of Chao Te-tsun, who in 1937 was elected an Executive Committee member of the National Liberation Vanguards of China at its first congress. In the post-1949 period in Manchuria, he held an impressive array of posts. Within the regional Party bureau headed by the ill-fated Kao Kang, Chao was bureau secretary-general, deputy director of the Organization Department, and director of the Rural Work Department. Moreover, he was both senior Party secretary and governor of Heilungkiang. Chao was clearly destined for bigger things, but his career abruptly ended in 1955 when he was cited as a coconspirator with Kao Kang and Jao Shu-shih in China's most celebrated pre-Cultural Revolution purge.

Ex-Peita student Han T'ien-shih was, as noted earlier, the Youth League secretary for all of Manchuria, and within the Party hierarchy he headed the regional bureau's Youth Work Committee and was senior secretary for Anshan, one of Manchuria's key industrial centers. Moreover, in the regional government structure, he was a member of the People's Supervision Committee. Han's seemingly burgeoning career came to a quiet halt in the mid-1950s: although there is no evidence to link him (possibly through Chao Te-tsun) with Politburo member Kao Kang, the possibility for such a relationship is obvious. Two promising careers were thus cut short, but others in the same region prospered.

The assignment of several December 9ers to Manchuria seems to have been based on native ties. Two cases in point are Yang Yü-min and Miss Yang K'o-ping, the former from Jehol and the latter from Liaotung. In 1936 they were two among a quintet in charge of National Liberation Vanguards of China headquarters. In the postwar period, both went to Manchuria.

As early as 1946, long before the Communists controlled all of Jehol Province, Yang Yü-min was its vice-governor; in later years, he was concurrently a vice-chairman of the provincial Economic Planning Committee and a member of the People's Supervision Committee. Yang K'o-ping was head of the Manchurian chapter of the National Women's Federation. She was also a member of the Northeast China People's Government Council, and in Anshan she served on the city's Supervision Committee and was later a municipal Party secretary.

Still another Yang—Yang I-ch'en—shared with Chao Te-tsun the distinction of having been both governor and senior Party secretary of a province—in Yang's case, his native Liaosi. He was later transferred to Heilungkiang where he became a vice-governor and a secretary of the Party committee.

Two other notable examples are Chang Hua-tung and Jao Pin, Northeasterners who were assigned to their native area. We last encountered Chang in Moscow where he went with Mao and Chou En-lai to negotiate the crucial 1950 treaty of alliance. Under the national government, Chang headed the Northeast Customs Control Bureau and, in the regional government, he held the related post of deputy director of the Trade Department. For a period in the early 1950s, Jao Pin held most of the key jobs in Sungkiang Province and Harbin, its capital city. In Harbin, he was the mayor and first deputy secretary of the Party; in the province, he was a vice-governor and the ranking Party secretary. In the regional government administration, he was secretary-general of the Economic Planning Committee, a post that apparently paved the way for his assignment as director of the Changchun No. 1 Motor Vehicle Works (one of China's best-known factories) and still later to vice-ministerial posts in Peking.

Nativity, of course, was not the only consideration for regional assignments in the Northeast (and even less so in other areas). For example, Kuo Ming-ch'iu was obviously there because of her marriage to Lin Feng, a Central Committee member and one of the three or four top leaders in Manchuria during the early 1950s. Other than Lu Ts'ui (Mme. Jao Shu-shih), Kuo Ming-ch'in was the only December 9 woman to marry a top Party leader of the P.R.C.'s early years. Kuo served on both the People's Supervision Committee and the Culture and Education Committee of the regional government. We noted earlier that December 9er Yang K'o-ping headed the Manchurian chapter of the National Women's Federation; Kuo initially served under her as a vice-chairman and later succeeded Yang as chairman.

This is not a complete listing of Manchurian-based December 9th participants, but it suffices to suggest at least one apparent assignment pattern—nativity. It is also enough to demonstrate that several December 9 participants were entrusted to be Party secretaries, governors and vice-governors, mayors, and frequently key officials in economic planning.

Another consideration for the posting of December 9 veterans (as well, of course, as other Communist leaders) was field army affiliation. The massive field armies emerged in the late 1940s as the PLA conquered China and ultimately they became the garrison force in the Northwest (the First Field Army), the Southwest (the Second), East China (the Third), and Central-South China (the Fourth). By 1949 more and more civilian cadres were attached to field armies to administer newly-conquered territories. In an early 1949 directive entitled "Turn the Army into a Working Force," Mao Tse-tung noted that 53,000 cadres were prepared to move south with the army,[10] and from that point on, we begin to hear about "south-bound work teams" (*nan-hsia kung-tso t'uan*). In 1937, Lin I-shan, a Normal University student in Peiping, was important enough to be included in a foursome sent to Yenan to attend a CCP national conference. During the war years, he led fellow students in guerrilla warfare in Shantung. Sometime in the late 1940s, he joined Lin Piao's vaunted Fourth Field Army and, in 1949, when Lin crossed the Yangtze and pushed all the way to Can-

---

[10] *Selected Works*, 4:337–39.

ton, Lin I-shan was named secretary-general of the field army's south-bound work team.

We have already encountered Lin I-shan as a senior official in two bodies under the Ministry of Water Conservancy—one to harness the Yangtze River and the other the Huai River. Technically, both posts were directly under the national government but, in practice, Lin worked at the regional level. There, in addition to his national offices, he was a logical choice to become deputy-director of the Water Conservancy Department under Lin Piao's Central-South Military and Administrative Committee (CSMAC). Moreover, he was also made a member of the CSMAC's Finance and Economics Committee and later, in 1953, a vice-chairman.

In another region, the Southwest, there were two other typical assignments based on field army affiliation. P'eng T'ao and Tuan Chün-i had both served in Liu Po-ch'eng's Second Field Army, and as a consequence spent the early post-1949 years in Szechwan. Tuan headed the Industry Department under the regional government administration. This was a heavy responsibility for a man still in his thirties. Even granting the economic underdevelopment of China at the time, Tuan was charged with restoring a war-torn industrial base in an area with a population far larger than the combined populations of France and Britain. His December 9 colleague P'eng T'ao was assigned to South Szechwan[11] where he was second secretary of the Party committee, head of the government's Finance and Economics Committee, and deputy political commissar of the local military district. He later transferred to Chungking, the capital of the Southwest Region, where he became second Party secretary for Chungking. Both men were later assigned to Peking as cabinet ministers. P'eng served until his death in 1961 as the first head of the Ministry of Chemical Industry. Tuan served as a vice-minister in the First Ministry of Machine Building un-

[11]From 1950 to 1952, Szechwan was divided into four sectors—North, East, South, and West Szechwan—but for administrative purposes these were regarded as provincial-level units.

der December 9 colleague Huang Ching, and in 1960 he succeeded to the ministerial portfolio.

Aside from birthplace and field army affiliation, past familiarity with an area was another factor for selection of December 9ers for assignments. Huang Ching, one of the movement's prime leaders, presumably went to Tientsin for this reason. There he dominated the political scene, serving as senior Party secretary, mayor, and head of the government's Finance and Economics Committee. It can also be assumed that Yao Chung-ming's guerrilla years in Shantung account for the fact that within a three-year period in the late 1940s he was successively mayor of Chefoo, Weifang, and finally the provincial capital at Tsinan.

In other instances, there are no apparent assignment criteria, but we can point to some noteworthy clusterings of December 9 men and women. One of the more strking examples occurred in the Central-South China Region. As youths in the 1930s, Ch'en Huang-mei and Ts'ui Wei had worked closely together. By the 1950s, they had become important figures in the Chinese Communist world of arts and were still together. Ch'en Huang-mei was deputy director of the regional Party's Propaganda Department, and he and Ts'ui Wei both served on the regional government's Culture and Education Committee. Subordinate to this body was the Culture Department, which Ts'ui headed with Ch'en as one of his deputies. Moreover, one more step down this same hierarchy, still another December 9er, Wu K'o-jen, was deputy-director of the Literature and Arts Office. Wuhan was the capital of the region, and in the municipal government administration there Wu K'o-jen served as deputy director of the Culture Department.

Although the general trend of service in the regions followed by a transfer to Peking in the mid-1950s has been stressed, there was one notable exception. T'ao Lu-chia, a prominent activist in the National Liberation Vanguards of China in the 1930s, was assigned to Shansi in the post-1949 period. Beginning as vice-chairman of the Culture and Education Committee in the provincial government and as Propaganda Department chief in the Party, he worked his way up to become a deputy secretary in the Party apparatus, then first deputy secretary, and finally first secretary from 1953 to 1965, an unusually long assignment for December 9ers and others alike. He was then sent to Peking to become a vice-chairman of the State Economic Commission.

THE NATIONAL GOVERNMENT: A SECOND LOOK

During the formative years of the People's Republic, the still youthful December 9ers tended to hold regional positions one or two levels below the top central posts. Thereafter, they gravitated steadily toward Peking. There were rather few cabinet changes between 1949 and the latter half of 1952, when several new ministries and commissions were created. In short, the bureaucracy expanded as the period of "reconstruction and rehabilitation" (1949–52) gave way to the era of national planning, which was partly institutionalized by the establishment of the State Planning Commission in November 1952 and the inauguration of the First Five-Year Plan in 1953. In August 1952, when sections of the Ministry of Heavy Industry were split off to become the First and Second Ministries of Machine Building, the December 9th group could point to its first minister. Huang Ching was transferred from his leading role in Tientsin to assume the portfolio of the First Ministry. (As already mentioned, Tuan Chün-i was brought from the Southwest to become a vice-minister under Huang.) At the same time, the Ministry of Trade was divided into the Ministry of Commerce and the Ministry of Foreign Trade. Yao I-lin was transferred from the post of vice-minister of the Ministry of Trade to the same one in the Commerce Ministry, and in the next year Li Che-jen was made a vice-minister of the Foreign Trade Ministry. Serving under Li as head of the ministry's Import Bureau was Chang Hua-tung. Both Li and Chang had been groomed for their new assignments by work in top positions in regional trade departments—Li in North China and Chang in the Northeast. Another of Li's subordinates, former Tsinghua student Chao Chi-ch'ang, was put in charge of the Ministry's Staff Office.

Still other December 9th men took up high-level central government offices during the 1952–53 partial reorganization. In 1952, Liu Ai-feng moved up from director of the Ministry of Education's Staff Office to vice-minister of the newly formed Ministry of Higher Education. Ma Hsu-lun, the professor who had helped the students in the mid-1930s, moved over from the Ministry of Education to the Ministry of Higher Education where he continued to be Liu's superior. The omnipresent Li Ch'ang also assumed his first central government post at this time when he became one of the vice-chairmen of the Commission to Eliminate Illiteracy. Still another newcomer to the vice-ministerial elite was Sung Ying, appointed to the newly formed Ministry of Geology. Like Tuan Chün-i, Sung transferred from the Southwest where he had been head of the Organization Department for the West Szechwan Party Committee and second secretary in Chengtu.

Central government changes of 1952–53 were only a preliminary to the major reorganization in the fall of 1954 in the wake of the first meeting of the National People's Congress. The cabinet, previously known as the Government Administration Council and now as the State Council, was considerably enlarged to conform to the complexities of the expanding economy. The need to draw upon emerging talent in 1952 was now even more notable. To focus on the rapid advance by December 9ers to ministerial and vice-ministerial levels, it is useful to contrast the pre-1954 period with the years from 1954 to the Cultural Revolution in 1966. In the 1949–54 period, seven December 9th men were either ministers or vice-ministers in nine different ministries. But in the 1954–66 period, 29 men held 43 ministerial, vice-ministerial, or assistant ministerial[12] rank in 24

---

[12]The post of assistant minister (*pu-chang chu-li*), sometimes rendered "assistant to the minister," was created in the fall of 1954 at the time of the cabinet reorganization.

different ministries or commissions. In this same period, an average of about 15 held these offices during any given year. This number rose to 22 in 1966, on the eve of the Cultural Revolution. These 22 persons worked in 15 different ministries or commissions, or nearly a third of the 49 ministries and commissions of that time. By 1966, December 9 veterans were about fifty years of age and at the peak of their careers.

Table 7 lists the ministerial, vice-ministerial, and assistant ministerial posts held by December 9ers from 1954 to the Cultural Revolution in 1966. (Because a few men held posts at more than one level in the same ministry, or positions in different ministries, the number of posts exceeds the number of

TABLE 7

DECEMBER 9TH GENERATION MINISTERS, VICE-MINISTERS, AND ASSISTANT MINISTERS, 1954–66

Ministry (or commission)	Posts	Ministry (or commission)	Posts
First Ministry of Machine Building	4	Agriculture	1
Cultural Relations with Foreign Countries	3	Allocation of Materials	1
		Communications	1
		Culture	1
Economic Commission	3	Chemical Industry	1
Education	3	Geology	1
Railways	3	Justice	1
Scientific and Technological Commission	3	Physical Culture and Sports	1
Commerce	2	State Planning Commission	1
Foreign Affairs	2	Public Health	1
Foreign Trade	2	Scientific Planning Commission	1
Higher Education	2		
Petroleum Industry	2	State Technological Commission	1
Supervision	2		

persons employed.) The ministries (or commissions) are ranked by the number of offices held by December 9 veterans.

Six of the men who held offices listed in Table 7 attained the rank of minister. Huang Ching, who was the first to do so, is also one of the very few men—in or out of the December 9th generation—to hold two ministerial portfolios concurrently. He headed the First Ministry of Machine Building from 1952 and the State Technological Commission from 1956 until his death in 1958. Moreover, in 1957–58, Huang was a vice-chairman of the Scientific Planning Commission. Thus, in the central government, no other December 9 man held such an impressive cluster of key posts. The other ministerial chiefs were P'eng T'ao, Chemical Industry, 1956 to his death in 1961; Yao I-lin, Commerce, 1960–66; Tuan Chün-i, First Ministry of Machine Building, 1960–66; Ho Wei, Education, 1964–66; and Chiang Nan-hsiang, Higher Education, 1965–66. The posts held by the last two, Ho and Chiang, gave them a "monopoly" over the cabinet's educational positions at the outset of the Cultural Revolution. However, both ministries, as well as the field of education in general, were hard hit during the Cultural Revolution.

There are probably other instances where December 9 vice-ministers or vice-chairmen held the real authority. For example, the Commission for Cultural Relations with Foreign Countries was headed from its establishment in 1958 until its dissolution early in the Cultural Revolution by non-Party member Chang Hsi-jo, a distinguished professor. Yet a former commission staff member has stated that December 9er Ch'en Chung-ching's authority exceeded Chang's.[13] Ch'en was secretary-general of the commission from 1958 to 1964 when he was promoted to a vice-chairmanship. Moreover, later in 1964, still another December 9 man, Li Ch'ang, became a vice-chairman; in view of Li's status as an alternate member of the Party Central Com-

---

[13]Interviews conducted by Donald Klein with former commission staff members, Hong Kong, May 1964 and Cambridge, Mass., June 1965, cited in Klein and Clark, *Biographic Dictionary*, 1:102.

mittee, it is safe to assume that he too outranked Chang in the commission.

There does not seem to be any particular pattern of types of ministries in which December 9 men held ministerial, vice-ministerial, or assistant ministerial posts. On the other hand, they were only marginally represented in defense or security-related ministries. For example, none ever served in the National Defense or Public Security ministries, and in the eight machine-building ministries (most of which are defense-related), December 9th veterans have only served in the First Ministry of Machine Building. To summarize and put this into the broadest perspective, it can be noted that December 9ers held the top three offices in 24 ministries (or commissions), but no comparable posts in 45 other ministries.[14]

Below ministerial levels (e.g., department directors), the most impressive clusterings of December 9th veterans were in the Ministry of Foreign Affairs and the Scientific Planning Commission. In the Foreign Ministry, during the 1949–54 period, only Huang Hua, Kung P'eng, and Kung P'u-sheng were departmental directors or deputy directors. However, after 1954, Huang and the Kung sisters were joined by six more December 9 colleagues who, at one time or another, achieved high rank in one of the Foreign Ministry departments.[15] In the Scientific Planning Commission, in addition to Vice-Chairman Huang Ching, four men (Liu Ai-feng, Liu Tao-sheng, Wu Heng, and Yü Kuang-yuan) were deputy secretaries-general and two others were commission members.

We have moved into the 1960s in our chronological treatment of the December 9ers in the central government bureaucracy. It

[14]The figure of 45 ministries is somewhat misleading, because several of them existed only a brief time. For example, the Ministry for the Purchase of Agricultural Supplies lasted only 16 months in 1955–56. In the 1954–66 period, the total number of ministries and commissions fluctuated from 35 to 49.

[15]In addition to those working in the Foreign Ministry in Peking, many others served in embassies abroad. See Chapter 7 below.

would be useful, therefore, to pause for an assessment of the Eighth Party Congress, clearly a landmark event in the post-1949 years.

VII

A Time to Rule: II

THE EIGHTH PARTY CONGRESS AND DECEMBER 9ERS

The Eighth Party Congress met in September 1956 in a period marked by high spirits, glowing optimism, and self-congratulation. In seven brief years of nationwide power there had been many notable achievements. Yet, monumental changes had occurred since the Seventh Congress 11 years before and political authority was still vested in 65-odd surviving members of the Seventh Central Committee.[1] It was obviously a moment to review the recent past, to plan for the future, and to elect a new hierarchy reflective of the myriad changes China was undergoing.

It is not known how Mao and his Politburo colleagues atop the political pyramid viewed the December 9ers. Perhaps they did not even perceive them as a coherent group; perhaps they saw them as tried and tested officials fully ready to play a key role in the future; or perhaps they viewed them with a touch of

[1] In 1945, 77 persons were elected full or alternate members of the Central Committee. In the intervening years, a few died natural deaths or were killed in air accidents, a few more fell into political limbo, and two—Kao Kang and Jao Shu-shih—were purged.

247

unease, fearful of an emerging elitist "clique" but willing to tolerate it for the short range because of its demonstrated skills.

The most indisputable fact about the Eighth Congress is the overwhelming dominance of the Long March generation.[2] This characteristic was strikingly evident among the 113 persons who spoke at the Congress or submitted written reports. Among the exceptions were some scattered speeches and reports by "model" workers and peasants. But the only exception that suggested a pattern was among the December 9th men. Five of them spoke at the meetings, and two others presented written reports. Chiang Nan-hsiang spoke on higher education, Huang Ching about the machine building industry, Hsu Li-ch'ün on the theoretical education of cadres, Jao Pin about the need to master manufacturing techniques, and Yü Kuang-yuan of scientific achievements and shortcomings. T'ao Lu-chia and Yao I-lin presented the written reports, the former on relations between industry and agriculture, the latter on problems in foodstuff distribution.

The new Central Committee elected at the Congress consisted of 97 full and 73 alternate members. Huang Ching became a full member, and two Tsinghua men, Chiang Nan-hsiang and Li Ch'ang, were elected alternates. A year and a half later, at the second session of the Eighth Congress, 25 additional alternates were elected. Three of them—P'eng T'ao, T'ao Lu-chia, and Yao I-lin—were from December 9th ranks.[3] At first glance, a mere six out of 195 does not seem very impressive. However, the Long March aura of the Congress must again be stressed. For example, *all* of the 97 full members were established Party members prior to the Long March and indeed most of them had been significant Party figures since the early or

[2]"Long March generation" is used here loosely. Some important Communists—P'eng Chen, for example—were already in the North when the march began and obviously were not participants. The term here refers simply to people who were established CCP leaders in the mid-1930s.

[3]Ironically, though among the youngest elected, two of the December 9ers were among the first to die—Huang Ching in 1958 and P'eng T'ao in 1961.

mid-1920s. Among the 98 alternates, the overwhelming majority were either of the same generation or only a trifle younger, either in age or Party seniority.[4]

Although December 9ers participated only minimally in Party Center activities during the early P.R.C. years, this situation gradually altered with the passage of time. The process was already underway before the Congress. In fact, of the December 9ers who spoke at the Eighth Congress, Yü Kuang-yuan and Hsu Li-ch'ün were then working in second-echelon posts in the Party Center's Propaganda Department. Yü headed the Science Office, and Hsu directed the Theoretical Propaganda Office. By 1961 Hsu had advanced to become a deputy director of the department. The only other December 9er to hold a senior Party Center position was Yao I-lin, a deputy director of the Finance and Trade Work Department by 1959 and director in 1964.[5]

THE MILITARY

One conventional scheme divides the Chinese political system into three major hierarchies—the Party, the government, and the military. Many Chinese leaders, of course, held posts in all three hierarchies, especially in the 1949–54 period. In fact, however, a close study of individual careers often reveals that one hierarchy clearly predominates and that the other two are subordinate, if not nominal. Moreover, titles can be misleading. For example, during the "takeover" period, P'eng T'ao was a

---

[4]Apart from the five December 9th alternates, 10 others have not been placed in either the pre- or post-Long March generation. In eight instances, there are no data. Two other men seem to be special cases—the Marxist historian Fan Wen-lan and the Sinkiang revolutionist Saifudin; prior to 1949, the latter was more closely tied to the Communist Party of the Soviet Union than to the CCP. Among the eight on whom information is lacking, two or three were students during the 1930s and it is quite possible that they were participants in the December 9th movement.

[5]In 1964, the name was slightly altered to Finance and Trade Political Department.

deputy political commissar in South Szechwan. But in P'eng's case, which is typical, the evidence strongly suggests that his major tasks were clearly in the government and the Party. Our data could support a list of a dozen-odd December 9ers in military posts, especially prior to the mid-1950s, but such a list would be disingenuous, if not spurious. And, as noted previously, the paucity of December 9 men in the military extended to defense-related industries.

The general lack of military careers among December 9ers might have been expected. There are no examples of a top-rank "fightin' general" among the December 9 men who emerged from the Sino-Japanese War or the civil war. Mao's military team was substantially set at the end of the Long March. A large number of these men had trained at the famed Whampoa Military Academy and had gained invaluable experience during the Northern Expedition, the "annihilation campaigns" of the Kiangsi Soviet era, and, of course, the Long March itself. The December 9ers had no hope, and probably less desire, to move up this hierarchy. The harsh necessities of war demanded that the Party fill its middle and lower military echelons with tough and hardened peasants who could live on a meager ration of rice. Moreover, December 9th talents during the war years were better utilized in civil administration, mass mobilization, education, and similar non-military tasks.

We can only speculate as to whether or not these historical factors caused the December 9th men to shy away from military careers, and thus create a subtle underlying dichotomy between "peasant" soldiers and "intellectual" administrators. Projecting ahead to the Cultural Revolution, there is the temptation to offer "proof" that the military types triumphed and the intellectuals lost. But that position would do violence to the fact that scores of military men were also purged, demoted, or simply disappeared from the scene. In any case, after 1949, the December 9th generation saw little military service and those who did more often than not soon transferred to nonmilitary assignments.

MASS ORGANIZATIONS

The Youth League, in which the December 9th generation played a pivotal role during the early years of the People's Republic, is, of course, but one of the many ostensibly "mass" or "people's" organizations that have worked to organize and mobilize virtually all sectors of society in China. Mass organizations can be divided into those that enroll millions of members (e.g., the China Peace Committee), and those more accurately categorized as professional bodies of more limited membership (e.g., the Political Science and Law Association). From another perspective, mass organizations can be divided into those with an essentially domestic orientation (the All-China Federation of Trade Unions), and those oriented toward foreign affairs (the Association for Cultural Relations with Foreign Countries). No Communist leader, regardless of his early ties to the CCP, has failed to hold a position within one or more of the mass organizations. And in this sense the December 9th generation is perhaps as typical as any clustering of Communist leaders.

The December 9th veterans have held posts in virtually all mass organizations at one time or another since 1949, but there are a few in which they seem to have had a particularly significant impact. The National Women's Federation is one of them. Lu Ts'ui was already a member of the Council of the Women's International Democratic Federation when the Chinese chapter (the National Women's Federation) was formed in 1949, and she headed the federation's International Liaison Department in the early 1950s. Lu was then in her early thirties and seemed headed for the chairmanship of the National Women's Federation. However, as noted before, her career was cut short in 1954 when her husband Jao Shu-shih was purged in the sensational "anti-Party" clique case of Kao Kang and Jao.

We have already noted the dominance of December 9ers in the Manchurian chapter of the National Women's Federation during the 1950s, when one December 9 woman, Yang K'o-ping, was succeeded by another, Kuo Ming-ch'iu. Another

December 9th activist, Kuo Chien, stood in the forefront at international peace and women's conferences during the early 1960s when China fought bitter verbal battles with Indian and Russian delegates. For example, in Moscow in mid-1963, Kuo caused an uproar among 2,000 assembled delegates when she insisted upon occupying the dais to reply to what she regarded as an affront by an Indian delegate.

The All-China Federation of Literary and Art Circles (ACFLAC) is another mass organization to which December 9 figures have contributed their talents. Lü Chi, for example, rose to become a federation vice-chairman. Subordinate to the federation are a number of member organizations. December 9th veterans have held senior posts in virtually all of them, including the Union of Chinese Writers, the Union of Movie Artists, the Association of Drama Workers, and the Union of Chinese Musicians. In the last-mentioned, Lü Chi has been chairman since its formation in 1949. During the Sino-Japanese War, Ch'en Huang-mei, Ts'ui Wei, and Miss Chang Jui-fang were active together in theatrical troupes that entertained Communist troops; a quarter of a century later, all three were members of the ACFLAC's National Committee, and each of them held at least one more senior post in one of the federation's subordinate organs.

One of the leading lights in the Chinese People's Association for Cultural Relations with Foreign Countries was the widely-traveled and American-educated Ch'en Chung-ching. This organization has hosted hundreds of cultural delegations visiting China and has sent abroad scores of cultural groups. Ch'en, named secretary-general of the association upon its establishment in 1954, advanced to a vice-chairmanship in 1961. In a closely related organization, the Chinese People's Institute of Foreign Affairs, senior diplomats Huang Hua and Shen Chien, both December 9 men, have played key roles—Huang during the 1950s and Shen in the 1960s. In the China Council for the Promotion of International Trade, the body charged with handling foreign trade with nations not having diplomatic relations with China, Chang Hua-tung became a vice-chairman in 1964.

Another mass organization in which December 9 members have been very active is the All-China Federation of Trade Unions, as well as its member unions. Most of this activity was confined to the 1950s, after which the December 9ers moved on to other tasks. Particularly notable is Lu P'ing, who was deputy director of the Youth Department in the national federation and was also a vice-chairman of the Railway Workers' Union. One of the few December 9 men still in union work in the 1960s was Chang Tse-sun. By 1964 Chang had worked his way up through the Textile Workers' Union to become a vice-chairman. Shanghai is the heart of China's textile industry, and it was there during the 1930s that Chang had been a student activist.

To cite a final example among many more, December 9th men have been involved in two related mass organizations, the All-China Federation of Supply and Marketing Cooperatives and the All-China Federation of Handicraft Cooperatives. Both have close links to the Ministry of Commerce, which probably accounts for the fact that Yao I-lin, a longtime senior ministry official, was a ranking figure in the Cooperatives Federation in the 1950s. Wang Nien-chi, one of the more active participants in the early days of the December 9th movement, became a vice-chairman of the Supply and Marketing Cooperatives in 1962 and a National Committee member of the handicraft organization in the next year. Within a year of the time Wang became a Supply and Marketing Cooperatives vice-chairman, he was joined by December 9th colleague Shih Li-te, who was also named to a vice-chairmanship.

HIGHER EDUCATION

Because December 9th veterans entered the revolutionary movement by way of universities, it might be expected that many would return to academic life after 1949. And so they did.

During any given year from the mid-1950s to the Cultural Revolution about 15 top-level posts were held by December 9 men, i.e., as presidents, vice-presidents, or deans of universities and colleges. During the decade as a whole, 12 men served as university presidents and 13 as vice-presidents (three of whom were later promoted to president). December 9th men have headed schools throughout China, but there is a clear concentration in Peking where many of them were students in the 1930s. At one time or another since 1949, they have held five senior posts at Peking University and four at Tsinghua, two of contemporary China's foremost schools.

In fact, some of the most significant December 9 leaders have served at these schools. Chiang Nan-hsiang headed his alma mater Tsinghua from 1952 until the Cultural Revolution, and by 1957 he was also secretary of the school's Party committee. Serving under Chiang on the Party committee was December 9er Li Shou-tz'u, who in 1962 was made one of Tsinghua's vice-presidents. Previously, from 1956 to 1958, Li had been a vice-president of the Peking Foreign Trade College. Another top December 9 figure, Lu P'ing, became a vice-president of Peking University in 1957, where he ostensibly served under Ma Yin-ch'u, a non-Communist and one of modern China's outstanding intellectuals. Then in 1960, by which time Ma was under attack for his outspoken views, Lu succeeded to the presidency. Like Chiang Nan-hsiang, Lu headed the school he had attended as a youth.

Shih P'ing, who had taken part in the December 9th movement at Chekiang University, was appointed a vice-president of Peking Agricultural University in 1954, and by 1958 he was secretary of the school's Party committee. By 1960 Shih was transferred to the directorship of the Office of Spare-Time Education in the Ministry of Education. One of his superiors in the ministry was Vice-Minister Chiang Nan-hsiang, a fellow member of the December 9 generation. Still another important school in the capital, the Peking College of Geology, was headed from 1958 by Kao Yuan-kuei. In the 1930s, Kao had attended

China College in Peking and during the Sino-Japanese War he led guerrillas in Shantung. Ch'ien Ying-lin was president of the Peking Railway College from 1960 to 1963, after serving in the same post at Tangshan Railway College from 1957 to 1960.

Probably the most important non-Peking school headed by a December 9 man was the Harbin Industrial University, one of China's leading technical schools. The oft-cited Li Ch'ang was appointed president in 1954, and it was his most important post when he was elected a Party Central Committee alternate in 1956. Li was one of the few men elected to the Central Committee who was then working primarily in the field of higher education. He remained at the Harbin school for nearly 11 years, and then, in the spring of 1965, he was named to the presidency of the Second Foreign Languages Institute in Peking.

SCIENCE

The December 9th movement activists are clearly among the best educated of the Communist elite, but with notable exceptions few of them went on for higher degrees. Nonetheless, the CCP has seen fit to place many of them in senior scientific administrative posts. Some have held posts in the Scientific and Technical Association of China or one of its subordinate societies (e.g., the China Geology Society). But more of them have been associated with the Academy of Sciences. A good example is Yü Kuang-yuan, who has held several scientific administrative posts, including membership on the Academic Committee of the Institute of Psychology, the Council of the China Physics Society, and who in 1955 was on an organizing committee to arrange popular lectures on atomic energy. In late 1960, Yü went to Moscow with the distinguished physicist Chou P'ei-yuan for one of the so-called Pugwash Conferences, a name derived from a village in Canada where the first Pugwash Conference was held under the auspices of American industrialist Cyrus Eaton. These meetings have brought together scientific leaders to discuss, among other things, the question of disarmament. Prior to 1971 it was one of the few forums in which Americans and Chinese participated. (As a consequence of the Sino-Soviet rift, China has boycotted these meetings since the 1960 conference).

Still other December 9th men who have worked in the field of science are Wu Heng, a deputy secretary-general of the Academy of Sciences from 1954 to the early 1960s and Ku Te-huan, who has been vice-chairman of both the China Electronics Society and the Research Institute of Radio Engineering and Electronics. Physicist Ch'ien Wei-ch'ang, almost certainly the best educated of the December 9th generation, has held a host of academic and scientific posts in the Academy of Sciences and several professional societies. Ch'ien is also distinctive in that he has probably undergone more ideological criticism from the Communist Party than another member of this generation. In 1957, he castigated the Party for meddling in science and the Party responded by categorizing him as a "rightist" element and stripping him of most if not all of his posts. Returned to duty about 1960, Ch'ien underwent another series of sharp criticisms during the Cultural Revolution.

The most obvious generalization about the involvement of December 9 men in science is that they have been popularizers of science or scientific administrators, but not practicing scientists. Ch'ien Wei-ch'ang is the exception, not the rule.

FOREIGN TRAVEL

In more normal times, given the generally well-to-do backgrounds of the December 9 generation, it is likely that many of them would have traveled abroad after their student days. History decreed otherwise, and most of these student activists were preoccupied with the Sino-Japanese War and then the civil war. Thus, in 1949, when they were in their mid-thirties, the overwhelming majority had never been outside China. Some of the exceptions have already been noted—such as Miss Lu Ts'ui, who spent several years in the United States and Europe, and the three friends, Shen Chien, Hsiung Hsiang-hui, and Ch'en Chung-ching, who studied in the United States in the 1940s. (Two of them are related by marriage, Shen having married Hsiung's sister in the United States in 1947.) Not surprisingly, as discussed in greater detail below, these three went on to have important diplomatic careers.

The relative paucity of pre-1949 foreign travel contrasts sharply with the next decade and a half when 63 December 9th men and women went abroad at least once. In fact, these 63 averaged three trips in the course of visiting 58 different countries. In rough terms, this meant visits to nearly every nation with which China maintained diplomatic relations between 1949 and the mid-1960s, and to a few others without formal ties to Peking (e.g., Japan, Saudi Arabia). If we deduct the 25 persons who went abroad only once, the remaining 38 averaged about four trips outside China. It should also be noted that some of these trips covered several countries and sometimes lasted for weeks or even months; moreover, several individuals were posted abroad for several years in diplomatic assignments.

From 1953, when China became more active on the international scene in the wake of the Korean War, to the onset of the Cultural Revolution in 1966, the total number of nations visited by the 63 December 9th veterans averaged about 20 a year. Travel peaked in the years 1963 and 1964 when they visited 32 and 34 countries, respectively. In view of China's strong orientation toward Communist nations in the 1950s, it is not surprising that December 9ers have visited Eastern Europe (61 visits to one or more countries by 31 persons) and the Soviet Union (25 persons on 39 trips) more frequently than any other areas. Not far behind, by order of frequency, were South and Southeast Asia, Africa, the Asian Communist countries, the Middle East (including Egypt), and West Europe, but trailing far behind were North and South America and Japan.

Ranked by purpose of visits, the broad category of diplomacy heads the list. (This includes diplomats posted abroad, a subject dealt with in detail in the next section.) Foreign trade is next, followed by cultural, scientific, youth, and women's groups. Other significant clusterings include athletics, friendship, journalism, peace, education, and "Afro-Asian solidarity."

Clusters and figures such as those above often distort reality by obscuring the preponderant role of one or two persons. An outstanding case in point is the peripatetic Kung P'eng; her trips to 25 countries on diplomatic missions represent nearly half the trips of all December 9 persons in the diplomatic category. The same can be said for Chiang Ming, whose trips represented a third of those in the category of foreign trade. Most striking of all, in this sense, is Jung Kao-t'ang, whose participation in athletic delegations constituted the entire December 9th input into this category. However, aside from these three cases, there are no other serious distortions in terms of purpose of visits.

The travel experience of December 9ers has inevitably differed from that of an earlier generation. Most December 9ers' foreign travels have inevitably been subjected to the strictures that characterize junkets by any government's officials: tight airport schedules, structured banquets, closed conferences with host government officials, tedious signing ceremonies. The December 9th travelers were older and less impressionable when they went abroad than were the students of the May 4th generation, and they missed the opportunities their forebears had to join in lively college-dorm bull sessions in London or New York or browse through Left Bank book stalls on the Seine. Moreover, the May 4th intellectual dissenters often studied for long years in the most developed nations—France, England, Germany, the United States, Japan—and while they did not always like what they saw, they did have the chance to see the economic strength of these nations and were clearly impressed. In sharp contrast, December 9ers' travel has focused mainly on the so-called underdeveloped world and least on the industrial nations. Furthermore, while the earlier generation produced countless numbers of men with advanced degrees from abroad, the war precluded this for all but a few December 9 men and women. Nevertheless, the December 9th veterans have probably been more useful to the Communist movement by their very lack of advanced, highly-technical training. In the barren Shensi hillsides, archeologists or biochemists would have been an un-needed luxury; better to have the useful enthusiasm of somewhat younger men with three or four years of general college than a Ph.D. fretting over the arts of the Shang dynasty. Indeed, this notion of training for service to the people still exists in China today and is nowhere better exemplified than in the "barefoot doctors" who are in far greater demand than brain surgeons.

DIPLOMACY

December 9ers have clearly played an important role in Chinese international relations. This is already evident from previous discussions of the Foreign Ministry, the foreign trade apparatus, various mass organizations involved in foreign affairs, and the wide-ranging travels of December 9ers since 1949. In this section, we turn more specifically to those diplomats posted abroad in diplomatic work.

The December 9th generation's contributions to Peking's diplomatic community were rather modest during the early years of the People's Republic. However, the embassy in Burma was an unusual exception. When former Peita student Yao Chung-ming arrived in Rangoon in September 1950 he was the second ambassador appointed to a non-Communist nation; when he was recalled in 1958 he had put in the longest single ambassadorial tour. Serving under Yao as deputy chief of mission was fellow December 9er Meng Ying, who held the rank of counselor. Still another December 9er, Li P'ing, was also a counselor who doubled as consul-general in Rangoon.

The only other December 9 veteran abroad in the early 1950s was Shen Chien, and few other cases better illustrate the swiftly changing fortunes of the December 9th generation. In 1948 he was still a student in the United States; two years later, he opened the most important P.R.C. diplomatic mission in South Asia. He was sent to New Delhi in mid-1950, several weeks before the arrival of Ambassador Yuan Chung-hsien, a former Red Army general. Shen held the rank of counselor, but during the next few years he frequently served as chargé d'affaires ad interim. He returned home to become deputy director and then director of the Foreign Ministry's American and Australian Department, and in 1960 he was appointed Peking's first ambassador to Cuba.

After Yao Chung-ming's ambassadorial appointment in 1950, the next December 9er to hold this rank was Ho Wei, a student in the mid-1930s at Huachung University, a missionary school in Wuchang, Hupei. From 1954 to 1957, he was an assistant minister in the Ministry of Foreign Affairs, and then from 1958 to 1962 he was ambassador in Hanoi. These years, of course, coincided with the dramatic escalation of the war in Vietnam. They also coincided with the period when China and Laos moved toward closer ties. In a rather unorthodox arrangement, Ho became the first head of the "P.R.C. Economic and Cultural Mission" in Laos in 1961. This special mission was not located in the capital at Vientiane, but rather in Xieng Khouang, where Communist influence had been strong for many years. Nonetheless, Ho formally presented his credentials to Prime Minister Souvanna Phouma and can thus be regarded as China's first "ambassador" to Laos.[6]

The only other December 9th men posted abroad during the rest of the 1950s were Counselor Hsu Ming and Commercial Counselor Chao Chi-ch'iang in East Germany, Commercial Counselor Chang Hua-tung in Moscow (the same man who had been in Moscow with Mao Tse-tung and Chou En-lai to negotiate the 1950 Sino-Soviet Treaty of Friendship, Alliance, and Mutual Assistance), and Meng Ying, who after his tour in

[6]In formal diplomatic terms, Liu Ch'un was appointed the first full-fledged ambassador in September 1962.

Burma served again with the rank of counselor in Mongolia.

In contrast to the 1950s, the 1960s witnessed a dramatic upturn of December 9er fortunes within the diplomatic community. This change is especially striking because, in effect, the December 9th men had barely more than half a decade to make their mark—the first phase of the Cultural Revolution brought diplomatic activity to a virtual standstill, and, by the winter of 1966–67, nearly all of Peking's first-rate diplomats had been recalled. Nevertheless, the three ambassadorships held by December 9th men in the 1950s and early 1960s (Yao Chung-ming in Burma and Ho Wei in Vietnam and Laos) had jumped to 12 ambassadorships[7] held by eight men by 1966. In 1964 alone, when China had diplomatic relations with 50 nations, December 9th men held almost one-seventh of the ambassadorships. In 1972, after the People's Republic had moved into high gear in the post-Cultural Revolution years, December 9th men could point to nine of their numbers who at one time or another since 1949 had been ambassadors to 16 different nations.[8] Two of the nine also held the rank of ambassador at the United Nations. If five more counselors who never reached ambassadorial rank are added, then December 9ers have been posted in 21 different countries between 1949 and 1972, plus the United Nations mission in New York.

A few persons clearly stand out. Yao Chung-ming, after his long tour in Rangoon, headed the Chinese side in the negotiations that led to the Sino-Burmese boundary treaty in 1961. He was then posted to Indonesia where he had the good fortune to take part in the high level of Sino-Indonesian ties during the early and mid-1960s, as well as the misfortune to be the ambassador in Jakarta when the abortive Communist coup of

---

[7]This figure included Hsiung Hsiang-hui, the chargé of the Office of the Chargé d'Affaires in London, and Ho Wei, chief of the Economic and Cultural Mission in Laos, both of which we regard as the equivalent of ambassadorships.

[8]In addition to the nine December 9 men who have been ambassadors, 124 other men have held this post between 1949 and mid-1972.

1965 led to the massive slaughter of Chinese residents in Indonesia. Yao's ambassadorship terminated in 1967 when Sino-Indonesian diplomatic relations were suspended.

Though never posted abroad, Kung P'eng merits special attention. As an adviser and spokesman, she was with Chou En-lai at the 1954 Geneva Conference, and she was again in Geneva in 1961 as an adviser to Foreign Minister Ch'en I for the conference on Laos. Among her other diplomatic missions, the most notable was the 10-week, 14-nation tour in 1963–64 led by Chou En-lai to the Middle East, Africa, Albania, and South and Southeast Asia. Kung took part in these activities as director of the Foreign Ministry's Information Department from 1949 to 1964 and from 1964 to her death in 1970 as an assistant minister.

A third standout is Huang Hua. After holding several key Foreign Ministry positions throughout the 1950s, Huang spent more than five years as ambassador to Ghana, China's most important diplomatic post in West Africa. From there he was sent to Cairo, and, as often noted, Huang was unique in being the only ambassador not recalled home during the Cultural Revolution. He twice gained world headlines in 1971—the first time when he went to Ottawa as the ambassador. He thus became the first top P.R.C. diplomat stationed in North America. Even this newsworthy event was far overshadowed in the fall of 1971 when he arrived in New York to become China's first Permanent Representative to the United Nations Security Council.

Huang Hua is the only December 9 man to serve in four ambassadorial posts, but five others have headed missions in two countries. As already noted, Yao Chung-ming was ambassador to Burma and Indonesia and Ho Wei was chief envoy in Vietnam and Laos. In addition, Meng Ying was ambassador in Zanzibar and the Central African Republic, Hsieh Pang-chih was chief envoy in Bulgaria and then Afghanistan, and Hsiung Hsiang-hui headed the mission in London and in Mexico.[9] Because of a special relationship to the United States, Hsiung merits further comment. In the fall of 1971, he was in New York, with the rank of ambassador, as a representative to the 26th United Nations General Assembly. This was his second time in the United States because, as noted earlier, he studied at Western Reserve University in Cleveland in the late 1940s.

The December 9 diplomats were not, of course, operating in isolation. The interdependence between men in the field and "desk" officers at home is a characteristic of all foreign affairs establishments. In the case of these Chinese diplomats, they were often reporting back to their December 9th colleagues and many of the men mentioned in this section served at one time or another in top jobs in the Foreign Ministry. In total, December 9 veterans have been directors of four area (e.g., West European) or functional (e.g., Treaty and Law) departments, and deputy directors of six departments. In addition, two of their numbers (Ho Wei and Kung P'eng) served as assistant ministers. When these people needed personal ties in closely related ministries, commissions, and bureaus, they could call upon numerous December 9ers in the Foreign Trade Ministry (including two vice-ministers), the Bureau (later Commission) for Cultural Relations with Foreign Countries, and the Bureau for Economic Relations with Foreign Countries.

In 1966, the rising stars of the December 9ers were suddenly eclipsed by the Cultural Revolution.

[9]The three December 9ers to hold ambassadorships in only one country are Shen Chien (Cuba), Wang Jo-chieh (Yemen), and Li Lien-pi, who is currently ambassador to Belgium. (Subsequent to the compilation of these data through the year 1972, Wang Jo-chieh received another ambassadorship—in Vietnam. Similarly, Li Lien-pi was made ambassador to Luxembourg. Both of these assignments are mentioned in Chapter 8.)

VIII

A Generation Disappears

The Great Proletarian Cultural Revolution of 1966–69 is the most recent of the revolutionary upheavals that have punctuated the history of Chinese communism. The past quarter century of this history can be viewed simply as a cyclical process: periods of moderation, bureaucratic growth, and ideological tolerance have been followed by outbursts of revolutionary extremism, revivals of anti-bureaucratism, and demands for the integration of ideology and conduct. The former included the zenith of the wartime united front (1937–39), the takeover (1949–50), the outset of the First Five-Year Plan (1953–54), and the era of Liuist "normalcy" between the Great Leap and the Cultural Revolution (1960–65). The latter included the *Cheng-feng* movement (1942–44), the thought reform, three-anti and five-anti drives (1951–52), the Antirightist and Great Leap movements (1957–59), and the Cultural Revolution (1966–69), as well as rectification campaigns in 1947, 1950, and 1954–55.

During periods of normalcy, the Party concentrated upon organizational development, establishment of rational bureaucratic procedures, and recruitment of educated men and women

264

essential for such operations. During revolutionary crusades, criticism of bureaucrats was accompanied by the ascendancy of less educated cadres of rural origins. In some instances these crusades also involved decentralization of power to county, commune, or village levels. As part of the rectification process, urban bureaucrats, professionals, teachers, and students were "sent down" to work on farms and in factories where, it was hoped, elitist habits would be eroded through close association with the working masses.

Until 1966 the December 9ers weathered these campaigns remarkably well. Though chastized and "sent down" during the *Cheng-feng* movement, they were too obscure to be singled out for denunciation and were young and malleable enough to resume their careers no worse for the experience. Subsequent rectification drives were aimed primarily at other targets: rural elements (1947), new recruits (1950), and high-level cadres (1954–55). The three-anti movement against corruption, waste, and bureaucratism bypassed the December 9ers. The thought reform campaigns of the early 1950s and the antirightist vendetta of 1957–58 were directed against non-Party intellectuals, including former teachers of the December 9ers and older associates from the National Salvation movement. Here, too, years of loyal Party service shielded the December 9th group.

Prior to 1966, only a handful of December 9ers were singled out for denunciation or purge. In 1954 Lu Ts'ui, the movement's "Joan of Arc," disappeared from sight when her husband, Shanghai city boss Jao Shu-shih, was purged in tandem with Manchuria's strongman Kao Kang.[1] Another possible victim of the Kao-Jao purge was Han T'ien-shih, who had been expelled from Peita in 1936 for helping to coerce a school employee during a phase of the movement that Communists criticized for "excessive leftism and reckless action."[2] In 1954–55, Han was dismissed from several important posts in

[1]See above, Chapter 2.

[2]Interview with a Peita alumnus who wishes to remain anonymous; *SNIC*, p. 145.

Manchuria, including the secretaryship of the Party committee from Anshan City. Han's fellow Peita alumnus, Ko P'ei-ch'i, a lecturer in physics and chemistry at Chinese People's University in Peking, was "sternly rebuked" for remonstrances against the Party during the Hundred Flowers movement of 1957.[3] Ko fell victim to the same antirightist backlash that brought down Tsinghua's tragicomic "Haile Selassie," Han Ming, a highly vulnerable member of the China Democratic League.[4]

During the Great Leap and commune experiments, local cadres were invested with some of the powers of the central bureaucracy. However, the December 9ers emerged from these traumatic social upheavals stronger than ever, for it was precisely these individuals who stood to gain when China turned from Maoist excesses of the late fifties to Liuist normalization of the early sixties. Thus, for thirty years, this remarkable generation survived both the physical dangers of war and the equally formidable perils of Communist campaigns.

In 1966 their luck ran out. The Cultural Revolution was a calculated gamble by Mao and his followers who saw the revolution endangered. Only extreme measures, they believed, would prevent China from sinking, like the USSR, into a bureaucratic inferno. The reality of this disturbing vision was substantiated by the December 9ers then occupying key positions in domestic administration, education, and foreign affairs. The Cultural Revolution, of course, claimed victims from all segments of China's ruling elite; not all of these individuals were equally guilty of anti-Maoist sins. As leaders of the discredited Party and state apparatus, however, the December 9 veterans were easy marks. Of all the organs of power, only the People's Liberation Army, where this group had virtually no foothold, was able to strike an offensive posture. Sanctified by Mao and spearheaded by a new generation of student rebels, the PLA enabled the masses to feel they could

[3] *Wen-hui pao,* June 30, 1957.
[4] See above, Chapter 2.

punish with impunity. Against this assault, the December 9ers were defenseless.

The fate of the December 9ers was exemplified by the case of Li Ch'ang. In many ways Li personified the experience of his generation. As a Tsinghua student, he attended the school that supplied the largest contingent to the ranks of the December 9ers. He also headed the most important organizational off-spring of the movement, the National Liberation Vanguards of China, and was one of the first to join the Youth League and the Party and to visit Yenan. In the post-1949 period, Li reached the Olympian political heights of the Party Central Committee. In 1964 he advanced to a new summit in his career, a vice-chairmanship in the Commission for Cultural Relations with Foreign Countries, and not long afterward became president of the Second Foreign Languages Institute. Li was soon off on foreign travels. In May 1965 he signed a Sino-Rumanian cultural agreement in Bucharest. The following March, he left for Syria, the United Arab Republic, Yemen, and Iraq and in each place signed cultural agreements. Early in June he returned to China.

But in Li's absence, his world had turned upside down. A superficially innocuous criticism of a historical play by Peking's vice-mayor had escalated into a high-level purge. Victims included the mayor of Peking, the chief of the army's general staff, and the entire editorial board of the *Jen-min jih-pao*. At Peking University, a group of student rebels was attacking President Lu P'ing in the name of Mao. The stage was set for the Red Guards, whose victims would include China's number two man, Liu Shao-ch'i. Li Ch'ang's happy homecoming was brief. His name was duly mentioned in the press when he arrived and again several days later. Since then, silence, broken only by strident accusations in 1967 that included Li's name among alleged foes of the Cultural Revolution. To the extent that press notices reflect political status in China, Li has become a non-person.

This brief recapitulation of a prominent December 9er's career could be repeated a hundredfold. For scores of others, nothing has been heard, for dozens more, denunciation: "capitalist roader," "renegade," "member of a counterrevolutionary organization," "royalist who tried to restore bourgeois dictatorship," "black henchman," "counterrevolutionary revisionist," the author of "poisonous weeds." So hyperbole-loaded are the accusations that the reader can draw few conclusions about underlying patterns of alleged malfeasances.

The bureaucrats of 1965 were unquestionably less revolutionary in political style than were the youthful demonstrators who confronted the established order in the winter of 1935–36. Yet it would be simplistic to explain that they had evolved "naturally" from revolutionaries to reactionaries because twenty-year-old radicals always grow into fifty-year-old conservatives. In fact, as we have noted, much of their post-December 9th training and experience might well have broadened and deepened their revolutionary commitment. One need not deny the truisms that fathers are generally better adjusted to the status quo than are their sons and that those highly placed in the power structure tend to be more conservative than those on the outside. The fact remains, nonetheless, that it was a dramatic and sudden social upheaval as much as gradual changes in themselves that gave the December 9ers a "conservative" image during the Cultural Revolution.

In terms of linkages with discredited senior leaders, the names of Liu Shao-ch'i and Peking's deposed mayor P'eng Chen crop up most frequently. Nowhere was Liu more deeply and personally involved than at Tsinghua University, China's leading center for scientific and technological studies. His daughter, Liu Tao, was a Tsinghua student, and his wife, Wang Kuang-mei, allegedly provided surreptitious support for the Liuist work team installed on campus from June 10 to July 31, 1966, to channel the surging tide of student rebellion.[5]

Famous December 9er Chiang Nan-hsiang was minister in

---

[5]William Hinton, *Hundred Day War: The Cultural Revolution at Tsinghua University* (New York: Monthly Review Press, 1972), pp. 49–51.

the Ministry of Higher Education and concurrently president of Tsinghua. Like his Peita counterpart Lu P'ing, Chiang was an early victim of the youthful uprising. He was driven from office under a barrage of accusations: he had allegedly built Tsinghua into a bastion of elitist expertise, discriminated against students of workers and peasant origins, denied the relevance of Resistance University's Maoist-style education, and turned Tsinghua's CCP branch into an exclusive club for professors and lecturers.[6]

Chiang's deviations were seen as part of Liu Shao-ch'i's scheme to subvert the revolutionary order from within. During the work team's visitation at Tsinghua, Liu is said to have veiled his identity behind a large face mask and visited the campus at night to oversee the machinations of his wife and daughter.[7] On at least two occasions, daylight appearances were made by Po I-po, Liu's top economic administrator, long associated with December 9ers. During one of these visits, Po verbally crossed swords with ultraleftist Red Guard leader K'uai Ta-fu, who called him "a fat old man." Since Tsinghua students were still under the sway of the work team, Po was able to parry the thrust, but the situation changed radically in succeeding months. On April 10, 1967, an estimated half million people crowded on and around the Tsinghua campus for a public denunciation of Liu Shao-ch'i's wife. Behind a grotesquely garbed Wang Kuang-mei, writes William Hinton, "stood six leading cadre who had played an adverse role in the history of the University."[8] Three were December 9ers or men closely associated with the movement: Chiang Nan-hsiang, Po I-po, and P'eng Chen. In accusing Mme. Liu and confessing their ties to her, these men helped to unravel the web of Liuist revisionism in which they had been enmeshed.

Numerous December 9ers unquestionably were "guilty" of long-established ties with Liu Shao-ch'i and P'eng Chen dating

[6]*Ibid.*, pp. 29, 33, 38.

[7]*Ibid.*, p. 64.

[8]*Ibid.*, p. 104.

from the student movement of 1935–36 and reinforced over the years by cooperation in a common cause. But many of the hundreds of non-December 9ers also linked to Liu and P'eng in denunciatory diatribes did not share this history of "criminal" association. There can be little doubt that the anti-Liuist campaign utilized ritualistic accusations and confessions, the hallmark of all crusades that seek to expose and exorcise the Devil's work.

When the Ninth Party Congress convened in 1969 it seemed that the December 9th generation had ceased to exist. The steady December 9er progress up the hierarchical ladder suggests that the six men elected to the Eighth Central Committee in 1956–58 might have easily doubled or tripled on the Ninth. Indeed, it is not extravagant to suggest that one or two might have been appointed to the select circle of the Politburo. Instead, there is no evidence that a December 9th veteran was even among the 1,500 delegates to the Ninth Congress and none, of course, was elected to the Central Committee. At that time, only two or three were even mentioned in the media.

By mid-1974, a few December 9ers were beginning to reappear on the political scene, yet this can scarcely be said to constitute a "trend." Eight years after the Cultural Revolution began, fewer than 30 December 9ers of some 200 who were active in the 1949–66 period are known to be back in circulation. Within this small contingent, there is a noteworthy pattern: five have been abroad as ambassadors in the early 1970s, and another dozen have been active in official or quasi-official diplomatic work in Peking. One of the latter is Kung P'eng. When she died in 1970 she was accorded press coverage in the *Jen-min jih-pao* appropriate to her political standing. Her obituary noted that she was an assistant minister of the Ministry of Foreign Affairs, and there was no hint that she had been involved in the Cultural Revolution. Her widower, Ch'iao Kuan-hua (Tsinghua, 1933), headed Peking's first four delegations to the United Nations General Assembly in 1971–74, and became foreign minister in late 1974. Kung

P'eng's sister, Kung P'u-sheng (a fellow December 9er) was long out of the news but returned to active life in 1972 and by 1973 was identified as an adviser to the Foreign Ministry's department concerned with international organizations and treaties. However, Kung P'u-sheng's husband Chang Han-fu, formerly the senior vice-minister in the Foreign Affairs Ministry, remains an unredeemed Cultural Revolution villain.

Other diplomats who have survived include Huang Hua, who remained at his ambassadorial post in Cairo during the Cultural Revolution and who in rapid succession in 1971 became the first Chinese Communist ambassador to Canada and then China's chief representative at the United Nations. Hsiung Hsiang-hui was Huang's deputy at the United Nations in 1971 and Peking's first ambassador to Mexico in 1972–73. Another man, Li Lien-pi, became China's first ambassador to both Belgium (1972) and Luxembourg (1973). Hsieh Pang-chih was ambassador in Afghanistan (1969–73) and then became the first P.R.C. ambassador to Upper Volta. Finally, Wang Jo-chieh left his post as chief envoy in Yemen in late 1972 and soon after became Peking's first ambassador to the Provisional Revolutionary Government of the Republic of South Vietnam. As these several "firsts" suggest, the People's Republic underwent a veritable diplomatic explosion in the early 1970s. Starting with the establishment of diplomatic ties with Canada in 1970 (and dramatized by entry into the U.N. in October 1971), between 1970 and 1974, Peking doubled the number of nations with which it had diplomatic relations. This expansion of relations, of course, necessitated the assignment of scores of diplomats abroad. And, given the sophisticated background of the December 9ers, it is not surprising that several of them were called back to service.

There seems to be no discernible pattern among the handful of other "returnees." A few are back in the Party or government apparatus, others in science and education. And, indeed, some have resumed quite significant posts. For example, Yao I-lin, long a key man in both domestic and foreign commerce, assumed a vice-ministership in the Foreign Trade Ministry in 1973, and Chu Mu-chih has headed the important New China News Agency since 1972. Moreover, Chu led a group of journalists to the United States in the spring of 1973 and was an active host for Henry Kissinger during the latter's November 1973 trip to China.[9] Another man, Tuan Chün-i, was a ranking figure in Szechwan in the early 1950s and on the eve of the Cultural Revolution was head of the First Ministry of Machine Building. By 1971, Tuan was back in Szechwan as second secretary of the provincial Party committee.

At the Party's Ninth Congress in 1969, as noted earlier, the December 9th generation was completely shut out. By the Tenth Congress, convened in August 1973, the story had altered somewhat. Four December 9 men—Chu Mu-chih, Huang Hua, T'ao Lu-chia, and Tuan Chün-i—were elected full Central Committee members, and Yao I-lin was elected an alternate member. While clearly an improvement over their showing in 1969, the true contrast is with the Eighth Central Committee (elected in 1956–58). On the Eighth Central Committee, the December 9ers had six men. Now, a decade and a half later—during which period this group should have reached the peak of its power and authority—the figure fell to five. Moreover, the size of the Central Committee had grown enormously—from 195 on the Eighth Committee to 319 on the Tenth.

Personal reports suggest that some of the less famous December 9ers are now leading normal, though obscure lives, and that others, criticized during the Cultural Revolution, have been quietly rehabilitated. Writing in April 1973, Han Suyin suggests that "The criticism during the Cultural Revolution, which was not always according to Chairman Mao's thinking, has not affected the lives of many; on the contrary, it seems

[9]During his trip to the United States, Chu revealed that he was a December 9er in conversation with a friend of the authors. Chu Mu-chih may, in fact, be a pseudonym for former Yenching student body president Chu Nan-hua.

much has been done to offset it."[10] Yenching December 9ers of whom she had news included Dr. Lee Yueh-lien, in 1969 reported practicing medicine in a hospital, probably in Shanghai; Dr. Chang Wei-hsun and his wife, Liang Szu-i ("both are doing extremely well, are very well thought of, and have had no trouble at all"); Han Kang-ling (similar reports); and Kung P'u-sheng ("doing very well" when Han saw her in 1972).[11] A Peita alumnus visiting Hong Kong in 1973 told a schoolmate that Ch'en Chung-ching was "safe and sound."[12] Swiss writer Alexander Casella, who visited Tsinghua University in October 1971, reports Chiang Nan-hsiang restored to the faculty, though not to the presidency, which had been replaced by a revolutionary committee. Chiang was spending part of his time at manual labor.[13]

Any discussion of December 9 "survivors" or "returnees" must take note of a methodological problem. Because of the dramatic intensification of foreign affairs since 1969, scores of second- and third-string officials dealing with foreign relations have appeared in the press. In contrast, many domestic sectors gain little if any press recognition, which may reflect the ongoing struggles and uncertainties that continue to mark the home scene. There is no way of gauging how many domestic officials may have been quietly returned to political life without the press coverage showered upon their diplomatic confreres.

What have the December 9ers been doing since charges were leveled against them in 1966–67 (or, more frequently, since their disappearance without charges)? Unfortunately, we have no specific information about the scores who apparently have not returned. And of the "returnees" we gain only fleeting glimpses. Edgar Snow recorded one such case during his 1970–71 trip to

[10]Letter to John Israel, April 9, 1973.

[11]*Ibid.*

[12]John Israel's interview with schoolmate, Hong Kong, December 11, 1973.

[13]Conversation with John Israel, Charlottesville, Virginia, May 3, 1973.

China.[14] Visiting a major Peking hospital, Snow met Chang Wei-hsun, an old friend and former deputy director of the institution. The late American journalist had known him since their Yenching days when Chang, in Snow's words, was a "radical student." In the intervening years, Chang had studied medicine, served on the Bellevue Hospital staff in New York, and returned to China about 1949 to work in public health. In the stormy spring of 1967, Chang was "struggled against" as a "Liu Shao-ch'i element," but none of this was mentioned in the Snow interview.

When Snow asked "what took you away from Peking?" Chang said that he had been at a production brigade in the countryside. "Who sent you there?" "No one sent me," Chang responded. He added:

I asked to go, to integrate with the peasants and to remold my ideology . . . I did not realize I was a reactionary until the Cultural Revolution. When I worked with the mobile medical teams I realized for the first time how much in need of medicine and doctors the peasants are. I went down as a cadre, to do manual labor, but the peasants learned that I was a doctor and they came to me for help.[15]

At first the peasants treated Chang deferentially, but now, he declared, "we are equals. I am very happy with them and determined to spend my life there." He visits his family in Peking once a month. Snow speculated: "Perhaps he will be called back to the city again when the new party needs him—and he has trained young people to carry on his work at the brigade. Or his family may move to the country, to join him."

Snow's prediction was a good one. On December 9, 1972, Chang, restored to his hospital directorship, was indeed called "back to the city" and lunching with the famous correspondent's former wife, Helen Snow, who had chronicled the student uprising 37 years earlier. Also present at the anniversary

[14]Edgar Snow, "Report from China, III," *New Republic*, May 1, 1971, pp. 20–23.

[15]Ibid., p. 23.

celebration were his wife (Liang Szu-i) and their fellow alumna Kung P'u-sheng. In 1973, Chang was posted to Geneva to become assistant director-general of the World Health Organization, a post that opened up following Peking's entry into the United Nations in 1971. Liang Szu-i fared equally well as an official of the International Red Cross. Early in 1973 she went to Geneva to attend a meeting of experts dealing with aspects of international law as they pertain to wartime periods. Her friend, Constance Chang, was at the U.N. headquarters in New York with her husband T'ang Ming-chao.

During her visit, Mrs. Snow also enjoyed reunions with other Yenching December 9ers in the capital. Her dear friend, Li Min, was teaching English and Chinese at foreign embassies. Ch'en Han-po, the skeptical young editor of the Yenching student newspaper who had first appeared on the Snow's doorstep in quest of enlightenment on fascism, was high up—possibly a department chief—in the government's publications department. Ch'en believed that his friend, former student body president Chang Chao-lin, was teaching at Kirin University in his native Manchuria, though others told Mrs. Snow that Chang had been killed years earlier in Sinkiang when warlord Sheng Shih-ts'ai executed a number of Communists, including Mao Tse-tung's brother.[16] To the delight and surprise of the authors, an inquiry addressed to "Professor Chang Chao-lin, Kirin University, Changchun, PRC" elicited a typewritten English-language reply. "In compliance with the needs of Party work I worked at different posts in various places all these years," reported Chang. "Early in the 1960s I was transferred to the educational front." Chang expressed gratitude to Edgar and "Peg" Snow for their contributions to the Chinese revolution and wished us success in conveying the significance of the December 9th movement to our readers.[17]

[16]Helen F. Snow to John Israel, August 24, 1974, Chang Chao-lin to John Israel, January 30, 1975. For background to the Sheng Shih-ts'ai episode, see Klein and Clark, *Biographic Dictionary*, 2:675.

[17]Chang Chao-lin to John Israel, January 30, 1975.

How many Chang Wei-hsuns are there? How many high-ranking December 9ers "voluntarily" work in the countryside? And how long are they likely to remain there? This is not, of course, the first time that officials have been "sent down" to the farms and factories, but it may not be so easy for these people, as it was in earlier years, to return to the status quo ante. For China's urban political elite, the Cultural Revolution, more than any previous campaign, was a total assault on existing modes of life, society, thought, and governance. To revert to anything like the situation in 1965 would be to confess failure, something that China's leaders are loathe to do. Not all officials, of course, spend their time on farms and in factories. Instead, many are sent for multi-month re-education in the more structured milieu of "May 7th schools." There they erect their own living quarters, produce their own food, and thereby, presumably, keep in touch with the earthy problems of the working masses. Though the May 7th sojourns have apparently been taken very seriously, they may become institutionalized sabbaticals serving as conventional outlets through which bureaucrats may do penance for ideological sins. Alumni of such institutions may conceivably return to official positions to transgress once again. Hence it is possible that December 9ers, having been "sent down" in some fashion, will bounce back again.

Possible but improbable. After more than half a decade in disgrace, or at least in eclipse, the December 9ers will not easily rebound to the posts they once occupied, much less to the commanding heights to which they may have aspired. It is known that a large number of them have not returned to their former positions because these posts were eliminated in the radical pruning of the governmental apparatus that followed the Cultural Revolution. For example, K'ang Shih-en, a vice-minister of the Ministry of Petroleum Industry in 1966, was sharply criticized in 1967. In 1971 K'ang was identified as a "responsible person" in an unspecified ministry, and then in January 1975 he was named to head the Ministry of Petroleum and Chemical Industries.

The December 9ers no longer are the bright, young, freshly rectified officials who rode out the *Cheng-feng* movement 30 years ago. They are approaching their sixties, scarcely an age at which renewed upward mobility is likely. Even if they have the will, it is unlikely that they can overcome opposition from those who have seized power from them since 1966—military leaders, representatives of the "masses," local potentates, and other rivals. At most the December 9ers may hope to gain positions that draw upon their expertise and experience without offering access to the levers of power.

As student insurgents, December 9ers were counterparts of young intellectuals in emerging nations of the mid-twentieth century; their mission was first to foment revolution and then, if they could, to transform it into bureaucratic rule. The propensity of revolutions to devour their own children has been underscored in the histories of myriad African and Asian nations; in Latin America, it is a century-old story. Student rebels time and again have been thrust aside once the citadels of power were in insurgent hands. But the Chinese upheaval was not like other revolutions, and the December 9ers differed from their counterparts in significant respects. No other revolutionary movement has had the opportunity to rule vast and populous areas for more than a decade before seizing power. In China, unlike most other countries, revolution and rule were not separate stages but overlapping and interwoven phenomena. Thus, by the time nationwide power was seized, this group had established a strong position based upon more than a decade of work and struggle. The December 9ers were entrenched insiders, no longer members of a mercurial but evanescent movement that could be stifled at a convenient moment. Hence, their purge after three decades of service was significantly different from the suppression of student rebels by postrevolutionary regimes in other lands.

Dedicated and loyal though they may have been, the December 9ers were vulnerable. Their relationship with Maoist elements in the revolutionary movement was an ambiguous one, marred by opportunism on both sides. Though united with the CCP in demands for "national liberation," the students understood this slogan in terms of their struggle for civil liberties and national sovereignty. The Communist Party was a vehicle for reaching these goals. As members of an urban elite, they were attracted to the Communists more by abstract principles than through a shared appreciation of the profound forces of rural revolution. The Communists, on the other hand, were committed to three propositions: (1) that conditions in China were ripe for revolution; (2) that the main force of this revolution would be the masses, especially those of the rural hinterland; and (3) that only a disciplined Leninist Party at the helm of a people's army could steer the revolution to victory. The December 9ers' talents and righteous moral indignation were useful commodities only insofar as they served revolutionary purposes as understood by the CCP. That is why the seasoned cadre Huang Ching regarded the students' November 1, 1935 petition for civil liberties as an outburst of puerile radicalism.

To the students, both the CCP and its dogmas served as an instrument for a higher goal—the liberation of the Chinese people from foreign domination. The populist side of Communist ideology, which sought to destroy China's old elites, including the intelligentsia, was absorbed, perhaps, grudgingly and superficially. Despite their inclination to romanticize the Communist leaders and the Red Army, and their willingness to assume the outward trappings of poverty, the students found it enormously difficult to identify with the masses. At very most they went to the people prepared to educate them, very seldom to learn from them. The nationalistic goals of these youths coincided with the populist revolutionary goals of the Party—up to a point. However, when populism turned out to be more than an instrument of nationalism and became an end in itself, these intellectuals parted company with the 100 percent Maoists. Writing of Peita professors and other high-level intellectuals during the Cultural Revolution, Marianne Bastid observed:

Among faculty members a high percentage of people adhered to Marxism out of nationalism, not out of faith in the absolute value of Marxist ideology itself. To them Marxism-Leninism and Mao Tsetung's thought were the best means, but only *means,* to achieve China's resurrection. Their attention focused on the end rather than on the means, and it was the idea of the end which enabled them to accept the hardships on the road. They were utilitarian Marxists.[18]

"Utilitarian Marxists"—the term fits the December 9ers like a glove.

Impressive talent, selfless dedication, and proven loyalty helped the December 9ers to survive and prosper in spite of these "contradictions." Equally important were the Maoist tenets (drawn from traditional Chinése precepts) that most men are fundamentally good, that all are educable, and that even human material corrupted by reactionary family backgrounds and imperialistic education could be purified by moral instruction and put to use. Hence the efficacy of periodic rectification movements. But there were limits to the redemptive process. More for practical than for philosophical reasons, the more prominent the man the less likely the rehabilitation. Thus, high-level officials accused of crimes seldom have reappeared. Kao Kang and Jao Shu-shih in 1954, P'eng Te-huai in 1959, Liu Shao-ch'i in 1966, Lin Piao in 1971—these men and their followers were permanently (and sometimes mortally) removed from the scene. Only a single echelon away from such towering figures, the December 9ers now face enormous obstacles to political recovery.

Americans may be saddened to see the December 9ers go. Even though it now appears that we can "do business" with old-line Communists, we harbor a residual longing for Chinese leaders created in our own image, men who literally and figuratively speak our language. For more than a century we

[18]Marianne Bastid, "A Triptych in Honor of the Cultural Revolution," *Bulletin of Concerned Asian Scholars* 2, no. 3 (April-June 1970): 85. Italics in original.

have assumed that somewhere in China such men existed or could be manufactured. This was an underlying assumption of the missionary education movement that established Yenching. It was part of the motivation behind the remission of the Boxer Indemnity which supported Tsinghua and enabled Chinese students to come to the United States for schooling. Still unfulfilled, this dream found new voice in January 1947 in the words of George Marshall when the parting American envoy bemoaned the powerlessness of "splendid" Chinese liberals, Western-educated and democratically-inclined, who stood between intransigent KMT and CCP forces. Prior to the Cultural Revolution, our folklore on the People's Republic came to include the notion that a generation of reasonable, moderate, technocratic modernizers—not ideological fanatics—might succeed Mao Tse-tung, opening the way to a Sino-American dialogue, détente, and world peace. Exactly who these leaders were or how they would come to power was never spelled out, but few doubted their existence.

The December 9ers, of course, never measured up to these romantic expectations. To be sure, they had been trained mainly under Western-educated professors in modern universities. For many of them English was a second language. Yet they were far less exposed to life and learning in the West than were their May 4th antecedents such as Chou En-lai and other Party elders. Aroused by patriotic ardor, they had swarmed into remote border areas and spent formative years isolated from foreigners and China's modern cities. By the time they reached power, they were part of a popular movement that had grown and reached fruition in native Chinese soil.

During the Korean War, when China's mortal enemy no longer was Japan but the United States, the intelligentsia was under strong pressure to renounce past American ties. Denunciation of cultural imperialism and confession by its alleged understudies became *de rigeur* for prominent alumni of Yenching, Tsinghua, and other Chinese universities, as well as for those who had studied abroad. Nor should we assume that such testimonials were merely a ruse to disguise deeply-rooted pro-American sentiments. There is no evidence that the December 9ers were ever so transfigured by higher education and foreign associations that their ascendency would have automatically smoothed the path of Sino-American relations. Chinese by birth, patriots through experience, and Communists by choice, they could never have accepted American encirclement, isolation, or even "containment" of China. Their failure to succeed the generation of Mao may make less difference than we had assumed, so far as Sino-American relations are concerned.

Nonetheless, the reader who first encountered the December 9ers as courageous young patriots may well feel that history has dealt a cruel blow to these men and women. The element of individual tragedy in their saga is, indeed, undeniable. Developmental theorists, moreover, might view the loss of talent as a tragic waste or a typical example of the turbulence that characterizes any developing nation. But in another sense, the December 9ers, in their demise, may have unwittingly contributed to the revolution. Whatever their manifest virtues and good intentions, officials of this generation had become part of a staid and aging ruling structure, in need of overhaul if the creative energies of the Chinese revolution were to be released. Testimony of recent visitors to China suggests that the Cultural Revolution, chaotic and destructive though it may have been, cleared the way for constructive forces. A renewed spirit of populism, community self-help, and national pride has been evident. No longer does the Chinese revolution seem destined to undergo the grey bureaucratic fate of its Soviet precursor.

The future, nonetheless, remains uncertain. The tortuous course of China's on-going revolution provides little comfort for political prognosticators. Chinese history now unfolds in two realms, the jet age universe of Ambassador Huang Hua and the earth-bound world of the communes. Central to this confusing picture is the enigmatic Chou En-lai, urbane and sophisticated, yet seemingly prepared to preside over the perpetuation of populist values. Significantly, most of the small band of December

9ers now prominent are associated with Chou's foreign policy establishment. But some 90 percent of this remarkable generation appears consigned to obscurity. If so, China has lost the services of a talented group of people. What it has gained remains to be seen. Does the elimination of these powerful bureaucrats mark a departure from two millenia of bureaucratic rule, or does it signify only the replacement of one elite by another? The fate of the December 9ers may have been sealed; China's fate still hangs in the balance.

Bibliographic Note

In tracing the lives and careers of some two hundred individuals, we have unearthed bits and pieces of information in a great variety of places. To list these seriatim in a "Bibliography" would do little to advance the interests of scholarship. Instead, we hope that this note will provide a point of departure for readers interested in further exploration of the December 9th movement and the December 9ers.

Major secondary works on the December 9th movement are: Hubert Freyn, *Prelude to War: The Chinese Student Rebellion of 1935-36* (Shanghai: China Journal Publishing Co., 1939); John Israel, *Student Nationalism in China, 1927–1937* (Stanford, Calif.: Stanford University Press, 1966, chapters 5 and 6) and "The December 9th Movement: A Case Study in Chinese Communist Historiography," *The China Quarterly*, no. 23 (July–September 1965), pp. 140–69; and Jessie G. Lutz, "December 9, 1935: Student Nationalism and the China Christian Colleges," *Journal of Asian Studies* 26, no. 4 (August 1967): 627–48.

For further bibliographic information, the reader is directed to bibliographies and notes in the above-mentioned works as well as to John Israel, *The Chinese Student Movement, 1927–1937: A Bibliographic Essay Based on the Resources of the Hoover Institution* (Stanford, Calif.: Hoover Institution on War, Revolution, and Peace, 1959) and Chün-tu Hsüeh, *The Chinese Communist Movement, 1921–1937* and *The Chinese Communist Movement, 1937–1949 (Stanford, Calif.: Hoover Institution on War,*

Revolution, and Peace, 1960 and 1962).

The richest collection of source material on the December 9th movement is Nym Wales (Helen F. Snow), *Notes on the Chinese Student Movement, 1935–36* (Madison, Conn.: mimeographed, 1959; reprinted by Scholarly Press, 1973). Also very useful are reminiscences and articles in Chiang Nan-hsiang and others, *The Roar of a Nation; Reminiscences of the December 9th Student Movement* (Peking: Foreign Languages Press, 1963) and Jen-min ch'u-pan she, ed., *I-erh chiu yun-tung* [The December 9th movement] (Peking: Jen-min ch'u-pan she, 1954). The Chinese-language collection from which the items in this volume are extracted is Li Ch'ang and others, *"I-erh chiu" hui-i lu* [Reminiscences of December 9th] (Peking: Chung-kuo ch'ing-nien ch'u-pan she, 1961). The most important item in this compilation, Li Ch'ang's "Recollections of the National Liberation Vanguard of China," is translated in *SCMM*, Part I, no. 296 (January 15, 1962), pp. 27-36, and Part II, no. 297 (January 22, 1962), pp. 28–43.

The close observer of footnotes will notice that the post-1949 portion of this book has far fewer footnotes than earlier chapters. The difference or imbalance is not frivolous. Rather, it is due to the approach and methodology. In the broadest sense, the post-1949 period concentrates on aggregate elite analysis. To take one of many examples, we have asserted that from 1953 to 1966 the December 9th veterans visited an average of about 20 nations a year. Clearly, it would take a dozen-odd pages to list—in conventional footnote fashion—each and every trip. Such pedantry would serve few purposes.

In addition to aggregate analysis we have, of course, many more specific facts—for example, a ministerial appointment. In this case, we could have used more conventional footnotes. But our thinking is that this would have larded the footnotes with a huge amount of readily available material. More specifically, virtually all these facts can be checked in Union Research Institute, *Who's Who in Communist China* (both the 1966 edition and the two-volume revised version of 1969 and 1970 were published by the URI in Hong Kong) or in Donald W. Klein and Anne B. Clark, *Biographic Dictionary of Chinese Communism, 1921–1965* (Cambridge, Mass.: Harvard University Press, 1971). Anyone wishing to probe the question still further should consult Donald W. Klein, "Sources for Elite Studies and Biographical Materials on China," in Robert A. Scalapino, ed., *Elites in the People's Republic of China* (Seattle: University of Washington Press, 1972), pp. 609–56.

INDEX

290

294

Marxism, 40, 133, 279; and Christiani-
ty, 27–28
Marxism-Leninism, 279
Marxism-Leninism-Maoism, 221
Marxist, 48, 62, 101, 279
Marxist-Leninist, 33, 81, 189–190
Marx-Lenin Academy, 182
May 4 movement (1919), 4, 12, 22,
66–69, 70, 71–72, 92, 98, 177, 280;
generation of, 20, 258
May 7th schools, 276
May 30th movement (1925), 151
Mei I-ch'i, 52, 62, 65, 210; quoted,
19–20
Meng Ying, 259, 260–261, 262
Mexico, 262, 271
Mentoukou, 142
Middle East, 257, 262. *See also* Egypt;
Saudi Arabia; Syria; Yemen
Military Academy, 182
Military Affairs Commission, 159, 165
Mining, Sino-Soviet stock companies,
228
Ministry of Agriculture, 243
Ministry of Allocation of Materials,
243
Ministry of Chemical Industry, 83–84,
238, 243, 244
Ministry of Commerce, 64, 241, 243,
244, 253
Ministry of Communications, 243
Ministry of Culture, 243
Ministry of Economic Affairs
(Nationalist government), 210
Ministry of Education, 226, 242, 243,
244, 254
Ministry of Foreign Affairs, 36, 42, 45,
48, 78, 227, 243, 245, 259, 260, 262,
263, 270, 271
Ministry of Foreign Trade, 241–242,
243, 263, 272
Ministry of Fuel Industry, 226
Ministry of Geology, 242, 243
Ministry of Heavy Industry, 241
Ministry of Higher Education, 242,
243, 244, 269
Ministry of the Interior, 226, 229
Ministry of Justice, 243
Ministry of Machine Building, First,
239–240, 241, 243, 244, 272
Ministry of Machine Building, Second,
241
Ministry of National Defense, 245
Ministry of North China Affairs, 227

Ministry of Petroleum and Chemical
Industries, 276–277
Ministry of Petroleum Industry, 276
Ministry of Public Health, 243
Ministry of Public Security, 245
Ministry for the Purchase of Agricul-
tural Supplies, 245n
Ministry of Railways, 76, 227–228, 243
Ministry of Supervision, 243
Ministry of Trade, 226, 229, 241
Ministry of Water Conservancy, 239
Missionary education movement, 53,
83, 280. *See also* Christianity; United
Board for Christian Higher Educa-
tion in Asia
Missionary schools, 23, 26–28, 40, 78,
260. *See also* Yenching University
Modern Lecture Society, 21
Mongolia, 261
Moscow, 222, 228, 237, 252, 255, 260
"Mosquite press," 174
Mukden (Shenyang), 84, 207
Mukden Incident (1931), 84, 101, 118,
150, 151

Nan Han-ch'en, 151
Nankai University (Kunming), 165,
188
Nanking, 63, 147, 180, 212; fall of,
150–151; government, *see* Kuomintang; National Liberation Vanguards of China in, 149–151
Nanking conference (January 1936),
104–105
Nanking student uprising (1931), 20,
22, 68–69
Nanyuan Barracks (1937), 86, 139
National Liberation Vanguards of
China (*Min-hsien-tui*), 2, 7, 44, 54–55,
60, 63, 72, 75–76, 85, 87, 93, 94,
102–104, 107, 113, 114–119,
119–122, 128, 129–132, 138, 140,
144, 148, 163, 166, 167, 177, 181,
193, 223, 236, 240, 267; chorus, 150;
and Communist Youth League,
196–199, *see also* Communist Youth
League; congress (April 1938), 195;
dissolution of, 195–203; guerrillas,
148–149; in Kweiyang, 171, 209; loss
of urban base, 149–156; Military
Department, 120; and National
Salvation Youth Corps, 165;
nationwide congress (1937),
129–130; Northwest Bureau, 156,

Studies of the
East Asian Institute

The Ladder of Success in Imperial China, by Ping-ti Ho. New York: Columbia University Press, 1962.

The Chinese Inflation, 1937–1949, by Shun-hsin Chou. New York: Columbia University Press, 1963.

Reformer in Modern China: Chang Chien, 1853–1926, by Samuel Chu. New York: Columbia University Press, 1965.

Research in Japanese Sources: A Guide, by Herschel Webb with the assistance of Marleigh Ryan. New York: Columbia University Press, 1965.

Society and Education in Japan, by Herbert Passin. New York: Bureau of Publications, Teachers College, Columbia University, 1965.

Agricultural Production and Economic Development in Japan, 1873–1922, by James I. Nakamura. Princeton, N.J.: Princeton University Press, 1966.

Japan's First Modern Novel: Ukigumo of Futabatei Shimei, by Marleigh Ryan. New York: Columbia University Press, 1967.

The Korean Communist Movement, 1918–1948, by Dae-Sook Suh. Princeton, N.J.: Princeton University Press, 1967.

The First Vietnam Crisis, by Melvin Gurtov. New York: Columbia University Press, 1967.

Cadres, Bureaucracy, and Political Power in Communist China, by A. Doak Barnett. New York: Columbia University Press, 1967.

The Japanese Imperial Institution in the Tokugawa Period, by Herschel Webb. New York: Columbia University Press, 1968.

Higher Education and Business Recruitment in Japan, by Koya Azumi. New York: Teachers College Press, Columbia University, 1969.

The Communists and Chinese Peasant Rebellions: A Study in the Rewriting of Chinese History, by James P. Harrison, Jr. New York: Atheneum, 1969.

How the Conservatives Rule Japan, by Nathaniel B. Thayer. Princeton, N.J.: Princeton University Press, 1969.

Aspects of Chinese Education, edited by C. T. Hu. New York: Teachers College Press, Columbia University, 1970.

Documents of Korean Communism, 1918–1948, by Dae-Sook Suh. Princeton, N.J.:

Princeton University Press, 1970.

Japanese Education: A Bibliography of Materials in the English Language, by Herbert Passin. New York: Teachers College Press, Columbia University, 1970.

Economic Development and the Labor Market in Japan, by Koji Taira. New York: Columbia University Press, 1970.

The Japanese Oligarchy and the Russo-Japanese War, by Shumpei Okamoto. New York: Columbia University Press, 1970.

Imperial Restoration in Medieval Japan, by H. Paul Varley. New York: Columbia University Press, 1971.

Japan's Postwar Defense Policy, 1947–1968, by Martin E. Weinstein. New York: Columbia University Press, 1971.

Election Campaigning Japanese Style, by Gerald L. Curtis. New York: Columbia University Press, 1971.

China and Russia: The "Great Game," by O. Edmund Clubb. New York: Columbia University Press, 1971.

Money and Monetary Policy in Communist China, by Katharine Huang Hsiao. New York: Columbia University Press, 1971.

The District Magistrate in Late Imperial China, by John R. Watt. New York: Columbia University Press, 1972.

Law and Policy in China's Foreign Relations: A Study of Attitudes and Practice, by James C. Hsiung. New York: Columbia University Press, 1972.

Pearl Harbor as History: Japanese-American Relations, 1931–1941, edited by Dorothy Borg and Shumpei Okamoto, with the assistance of Dale K. A. Finlayson. New York: Columbia University Press, 1973.

Japanese Culture: A Short History, by H. Paul Varley. New York: Praeger Publishers, 1973.

Doctors in Politics: The Political Life of the Japan Medical Association, by William E. Steslicke. New York: Praeger Publishers, 1973.

Japan's Foreign Policy, 1868–1941: A Research Guide, edited by James William Morley. New York: Columbia University Press, 1974.

The Japan Teachers Union: A Radical Interest Group in Japanese Politics, by Donald Ray Thurston. Princeton, N.J.: Princeton University Press, 1973.

Palace and Politics in Prewar Japan, by David Anson Titus. New York: Columbia University Press, 1974.

The Idea of China: Essays in Geographic Myth and Theory, by Andrew March. Devon, England: David and Charles, 1974; New York: Praeger Publishers, 1974.

Origins of the Cultural Revolution, by Roderick MacFarquhar. New York: Columbia University Press, 1974.

Shiba Kokan, by Calvin L. French. Tokyo: John Weatherhill, Inc., 1974.

Embassy at War, by Harold J. Noble, edited by Frank P. Baldwin, Jr. Seattle: University of Washington Press, 1975.

Insei: Abdicated Sovereigns in the Politics of Late Heian Japan, 1086–1185, by G. Cameron Hurst. New York: Columbia University Press, 1975.

Rebels and Bureaucrats: China's December 9ers, by John Israel and Donald W. Klein. Berkeley: University of California Press, 1975.